Marketing for Competitiveness

ASIA TO THE WORLD!
IN THE AGE OF DIGITAL CONSUMERS

Asia Marketing Federation

Marketing for Competitiveness

ASIA TO THE WORLD!
IN THE AGE OF DIGITAL CONSUMERS

PHILIP KOTLER
Northwestern University
USA

HERMAWAN KARTAJAYA
MarkPlus, Inc.
Indonesia

HOOI DEN HUAN
Nanyang Technological University
Singapore

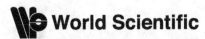 **World Scientific**

NEW JERSEY · LONDON · SINGAPORE · BEIJING · SHANGHAI · HONG KONG · TAIPEI · CHENNAI · TOKYO

Published by

World Scientific Publishing Co. Pte. Ltd.

5 Toh Tuck Link, Singapore 596224

USA office: 27 Warren Street, Suite 401-402, Hackensack, NJ 07601

UK office: 57 Shelton Street, Covent Garden, London WC2H 9HE

British Library Cataloguing-in-Publication Data
A catalogue record for this book is available from the British Library.

MARKETING FOR COMPETITIVENESS: ASIA TO THE WORLD
In the Age of Digital Consumers

ISBN 978-981-3201-95-8
ISBN 978-981-3201-96-5 (pbk)

Desk Editor: Sandhya Venkatesh

Typeset by Stallion Press
Email: enquiries@stallionpress.com

Printed in Singapore

ACKNOWLEDGMENTS

We deeply appreciate the invaluable help given by all staff of MarkPlus including Michael Hermawan, Chief Executive Officer; Dr Jacky Mussry, Deputy Chief Executive Officer; Iwan Setiawan, Chief Operations Officer; Hendra Warsita, Chief Corporate Officer; Stephanie Hermawan, Chief Business Officer; and, in particular, Ardhi Ridwansyah and Priyanka Shekhawat who were deeply involved in this project.

We specially acknowledge Ardhi for his immense efforts for this book.

We are also grateful for the support from Goto-san, the president of the Asia Marketing Federation; Pak Junardy, Chairman of the Asia Marketing Federation Foundation; and our colleagues from all the national marketing associations who are members of the Asia Marketing Federation.

Last but not least, we are ever grateful for the support and encouragement from all our loved ones.

ABOUT THE AUTHORS

Philip Kotler

Dr Philip Kotler is the S.C. Johnson Distinguished Professor of International Marketing at the Kellogg School of Management. He has been honored as one of the world's leading marketing thinkers. He earned his M.A. degree in Economics (1953) from the University of Chicago and his PhD degree in Economics (1956) from the Massachusetts Institute of Technology (MIT), and has received honorary degrees from 20 foreign universities. He is the author of over 58 books and over 150 articles. He has been a consultant to IBM, General Electric, Sony, AT&T, Bank of America, Merck, Motorola, Ford, and others. *The Financial Times* included him in its list of the top 10 business thinkers. They cited his *Marketing Management* as one of the 50 best business books of all times.

Hermawan Kartajaya

Hermawan Kartajaya is the founder of the Asia Marketing Federation and the president of the Asia Council for Small Business. In 2003, he was named as one of the "50 Gurus Who Have Shaped the Future of Marketing" by CIM-UK. In 2009, he received the Distinguished Global Leadership Award from the Pan-Pacific Business Association. He is both a strategic business thinker and a marketing practitioner. He has written five international books with Philip Kotler — the father of modern marketing. His latest book, *Marketing 3.0* is widely acknowledged globally and is published in 25 languages. Hermawan is the executive chairman and founder of MarkPlus Inc., a leading integrated marketing solution provider that provides comprehensive consulting, research, training and media services with branches in 18 cities in Indonesia. He received an honorary doctorate degree from ITS Surabaya.

Hooi Den Huan

Dr Hooi Den Huan is the director of Nanyang Technological University's Nanyang Technopreneurship Center and an Associate Professor at the Nanyang Business School. He is a supervisor of the Asia Marketing Federation Foundation a Vice-President of the Asian Council for Small Business, an honorary consultant for the CCPIT Commercial Sub-Council, and an advisory board member of the Times Higher Education, *Times of India*. Den received his BSc (Hons) in Business Studies from the University of Bradford, his PhD from the University of Manchester, and was a visiting scholar at the Sloan School of Management, MIT. He is a Chartered Marketer (CIM-UK), a Chartered Accountant (ICAEW), a Chartered Management Accountant (CIMA), and a Babson TETA Fellow. Den was conferred the Distinguished Global Leadership Award by the Pan-Pacific Business Association in 2011, the ICSB President's Award in 2014, and a Fellowship by the Marketing Institute of Malaysia in 2016.

DEDICATION

To my lovely wife, Nancy Kotler
Philip Kotler

To Darren Dominique Hermawan, the next Great Marketeer
Hermawan Kartajaya

To my wonderful wife, Wan Fei, and daughters, Ren Yi and Ren Syn
Hooi Den Huan

FOREWORD

Today we witness a world of rapid changes, volatility, uncertainty, complexity, and ambiguity. This is characterized by dynamic and disruptive forces that significantly shape the total business landscape.

No organization, however big or small, public or private, profit-oriented or otherwise, can ignore these forces that exert a profound impact on its success and sustainability. Such dynamism permeates not only organizations but individuals too, resulting in significant changes not just in consumer behavior but also in organizational behavior.

To cope with such challenges and leverage on the opportunities, marketing is arguably one of the most suitable disciplines, if not the most suitable, because marketing invariably touches the minds, hearts, and spirit of everyone. According to an article by Regis McKenna, "Marketing Is Everything."

If we may also further emphasize, "Marketing Is Everywhere" too and not least in the Asian region, which is arguably one of the most dynamic regions in the world, whether measured by size, growth rate, diversity, or any other conceivable criteria. Indeed, Asia has experienced such rapid changes especially in the last half century or so that some even call the 21st century, the Asian century.

Given the importance of Marketing as a discipline and Asia as a region, it will be a failure on our part if we do not take upon ourselves the duty to help further develop the marketing profession by drawing useful theory and practices from within and outside Asia and sharing such experiences and knowledge with all.

In this world of connectivity, we cannot, and neither is it good to, try to do things alone. Through the Asia Marketing Federation, we foster intra-region and international collaborations.

Hence we are pleased to support this book initiative by Professor Philip Kotler, Pak Hermawan Kartajaya, and Associate Professor Hooi Den Huan, all of whom are key members of the Asia Marketing Federation. We trust this further enhances our primary goal — to help develop a body of knowledge of the art and science of marketing theory and practice that will contribute toward uplifting the standards of marketing professionalism — globally, regionally, and locally.

- President, Asia Marketing Federation
- Chairman, Asia Marketing Federation Foundation
- CCPIT Commercial Sub-Council
- Hong Kong Institute of Marketing
- Indonesia Marketing Association
- Institute of Marketing Malaysia
- Japan Marketing Association
- Marketing Association of Cambodia
- Marketing Association of Thailand
- Marketing Institute of Singapore
- Marketing Society of Bangladesh
- Marketing Society of Korea
- Mongolian Marketing Association
- Myanmar Marketing Society
- Philippine Marketing Association
- Sri Lanka Institute of Marketing
- Taiwan Institute of Marketing Science
- Vietnam Marketing Association

CONTENTS

Preface

The Anatomy of Change

Asia is the world's most populated region, accounting for over 60 percent of the population. Asia's young population, an expanding middle class, and high economic growth across various countries make it a very lucrative market. In fact, the evolving market dynamics in the region are not inferior in any way when compared with those of the more mature regions including Europe or North America. Marketers aiming to run successful businesses in the region should understand how the anatomy of change is really happening in this region.

Part I of this book discusses the dynamic business landscape, influenced by indigenous as well as external forces, the factors shaping these forces, the various challenges facing businesses, and the opportunities galore, which can be exploited. Even as the market has long been evolving, some variables, such as the fast-developing technological advances, rapid progress of globalization, and how an expanding section of well-informed customers are responding to these phenomena that have come into play over the past decade, have caused the speed of change to increase. Old rules of doing business will have to morph to stay relevant and competitive in the changing markets. There will be sacrifices and compromises, winners and losers, and no one in the quest for progress and prosperity would want to be left behind.

Change is the dynamic factor that determines the external macroeconomic environment, which in turn influences an organization's strategy formulation. In our book *Rethinking Marketing: Sustainable Market-ing Enterprise in Asia*, we concluded, that the anatomy of change consists of five elements — technology, political legal, social-cultural, economy, and market (see Fig. A). Technology is the primary force of change that directly impacts the way we live and work. It influences political and legal

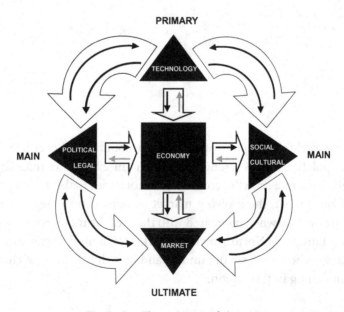

Figure A: The anatomy of change.

systems, economic development, and sociocultural standards. These changes indirectly create new markets and eliminate old ones.

Chapters 1–3 in this book elaborate on the dynamics of the macro-environment in Asia, especially the rapidly unfolding digital technology revolution in the region and its influence on other elements. These changes, in turn, further affect all the existing stakeholders: governments, companies, customers, and many more. Understanding these changes and their consequences will enable a marketer to gauge opportunities when its rivals may still be preoccupied with tackling existing challenges.

CHAPTER 1

TECHNOLOGY
AS THE PRIMARY DRIVER

Mobile, mobile, mobile!
Internet users in Asia are predominantly connecting via mobile.
Most of them are not migrating to mobile,
that's where they're starting.

Michelle Guthrie, Former Managing Director of Agencies
Asia Pacific — Google

The industrial revolution of the 19th century justifiably puts the spotlight on technology as a powerful force of change. The invention of the steam engine and its eventual application in power machinery and locomotives prompted a major transformation in agriculture, manufacturing, mining, transportation, and politics around the world.

Another revolution that has been underway over the past half a century or so is the digital revolution. Starting with the transition from mechanical and electronic technology to digital and eventually mobile, it has stimulated remarkable development across industries, while at the same time, overturning the conventional order in various fields.

Some prefer to call it disruption. Whether we recognize it or not, the digital revolution would mark a powerful transformation in the way businesses and societies function. The impact is simply evident from the incredible speed at which advancements in digital and mobile technologies have taken place, especially in light of the technological changes in the previous era. For example, it took more than 50 years for half of the homes in the United States to install a telephone, while the same percentage acquired smartphones in a little more than five years. It took 30 years for the radio to attract an audience of 50 million people, while Facebook did so in 12 months and Twitter in nine months. WeChat, the mobile text messaging and voice communication service developed by China's Tencent, added 400 million users in two years (Thompson *et al.*, 2015).

In addition to unparalleled speed, the digital revolution has also created pivotal changes in many aspects of our lives in unimaginable ways. In the business world, industries are being torn apart and economies reshaped overnight. Banks today are competing with telecoms' players offering payment services. The hospitality industry is losing sleep over guarding its turf against the much-palpable threat from online room-letting and rent-lodging services — such as Airbnb, and Couchsurfing. Conventional transport companies are beginning to panic because of declining market shares in view of emerging online transportation networks such as Uber, China's Didi Chuxing (formerly known as Didi Kuaidi), Malaysia's Grab, and Indonesia's GoJek. Brick-and-mortar retailers are struggling to attract visitors to their stores in view of the rise in e-commerce and online market places. The face of competition has changed drastically.

Digital disruptions have affected consumer behavior: from how they search to the way they buy, pay for, use, and dispose products. Their media consumption habits have dramatically evolved, forcing marketers to think hard about finding alternative channels, which are more effective in engaging with them. And hence, we have an influx of various online interactive platforms, aimed at creating a two-way and multiple-way dialogue. Consumers' decision-making process is also much more complex because of the various influencing voices around them — both offline and online.

For businesses operating in the Asian region, the ongoing evolution of industries as well as consumers is even more pertinent and calls for a proactive approach in responding to the changes. As the most populous region in the world, Asia makes for a highly attractive consumer market. Yet, it poses big challenges for businesses as they face the realities of this melting pot of various cultures, languages, consumers' distinct behaviors, and nuances. This chapter covers various technological developments in the region, the challenges faced by policy makers and marketers, as well as the impact of such changes on the macro and business perspectives.

Digital Revolution in Asia: Growth and Challenges

The Asian region has the highest population in the world, with China, India, and Indonesia being the most populous countries in that order. Overall, mobile phone penetration in the Asian region is as high as 93 percent, only slightly below the global average penetration of 97.7 percent (see Table 1.1). In fact, more than half the countries in Asia have witnessed mobile penetration above 100 percent, which means that the average population owns more than one mobile phone unit (see Table 1.2).

There are two reasons for this high mobile penetration in Asia: increased mobile broadband coverage as well as the increasing number of affordable mobile devices. The increased coverage in the region is a result of strengthening collaboration between governments and private sectors (network operators), aimed at building an infrastructure that supports expansion of the reach of mobile communication. Greater affordability of mobile devices could be attributed to a mix of both, increasingly disposable incomes of a fast-expanding middle class and innovation in technology and manufacturing from handset manufacturers in the region. Based on data from GSMA Intelligence (2015), approximately 90 percent of the handsets that were shipped in 2014 came from Asia-based vendors. This has led to mobile phones becoming a mass product in Asia.

The high usage of the mobile phone does not seem uniformly spread across the region. There are still countries such as Myanmar and North Korea which lag far behind their counterparts (see Table 1.2), partly as a

Table 1.1: Internet and mobile users: Asia and rest of the world.

	Population (2015 Est.)	Population (% of World)	Internet Users (2015)		Mobile Phone Users (2015)	
			In Numbers	Penetration (%)	In Numbers	Penetration (%)
Asia*	3,915,876,022	53.9%	1,580,740,616	40.4	3,639,947,757	93
Non-Asia	3,344,026,221	46.1%	1,785,520,540	53.4	3,450,052,243	103.2
World	7,259,902,243	100%	3,366,261,156	46.4	7.090.000.000	97.7

*Not including Middle East countries and former Soviet Union.

Source: Data on population and Internet users from internetworldstats.com; data on mobile phone users from GSMA Intelligence, Wikipedia, wearesocial.sg, internetworldstats.com.

result of political regression in the two states. Even among the politically stable states, mobile penetration varies widely due to socio-economic disparities. In some countries, government policies on investments for the development of mobile broadband infrastructure are not yet optimal. Myanmar, has made considerable progress in this regard, despite since traversing through a bumpy ride of democratic mandate over by half a

Table 1.2: Digitalization in Asian countries.

Country Name	Population (2015 Est)	Internet Users (2015)		Mobile Phone Users (2015)	
		Number of Users	Penetration (%)	Number of Users	Penetration (%)
Bangladesh	168,957,745	53,941,000	31.9	133,720,000	79.1
Bhutan	741,919	254,998	34.4	570,000	76.8
Brunei	429,646	318,901	74.2	495,000	115.2
Cambodia	15,708,756	5,000,000	31.8	24,200,000	154.1
China	1,361,512,535	674,000,000	49.5	1,276,660,000	93.8
Hong Kong	7,141,106	5,751,357	80.5	12,700,000	177.8
India	1,251,695,584	375,000,000	30.0	1,017,968,757	81.3
Indonesia	255,993,674	78,000,000	30.5	308,200,000	120.4
Japan	126,919,659	114,963,827	90.6	155,600,000	122.6
Korea, North	24,983,205	7,200	0.0	2,800,000	11.2
Korea, South	49,115,196	45,314,248	92.3	56,000,000	114.0
Laos	6,911,544	985,586	14.3	7,000,000	101.3
Macao	592,731	413,608	69.8	1,700,000	286.8
Malaysia	30,513,848	20,596,847	67.5	41,800,000	137.0
Maldives	393,253	230,000	58.5	673,000	171.1
Mongolia	2,992,908	1,300,000	43.4	3,100,000	103.6
Myanmar	56,320,206	7,100,000	12.6	13,300,000	23.6
Nepal	31,551,305	5,700,000	18.1	25,200,000	79.9
Pakistan	199,085,847	29,128,970	14.6	149,200,000	74.9

(*Continued*)

Table 1.2: (*Continued*)

Country Name	Population (2015 Est)	Internet Users (2015)		Mobile Phone Users (2015)	
		Number of Users	Penetration (%)	Number of Users	Penetration (%)
Philippines	109,615,913	47,134,843	43.0	114,600,000	104.5
Singapore	5,674,472	4,653,067	82.0	8,300,000	146.3
Sri Lanka	22,053,488	5,689,800	25.8	27,400,000	124.2
Taiwan	23,415,126	19,666,364	84.0	32,600,000	139.2
Thailand	67,976,405	38,000,000	55.9	97,000,000	142.7
Timor-Leste	1,231,116	290,000	23.6	861,000	69.9
Vietnam	94,348,835	47,300,000	50.1	128,300,000	136.0
Total Asia	**3,915,876,022**	**1,580,740,616**	**40.4**	**3,639,947,757**	**93.0**

* Not including Middle East countries and former Soviet Union.

Source: Data on population and Internet users from internetworldstats.com; data on mobile phone users from GSMA Intelligence, Wikipedia, Wearesocial.sg, internetworldstats.com.

decade. The government initiated a series of economic reforms by opening up the country to the outside world. This has prompted, among other industries, several mobile operators and handset manufacturers in Asia to begin expanding in Myanmar. The country was named the fourth fastest growing mobile market in the world, behind China, India, and the United States in a recent report by Ericssion in 2015.

The second challenge facing Asia is inadequate Internet access, which somewhat stunts the potential of the growing use of mobile phone in the region. As shown in Table 1.1, penetration of Internet users in Asia has reached only 40.4 percent. It is an indication of how a vast majority of mobile phone users in Asia continue to use outdated handphones, or basic feature phones with limited technology. For example, in India — one of the most densely populated countries in Asia — smartphones users, as of 2015, totaled about 167.9 million or only about 16.5 percent of total mobile device users (Statista, 2016).

A closer look at the data on Internet users in each country points to the persistence of the looming digital divide in the region. Only about a quarter has Internet penetration above 60 percent, the majority of which covers only a small number of countries with relatively low populations, including Hong Kong, Singapore, South Korea, and Taiwan. The contemporary Asian countries are actually lagging behind, in terms of mobile and Internet penetration. For example, in India and Indonesia, whose combined population exceeds one-third of the population of Asia, the penetration of Internet is around 30 percent (see Table 1.2). Such inequality should be of concern to every policy maker and marketer in Asia.

Asia's Digital Ecosystem

The development of digital technology in Asia would not have progressed without the existence of a supporting ecosystem. It comprises various parties from both government and private sectors to deliver mobile and Internet services to customers (see Fig. 1.1). Ultimately, the onus is on this ecosystem to be instrumental in improving digital literacy, while reducing the digital divide in Asia.

Based on the research conducted by the GSM Association, in 2014, the total value added — the total income generated by the industry to its employees (through payment of wages), to government (through tax contributions), and to shareholders (through profits) — by the ecosystem in Asia Pacific (Asia plus Australia and New Zealand) was US$395 billion (1.6 percent of gross domestic product [GDP]). It also provided direct employment to 6.5 million people in Asia Pacific and this is expected to increase to eight million by 2020. The greatest economic contribution among all digital ecosystem players in the region was from mobile operators, around 1.2 percent of GDP across the region, or more than 70 percent of the total contribution of the ecosystem.

- **Infrastructure and Support Services**

  Information and communication technology (ICT) infrastructure is an obvious and essential foundation to the Information Society (Sharma and Mokhtar, 2006). The government — supported by the private sector — works on a unified approach that is expected to vastly improve public

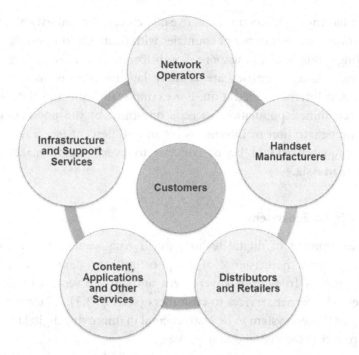

Figure 1.1: Digital ecosystem.

access to Internet through mobile technology and related infrastructure improvements. Almost all countries in Asia have already devised a master plan or a national initiative to support digitalization in various aspects of life. For example, Singapore developed eGov2015 to build an interactive environment where the government, private sector, and people work together seamlessly through the enabling power of information technology. Thailand, on the other hand, aims to achieve similar ICT objectives through its 2020 blueprint and Smart Thailand project (Kotler *et al.*, 2014).

- **Network Operators**

A healthy competition among mobile and Internet service providers in Asia has resulted in reduction in IT usage fee. It is evident from market trends that the cost of both mobile phone usage and short message service (SMS) has been on a decline, resulting in the mobile technology being more accessible to a larger section of consumers. As a result, between 2008 and 2015, the average revenue per user (ARPU) in almost all Asian countries dropped and is expected to drop further (ROA Holdings, 2012). It is both a challenge and an opportunity for network operators to be able to sell extra services outside their traditional business model.

- **Handset Manufacturers**

Smartphone adoption in Asia Pacific continued to grow though 2015 and reached 40 percent of total connections. The data is consistent with the statistics on Internet penetration in Asia, which reached a total of 40.4 percent (see Table 1.2). It can, therefore, be assumed that rising penetration of smartphones will directly support an increase in the number of Internet users in Asia. The digital divide that exists between advanced markets (such as Japan and South Korea) and a large number of Asian countries can be attenuated with the growing supply of smartphones from local manufacturers, which are fast gaining foothold in their respective markets, including Xiaomi (China), Huawei (China), Samsung (South Korea), Micromax (India), Advan (Indonesia), Ninetology (Malaysia), Cherry Mobile (Philippines), and many more (see Box 1.1).

- **Distributors and Retailers**

The existence of distribution companies is vital to mobile and Internet penetration in Asia. Through an extensive network, they help people in rural areas acquire mobile handsets and SIM cards. But over time, these physical channels of distribution have started to transform into e-channels which are much easier to maneuver in terms of investment and infrastructure. The growth of e-commerce and online market places has stimulated smartphone penetration in urban areas at more affordable prices. Xiaomi's successful collaboration with e-commerce companies Lazada and Flipkart in India has given it a relatively cost-efficient and wide-reaching launchpad and distribution platform, leading to massive sales across Asian markets.

- **Content, Applications, and Other Services**

The industry is inarguably growing at an extraordinary rate and speed, as evident from the proliferation of online news services, social media, instant messengers, apps developers, and so on. In addition to multinational companies such as Google, Yahoo, and Facebook, local players and even start-up companies have been offering applications, online news services etc. In China, the number of monthly active users of Weibo, a microblogging social media site, reached 198 million in March 2015, up by 38 percent from the previous year. (The Economist Corporate Network, 2015). Application developers have also flourished in the developing countries of Asia with a massive injection of funds from venture capitalists across the globe. The existence of local players is necessary to increase the local content that is relevant and can be understood by the Asian community at large.

Box 1.1: Inexpensive Smartphones Flood the Asian Market

Handphone manufacturers are proliferating the Asian market with low-cost smartphones. In view of rising disposable incomes and increasing affordability, smartphone sales are flourishing and local manufacturers in various regions are dominating the markets. Half a decade into operations, Chinese smartphone maker Xiaomi already maintain a strong foothold in the home market, and has been striding ahead in other Asian markets. Its high-quality, inexpensive smartphones are becoming quite a rage among buyers and at the end of 2014, Xiaomi already became the top smartphone supplier in China, ahead of Samsung and Lenovo. Data from the International Data Corporation (IDC) shows that two other Chinese mobile phone makers, Oppo and Vivo, are now the world's fourth and fifth largest phone sellers, respectively, behind Samsung, Apple, and Huawei — another big Chinese hardware maker.

Other Asian device manufacturers making big inroads into the smartphone market in Asia include Cherry Mobile in the Philippines, Micromax in India, and Q-Smart in Vietnam. These companies have optimally taken advantage of technological innovation, resulting in prices of their smartphones dropping to as low as US$35 without subsidies. Other device makers producing low-cost smartphones in Asia include Ninetology in Malaysia, Smartfren Telecom in Indonesia, Q Mobile in Pakistan, and I-Mobile in Thailand.

Since the smartphone market is quite mature in the developed world, including countries in Asia such as Japan, Taiwan, Singapore, and South Korea, it is in the developing economies that smartphones

(Continued)

Box 1.1:   (*Continued*)

sales are booming due to rollouts of wireless broadband and availability of low-cost devices. An Ericsson report states that almost two-thirds of mobile phone subscriptions in Southeast Asia and Oceania regions would be smartphones by 2020, reaching as many as about 800 million people.

Let's look at some of the facts which substantiate the meteoric growth in smartphone adoption in Asia:

- In Malaysia, the number of smartphone users, as part of mobile users, rose from 47 to 63 percent from 2012 to 2013. By the end of 2014, 74 percent of mobile users in Malaysia were using smartphones.

- In Sri Lanka, smartphone sales rose over 100 percent in 2014 compared to the prior year.

- Smartphone penetration rate stood at 34 percent in the Philippines at the end of 2014 (doubled from year before) and is projected to increase to 54 percent by the end of 2016.

- At the end of 2014, 38 percent of Vietnam's population owned a smartphone, 20 percent more than the year before. The number of smartphone users is around 22 million, predicted to reach 26 million in 2016.

- In Indonesia, full-year smartphone shipments in 2015 grew 17.1 percent to 29.3 million units in 2015. The number of smartphone users in Indonesia is expected to grow by a compound annual growth rate (CAGR) of 33 percent between 2013 and 2017, growing from an estimated 52 million in 2015 to 87 million in 2017.

- By the end of December 2014, barely 5 percent of mobile subscribers in Pakistan used smartphones on wireless 3G and 4G networks; yet growth is rapid, at about two million people a month. By the end of 2016, there will be an estimated 40 million smartphone users in Pakistan.

Source: Sam (2015).

The Impact of Digitalization

The impact of the rising usage of mobile and Internet is profound. Consumers can carry around powerful, Internet-enabled devices with them wherever they go. They are always connected, always reachable, and even their precise position is traceable. Mohd Khairil Abdullah, CEO of digital services at Axiata, a Malaysia-based telco with operations across Asia, argues:

> Mobile is becoming the platform on which people manage their lives. People are migrating whole sets of behavior from the non-digital world onto mobile environments, from booking taxis, to shopping, paying for services, watching videos or connecting with families (The Economist Corporate Network, 2015).

The profound impact of mobile and Internet technologies is not limited to consumers' lifestyles. Economically too, digitalization contributes significantly to countries in Asia and beyond. In 2014, mobile technologies and services generated 4.7 percent of the GDP in Asia Pacific — a contribution that amounted to over US$1 trillion of economic value across 50 different countries and territories (GSM Association, 2015). There is naturally a strong correlation between digitalization and economic growth. According to infostate — an index by the United Nations Educational, Scientific and Cultural Organization (UNESCO) that measures the digital divide, the countries with the highest infostate (the degree of digitalization in a country) are the same countries with the highest GDP; similarly, the lowest infostate countries rank the lowest based on GDP. Research by the International Telecommunication Union (2008) shows how Internet penetration correlates positively with GDP per capita in the Association of Southeast Asian Nations (ASEAN) member states (Kotler et al., 2014).

Digitalization also contributes directly to reduction in poverty and unemployment in developing countries. In 2014, the mobile ecosystem provided direct employment to 6.5 million people in Asia Pacific, and the number is estimated to grow to nearly eight million people by 2020. The economic activity generated by the ecosystem also indirectly supported around six million jobs in the broader economy in 2014, and this figure is also expected to increase to nearly seven million by 2020 (GSM Association, 2015).

The societal gap that typically exists between urban and rural regions can also be reduced through appropriate use of digital technology. Technology transcends geographical barriers and allows rural populations across the world to access products and services that have traditionally been beyond their reach. Mobile banking and mobile payments are expanding financial inclusion and e-commerce is fueling consumption in regions with little brick-and-mortar retail (Thompson *et al.* (2015). It is no wonder then that we have global technology giants — the likes of Google and Facebook — launching dedicated initiatives aimed at improving connectivity among millions of rural residents across the world. The biggest role, however, in expanding connectivity among the rural population will be that of the governments. The higher the government's commitment to build mobile and Internet insfrastructure in regions lagging behind, the greater will be the positive impact that can be leveraged from this digitalization trend.

For businesses, digitalization creates opportunities in times of unforeseen challenges. The company benefits from a multitude of new technologies — there is a newer, cheaper selection of channels to reach customers. Emerging trends such as big data and artificial intelligence are making it easier for companies to do better customization, based on customer behavior patterns. Technology has resulted in the relationship between the company and customers becoming more horizontal. Customers can no longer be treated as passive objects. They must be involved and engaged actively by the companies.

On the flip side, digitalization has encouraged the creation of unfamiliar competition. Traditional print newspapers must compete with online news sites which can break stories on the click of a button. Conventional transport companies are increasingly threatened by the widespread use of online transportation services available through mobile applications. Big retailers are concerned with the emergence of online stores and marketplaces managed by numerous small-time vendors. This calls for a fundamental transformation in the perspectives and strategies of managing businesses.

Three Paradoxes of Digitalization

More than 20 years ago, Handy (1995) in the book *"The Age of Paradox"* called many world events, including the development of technology, a

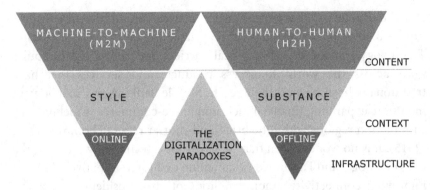

Figure 1.2: Three paradoxes of digitalization.

paradox. Many of those epiphanies stand true today — policy makers and marketers are witnessing several transformations, most notably in the world of technology. In order to be competitive in this new era, businesses need to understand and manage the following three paradoxes appropriately (see Fig. 1.2).

Online versus offline

Internet technology offers convenience and high efficiency. The interaction between the company and the customer can take place anytime and anywhere. This is prompting companies in Asia to flock to the online world, build their official websites, nurture online communities, and set up special social media teams to build relationships with customers. But as a matter of fact, the online world still has limitations which means that conventional approaches of the offline world cannot be completely replaced. Despite growing Internet usage and the seemingly improving tech-savviness among Asians, most consumers may not yet be fully familiar with digital services or simply not be sufficiently confident to take a jump on to the digital bandwagon. In order for companies to go digital, there is ostensibly a growing need to pay special attention to customer education in the online world this.

As a case in point, e-commerce companies in Asia are beginning to realize the importance of integration between the online and offline experience for shoppers. Even though rising e-commerce adoption is encouraging, a hard-hitting business reality is that a large section of Asian customers is still wary of online payment methods. Moving beyond the conventional cash-on-delivery model, Zalora, a Singapore-based online fashion retailer, offers a unique payment method. The Zalora website provides a cash-on-collection option, a concept that has already gained popularity in Taiwan and Japan. Collaborating with some convenience store chains, Zalora gives its customers an option of picking up and paying for their items at an outlet of their choice (Kotler *et al.*, 2014).

Commenting on this integration of online and offline interaction, Kasireddy from Fonterra in China says: "differentiating online and offline is really a false distinction. It's much more important to get the offline and the online working together seamlessly" (The Economist Corporate Network, 2015).

Substance versus style

The Internet has created new patterns of information consumption. If, in the print media, readers have conventionally been familiar with a writing style that's more elaborate, focusing on features, and in-depth stories, readers of online news sites are more accustomed to shorter, crispier write-ups. On smaller mobile phone screens, too much written content is perceived not only as un-user friendly but boring too. Visual factors — images and illustrations — frequently used by content providers to develop more engaging online content help improve the design. Ries (2012) in the book *Visual Hammer* stressed the importance of the visual aspect as a verbal positioning booster to inculcate a certain perception in the minds of customers. This trend in the digital world requires producers to include "style" in the content developed.

However, companies cannot rely solely on style aspects (visuals, audio, design, etc.) to provide information that touches a chord with customers, both rationally and emotionally. Digital content producers will have to strike a balance in creating content that is concise and interesting, yet does not lose its core substance. For example, the makers of video advertisements on YouTube must be creative enough to design a message that attracts the attention of viewers within the first five seconds, so that they will not skip the video. It is about style. But a compelling message will still be able to convey information about an advertised product effectively, and that is termed as 'substance'.

Machine-to-machine versus human-to-human

Digitalization has enabled "interactions" between various technology products. Existing data on our handsets can be transferred to other technology products in the form of instructions that produce a specific action or output. This is known as the Internet of things (IOT) or machine-to-machine (M2M) technology. The consumer space is a significant sector within the M2M universe that a range of players, including mobile operators and hardware manufacturers, are trying to address. For example, there is a particular focus, at present, on both wearable devices and the potential of "smart homes" (GSM Association, 2015).

A range of new wearable devices have been launched over the past years, including the Samsung Gear and the LG Lifeband. Connected devices and sensors allow customers to employ a smarter, more efficient lifestyle, with their personal devices such as smartphones and tablets connected with devices in their homes to enable automation. This helps users to remotely control functions, from lighting to basic security systems. Samsung Electronics has announced that 90 percent of its products — ranging from smartphones to refrigerators — would be able to connect to the Web by 2017. And by 2020, all of its products will be Internet connected (CNET, 2015).

But technology does not make man into a machine without emotions. Instead, digital technology, particularly social media, has turned customers into more emotionally expressive beings. This is why the human-to-human (H2H) touch must not be forgotten. Technology must be optimized to create a H2H interaction that is more flexible (not constrained by space and time), and not quite create a separate space that ends up replacing the intimate conventional ways of interaction.

Zappos, an online retailer Amazon acquired in 2009 for US$1.2 billion, has a unique way of building H2H interaction with its customers. Although Zappos actively uses social media including Twitter, YouTube, and Facebook to communicate with its customers, the company has not abandoned the use of the telephone. Tony Hsieh, CEO of Zappos once said: "We do not really look at Twitter as a marketing vehicle, so we do not look at how it translates into the bottom line. What we care about is being able to connect with our customers on a more personal level. We do that through the telephone as well as through Twitter. Nobody writes about the telephone because it's not an interesting news story, but we believe it's actually one of the best branding devices out there".

The telephone allows Zappos call center staff to establish a personal (H2H) connection with its customers. The staffs' performance is evaluated based on customer satisfaction on the calls they handle, without being limited by time. The longest customer service call took almost 6 hours. This makes Zappos one of the highly recommended brands by its customers (Frei *et al.*, 2009).

Therefore, these three paradoxes can actually be managed simultaneously, without having to negate each other. Companies need to be creative paradoxes in building integrated online and offline experiences, develop content that has substance with style, as well as M2M technology supported by H2H touch. A company's success in managing these three Paradoxes will create a strong competitive advantage to win the minds and hearts of digital consumers in Asia.

References

CNET (2015). Samsung Co-CEO: In 5 Years, All Our Products Will be Internet Connected. http://www.cnet.com/news/samsung-co-ceo-in-5-years-all-our-products-will-be-internet-connected/ (last accessed April 25, 2016).

Frei, FX, RJ Ely and L Winig (20 October 2009). Zappos.com 2009: Clothing, Customer Service & Culture. *Harvard Business School Case*.

GSM Association (2015). *The Mobile Economy: Asia Pacific 2015*. London: GSM Association.

Handy, C (1995). *The Age of Paradox*. Boston: Harvard Business School Press.

Internet World Stats (2015). Internet Usage in Asia. http://www.internetworldstats.com/stats3.htm, (last accessed April 24, 2016).

Kotler, P, H Kartajaya and Hooi, DH (2014). *Think New ASEAN*. Singapore: McGraw Hill.

Ries, L (2012). *Visual Hammer: Nail Your Brand into the Mind with the Emotional Power of a Visual*. Georgia: Laura Ries.

ROA Holdings (2012). *Asian Mobile Market Forecast 2012–2015*. Tokyo: ROA Holdings.

Sam, SA (March 2015). The 2014–2019 Asia Mobile Learning Market. *Ambient Insight*.

Sharma, R and IA Mokhtar (2006). Bridging the digital divide in Asia. *International Journal of Technology Knowledge and Society*, 1(3) pp. 15–30.

Statista (2016). Number of Smartphone Users in India from 2013 to 2019. http://www.statista.com/statistics/467163/forecast-of-smartphone-users-in-india/ (last accessed April 24, 2016).

The Economist Corporate Network (2015). *Asia's Digital Disruption: How Technology is Driving Consumer Engagement in the World's Most Exciting Markets*. The Economist Intelligence Unit.

Thompson, *et al.* (2015). *No Ordinary Disruption: The Forces Reshaping Asia*. Singapore: McKinsey Global Institute.

CHAPTER 2

POLITICAL–LEGAL, ECONOMY, AND SOCIAL CULTURE AS THE MAIN DRIVERS

Today, technology is advancing citizen empowerment.
Technology is forcing governments to deal with massive
volume of data and generate responses
not in 24 hours but in 24 minutes.

Narendra Modi, Prime Minister of India

The world is rapidly changing. The revolution in digital technology is expected to cast a snowball effect, changing the order of factors at the macro level. This is happening everywhere, including in Asia. A wave of emerging Internet and mobile technology is rapidly sweeping across Asia, contributing directly or indirectly to changes in the political, legal, economic, social, and cultural aspects in the region. These aspects constitute the main drivers that affect people's lives in any country because they define the rules and norms governing the interactions between citizens.

Asia is a large market. With a population exceeding half of the total world population, Asia has tremendous business potential. Another reason for the Asian market optimism is the significant economic growth various countries have achieved over the last decade. Asia is not only vast but also hugely diverse, from the rich and aging Japan to less richer but also aging China to poorer but younger India and Indonesia, as well as emerging markets like Myanmar that are just opening up after decades of political isolation (The Economist Intelligence Unit [EIU], 2014). Marketers need to understand the diversity and dynamics of this region in order to formulate effective strategies to counter the challenges and seize the opportunities that arise.

This chapter includes an overview of the political and legal system, macro-economic conditions, and socio-cultural profile of Asia. The diversity that exists among Asian countries is portrayed as a general guide for businesses that want to grow successfully in this region. In addition, the changes in these aspects are highlighted and analyzed to assess how digital technologies contribute to changes in the region.

Asia's Political–Legal Challenges

Among the various factors driving the political dynamics in Asia, democratization is the one that has been always highlighted, especially by the Western observers. The perpetual debate over democracy exists because there is seldom any consensus on how to measure it; definitions of democracy are contested and are constantly evolving. For instance, although promotion of democracy is high on the list of priorities of American foreign policy, there is no consensus within the American government on what constitutes a democracy. As one observer put it, "the world's only superpower is rhetorically and militarily promoting a political system that remains undefined and it is staking its credibility and treasure on that pursuit" (Rodrik, 2012).

Polemics about the most ideal system of government for countries in Asia will continue in line with the political experimentation of the leaders in the region. Owing to differences in cultural backgrounds and varying standards of economic development, each country is also susceptible to creating different preferences regarding an ideal relationship between the ruling party and the people. This is evident from the many diverse political systems that exist in Asia — constitutional monarchies, absolute monarchies, one-party states, federal states, dependent territories, liberal democracies etc.

Even countries in Southeast Asia that are committed to building the ASEAN Political-Security Community (APSC) constitute a diverse set of political systems. Brunei Darussalam is a monarchy in which the Sultan has absolute power; Cambodia has undergone a transition from one-party rule to multiparty system; and Singapore has been ruled by the People's Action Party ever since it became a self-governing island colony of Britain in 1959. Similarly, Association of Southeast Asian Nations (ASEAN) member countries also have their unique political systems (Chong and Elies, 2011).

The adoption of democracy as defined by Western standards does not guarantee that Asian countries would do better politically and economically. Singapore is a case that despite being criticized by some media for a "less democratic" political system has showed a stellar economic performance and GDP per capita higher than most developed countries, not to mention low unemployment rates, stable prices, an efficient government, and a corruption-free environment. A more apt example is China. Though not practising the liberal democracy system of western countries, China has achieved excellent economic growth averaging at 7 percent over the last three years. This has led many observers to question the idea of democracy for developing countries, essentially opining that it may be undesirable in such regions where economic growth and reduction of poverty should be the top priorities (Wafawarova, 2013). Nevertheless, even as some lament the relevance of democracy in developing countries, there are others who believe in the benefit it brings in the form of decentralization, and this debate would continue to rage amid efforts to find the most ideal form of government for the developing world.

Digitalization and Political–Legal Changes

The revolution in digital technology, among other things, has undoubtedly made information more easily accessible to anyone. This also means corrupt or arbitrary governance practices can no longer thrive for long as the public is not oblivious to the functioning of governments anymore. On a fundamental level, disclosure of information enhances people's awareness of the political situation. In the next stage, information technology becomes an effective medium for opposition parties to join forces. When the masses outside the government harbor the same desire to drive a change, the status quo will be difficult to sustain.

For example, social media contributed greatly to the process of political change in Egypt that eventually toppled the president in power. Interestingly, those who took part in the revolutionary process did not just come from the military or a party with organized political machine. Anyone with access to Internet could play a role, including a young Google executive named Wael Ghonim who shared strong opinions on the subject through a Facebook page he built (Coker *et al.*, 2011). His name was eventually featured in the *Time Magazine 100*, making it to the names of the world's most influential people in 2011 (ElBaradei, 2011).

A similar trend swept Asia. The authoritarian regime that survived for 32 years in Indonesia finally collapsed in 1998. And it was not a mere coincidence that the mobile phone had just started to become a mass product being used by all classes in the country at the time. What has happened in Sri Lanka (see Box 2.1) and the Philippines hint at a pattern that is not much different. Shirky (2011), illustrating the effects of technology on the political changes in the Philippines, wrote in an article in *Foreign Affairs*:

> January 17, 2001, during the impeachment trial of Philippine President Joseph Estrada, loyalists in the Philippine Congress voted to set aside key evidence against him. Less than two hours after the decision was announced, thousands of Filipinos, angry that their corrupt president might be let off the hook, converged on Epifanio de los Santos Avenue, a major crossroads in Manila. The protest was arranged, in part, by forwarded text messages reading, "Go 2 EDSA. Wear blk." The crowd quickly swelled, and in the next few days, over a million people arrived, choking traffic in downtown Manila.
>
> The public's ability to coordinate such a massive and rapid response — close to seven million text messages were sent that week — so alarmed the country's legislators that they reversed course

Box 2.1: Sri Lanka's Political Transition and the Role of Technology

Lying off the southern tip of India, the tropical island of Sri Lanka has attracted visitors for centuries with its natural beauty. But it has been scarred by a long and bitter civil war arising out of ethnic tensions between the majority Sinhalese and the Tamil minority in the northeast. After more than 25 years of violence, the conflict ended in May 2009 when government forces seized the last area controlled by Tamil Tiger rebels. The victory granted Mahinda Rajapaksa — the country's president — more political power.

In January 2015, Sri Lanka went to the polls in a historic election. For the first time since the island became independent in 1948, an incumbent president was voted out of office. The election was initiated by Rajapaksa himself. The move was calculated to renew his mandate before a worsening economy began to eat into his electoral majority. With the opposition unable to produce a very strong candidate at that time, Rajapaksa expected to win.

But two days after announcing the election, Rajapaksa received a shock. His health minister, Maithripala Sirisena, defected and announced his own candidacy backed by the opposition. Over the course of the short campaign, Sirisena gathered a big-tent coalition of unlikely allies. And then Maithripala Sirisena surprised the world when he defeated his old boss Mahinda Rajapaksa in the country's presidential election. The nation was now set to turn its attention to a wide-ranging reform agenda.

What is interesting behind Sri Lanka's political transition is the fact that the Sirisena candidacy had been orchestrated using satellite phones to escape surveillance. Satellite communication is a method of communicating around the globe via a satellite. A satellite sent to space for the purpose of telecommunication receives and retransmits the signals sent from a satellite phone back to Earth. The ground area that receives the retransmission is called a satellite footprint.

Therefore, instead of using mobile phones, which are simple to track with modern technology, Sirisena and his coalition had used

(Continued)

Box 2.1:   (*Continued*)

satellite telephones, which are much harder to trace and intercept, especially, if the required technology is not available for the relevant authorities to use. The result was as expected: the majority of the members of the Sri Lankan Freedom Party (SLFP) did not know that Sirisena was to defect from the government along with several other prominent government ministers. He could then effectively run to contest against President Rajapaksa in the presidential election and won.

Sources: Cronin-Furman (2015), Dibbert (2016), Gunasekara and Gooneratne (2014), and Sri Lanka Country Profile (2015).

---

and allowed the evidence to be presented. Estrada's fate was sealed; by January 20, he was gone. The event marked the first time that social media had helped force out a national leader. Estrada himself blamed "the text-messaging generation" for his downfall.

The political changes occurring in Asia should be of concern to marketers looking to develop business in the region. Every process leading up to this political transformation in Asia should be monitored closely so as to take timely cognizance of the emerging threats and opportunities. A good example of a market that is opening up and garnering a lot of excitement is Myanmar. For foreign investors setting sights on the country, the progress that Myanmar has already made should serve as a point of optimism (Kotler *et al.*, 2014). If the opportunities emerging from this changing political landscape are not identified quickly enough, the competitors would likely get the first-mover advantages.

Digitalization and Asia's Economic Challenges

The economic pendulum began to swing back to the East in the second half of the 20th century as Japan developed a new industrial muscle. Political power once concentrated in the West slowly started shifting to

Asia on the back of improving economic conditions of the countries in the developing world. For several decades, the economies of the countries in this region experienced impressive growth and rapid development. This trend was dubbed by Zakaria (2008) as "the rise of the rest".

But what we have observed over the past 10 years is even more spectacular. The world's economic center of gravity has shifted at an unprecedented pace with the remarkable rise of China, India, and other emerging economies. Britain took 150 years to double output per person; industrialized China and India achieved this feat in only 12 and 16 years, respectively. This acceleration is roughly 10 times faster than the one triggered by Britain's Industrial Revolution (Thompson *et al.*, 2015).

Asia continues to be seen as the world's main growth engine in 2016 as it has been for the past several years. Since the global financial crisis, the world's average annual growth rate has been 4 percent, with developing Asia contributing 2.3 percentage points more or nearly 60 percent. For Asia as a whole, growth is projected at 6.3 percent in 2016 (Asian Development Bank, 2015). But if we look closely, there is a considerable gap in economic growth among Asian countries (Table 2.1). This gap is just one among a host of other major economic problems that plague Asia as a region.

Despite the data showing astounding economic growth, Asia is still a region facing many economic problems that are yet to be addressed. The economic challenges in Asia are those that constitute the classic issues in modern human civilization: poverty, high unemployment rates, and income inequality. In attempting to address these problems, both government and the private sectors in Asia have consistently undertaken a lot of initiatives. And digital technologies, both Internet and mobile, are crucial enablers to support the success of these initiatives.

McKinsey Global Institute (2015) research has shown that access to Internet is a powerful growth driver. A 2011 analysis of the economic impact of the Internet in 13 of the world's largest economies found that the Internet had generated 21 percent of GDP growth over the previous five years. A subsequent 2012 report on 30 "aspiring countries" (including Malaysia, Taiwan, and Vietnam) had found that Internet penetration increased by 25 percent annually over the previous five years.

In 2014, mobile technologies and services generated 4.7 percent of the GDP in the Asia Pacific, a contribution that amounted to over

Table 2.1: Asian countries' economic growth
(percent per year)

Subregion	2014	2015*	2016*
East Asia			
China	7.4	7.2	7.0
Hong Kong	2.3	2.8	2.9
South Korea	3.3	3.5	3.7
Taiwan	3.7	3.7	3.6
Japan	−0.1	0.6	1.0
South Asia			
Bangladesh	6.1	6.1	6.4
India	7.4	7.8	8.2
Pakistan	4.1	4.2	4.4
Sri Lanka	7.4	7.0	7.3
Nepal	5.4	3.4	4.4
Southeast Asia			
Indonesia	5.0	5.5	6.0
Malaysia	6.0	4.7	5.0
Philippines	6.1	6.4	6.3
Singapore	2.9	3.0	3.4
Thailand	0.7	3.6	4.1
Vietnam	6.0	6.1	6.2
Cambodia	7.0	7.0	7.2
Myanmar	8.5	8.5	8.4
Brunei	−2.3	−1.2	3.2
Laos	7.4	7.5	8.0

*Predictive data.

Sources: Asia Development Bank (2015) and International Monetary Fund (2015).

US$1 trillion of economic value across 50 countries and territories. This figure does not include additional socio-economic impacts, such as improved access to education and health services brought about by mobile applications. By 2020, the mobile's contribution is expected to grow at a faster rate than the rest of the economy, accounting for 5.9 percent of the region's GDP (GSM Association, 2015).

The link between economic performance and digitalization — particularly in Asia — is an early indication for policy makers and marketers of the importance of technology and its role in the resolution of economic problems in the region. Technology-supported collaboration between the two parties will go a long way in increasing financial inclusion, supporting rural communities to have access to information, creating new jobs, and solving other economic challenges. And when technology meets creativity, these problems can be resolved even earlier, while casting significant financial impact on the businesses involved.

Digitalization and New Social–Cultural Trends

Asia features different kinds of cultural heritages of many nationalities, societies, and ethnic groups in the region. Geographically, Asia is not a distinct continent, and culturally, there has been little unity or common history among many of the cultures and peoples of Asia. The region is commonly divided into some geographic and cultural subregions, including Central Asia, East Asia, South Asia, Southeast Asia, and West Asia.

East Asia consists of China, Japan, North Korea, and South Korea. Major characteristics of this region include shared Chinese-derived language characteristics as well as shared religions, especially Buddhism, Taoism, and Confucianism. In South Asia, four South India states and northern parts of Sri Lanka share a Dravidian culture while others are influenced by the Indo-Aryan heritage. The culture of Southeast Asian nations is no less diverse, ranging from tribal culture to sophisticated civilizations that created architectural wonders such as the Angkor of Cambodia and Borobudur of Indonesia. Furthermore, the arts and literatures of Southeast Asia are very distinctive as some have been influenced by the Islamic, Indian, Hindu, Chinese, and Buddhist literatures.

Although Asia is culturally quite diverse, we believe that there are three new subcultures that play an important role in the region. These include youth ("opposite" of seniors), women ("opposite" of men), and netizens ("opposite" of citizens) (see Fig. 2.1).

The first subculture is that of youth. This community is increasingly challenging the domination of the seniors amidst a declining population of baby boomers worldwide. Youth plays an important role in "leading the

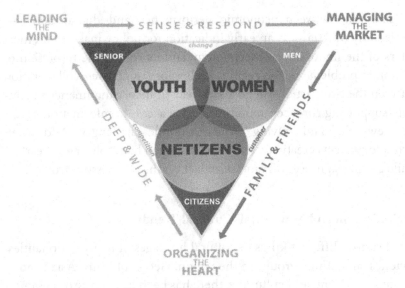

Figure 2.1:   The new subculture.

mind". And they are able to do so because they are more attuned to "sense and respond", instead of "command and control", as commonly done by the senior generation. The development of ICT indeed calls for a greater ability to sniff out the changes more quickly and respond appropriately faster. If not, then the other party will beat one to that. Another characteristic of the youth is dynamism; they quickly adapt to changes in the external environment which is getting increasingly difficult to predict and control. It is the youth who will lead the change in Asia in the future. What happened in Hong Kong in 2014 is a clear example of it. A series of sit-in street protests — known as the Umbrella Revolution — that occurred from 26 September to 15 December was mainly led by young students.

Women comprise the second subculture. The evolving social and cultural dynamics have lent greater importance to women in private as well as public spheres. In the family, a woman plays an increasingly dominant role in decision-making, especially in terms of purchase of goods and services. An EIU report on "Female Consumers in Asia 2014" shows increasing independence among women in handling finances. More than two-thirds reported having their own bank accounts (this ranged from a high of 76 percent in mainland China to a low of 47 percent in Macau), and 48 percent held their own credit cards.

Most women said they were in charge of the budgeting decisions on groceries, clothing and accessories, and children's products, and are at least co-decision-makers in most other product categories such as electronics and travel services.

While in the public space, the rising influence of women owes to the fact that they are able to lead a massive build-up of opinion through word of mouth, which comes from their natural trait of sharing information with friends and acquaintances. With the growing importance of word of mouth in decision-making of customers, women are naturally accorded more importance for their role. It is not wrong to say that women play a role in "managing the market".

The third subculture is of netizens whose role through the community in cyberspace is significantly transforming the role of citizens in the real world. Considering the high Internet and mobile penetration in Asian countries, public opinion is no longer directed by the mainstream media but influenced to a great deal by social media and active participation of netizens. Internet technology allows netizens to process information "deep and wide". In doing so, they are able to spread opinions that can move millions of people. Suffice it to say that netizens play a role in "organizing the heart".

The emergence of the third subculture needs strong attention from marketers in Asia. They should design strategies and marketing programs that can actively engage netizens in a participatory manner. The development of digital technology further eases this process of collaboration that may occur between the company and the netizen subculture.

References

Asian Development Bank (2015). *Asian Development Outlook 2015*. Manila: Asian Development Bank.

BBC (2015). Sri Lanka Country Profile. http://www.bbc.com/news/World-South-Asia-11999611 (last modified October 11, 2015; last accessed July 25, 2016).

Chong, T and S Elies (ed.) (2011). *An ASEAN Community for All: Exploring the Scope for Civil Society Engagement*. Singapore: Friedrich-Ebert-Stiftung.

Coker, M, N Malas and M Champion (February 7, 2011). Google Executive Emerges as Key Figure in Revolt. *Wall Street Journal*.

Cronin-Furman, K (January 12, 2015). Sri Lanka's Surprise Political Transition. *Washington Post*. https://www.washingtonpost.com/blogs/monkey-cage/wp/2015/01/11/sri-lankas-surprise-political-transition/ (last accessed May 2, 2016).

Dibbert, T (April 21, 2016). Sri Lanka, Lost in Transition. *Foreign Affairs.*

ElBaradei, M (2011). Wael Ghonim: Spokesman for a Revolution. http://Content.time. com./time/specials/packages/article/0,28804,2066367-2066369,00.html (last modified April 21, 2011; last accessed July 25, 2016).

GSM Association (2015). *The Mobile Economy: Asia Pacific 2015*. London: GSM Association.

Gunasekara, S and L Gooneratne (2014). Maithripala Sirisena Used Satellite Phones to Avoid Detection by Govt Intelligence While Planning Defection Moves. http:// dbsjeyaraj.com/dbsj/archives/35569 (November 30, 2014; last accessed May 2, 2016).

International Monetary Fund (2015). *Regional Economic Outlook 2015*. Washington: International Monetary Fund.

Kekic, L (2008). The Economist Intelligence Unit's Index of Democracy. http://www. economist.com/media/pdf/DEMOCRACY_INDEX_2007_v3.pdf (last accessed May 2, 2016).

Kotler, P, H Kartajaya and Hooi, DH (2014). *Think New ASEAN*. Singapore: McGraw-Hill.

Rodrik, D (2012). *The Globalization Paradox: Democracy and the Future of the World Economy*. New York: W. W. Norton.

Shirky, C (January/February 2011). The Political Power of Social Media. *Foreign Affairs.*

The Economist Intelligence Unit (2014). *On the Rise and Online: Female Consumers in Asia*. London: The Economist.

The Economist Intelligence Unit (2016). *Democracy Index 2015: Democracy in an Age of Anxiety*. London: The Economist.

Thompson *et al.* (2015). *No Ordinary Disruption: The Forces Reshaping Asia*. Singapore: McKinsey Global Institute.

Wafawarova, R (2013). Head to Head: African Democracy, http://news.bbc.co.uk/2/hi/ africa/7671283.stm (last modified October 16, 2013; last accessed May 2, 2016).

Zakaria, F (2008). *The Post-American World*. New York: W. W. Norton.

CHAPTER 3

MARKET AS THE ULTIMATE DRIVER

*People are migrating whole sets of behaviour from
the non-digital world onto mobile environments,
from booking taxis, to shopping, paying for services,
watching videos or connecting with families.*

Mohd Khairil Abdullah, CEO of Digital Services at Axiata

The market is a place where forces of supply and demand operate. This is a place where companies — as value suppliers — compete to win the minds and hearts of the customers — as value demanders. In the business world, the market acts like an estuary for the changes that occur at the macroscale. The technological revolution further drives economic, political-legal, and socio-cultural changes, all of which influence the market.

Several Asian countries have experienced a structural change in the market, inevitably resulting in greater competition. The development of technology, which has led to greater information availability, has prompted profound changes in the political system in several countries. Such an open economy means the boundaries of monopoly restrictions have diminished to a large extent. In some important industries as telecom and banking, we witness an influx of private players, both indigenous and foreign, entering the markets. The increasingly competitive business environment has forced players to continue to innovate and improve efficiency. The customer has largely benefited from the development, not least with a more varied selection of products and services.

Technology also continues to evolve. The emergence of the Internet and related technologies has made the "whole world flat", as claimed by Friedman (2005) in his book *The World Is Flat*. The barriers between countries are seemingly engulfed in the wave of change that is called globalization 3.0. In this context, Sirkin *et al.* (2008) stated that the business world will be faced with a phenomenon called "globality", in which a company will compete with everyone, from everywhere, for everything. He wrote, "You are looking at the future, when US, European, Japanese companies, and companies from other matured markets will be competing not only with each other, but with Chinese companies and with highly competitive companies from every corner of the world: Argentina, Brazil, Chile, Egypt, Hungary, India, Indonesia, Malaysia, Mexico, Poland, Russia, Thailand, Turkey, Vietnam and places you'd never expected".

But the only constant thing is change. The ongoing technological revolution continues to trigger new market dynamics, especially in Asia. This chapter discusses how the digital revolution has changed the face of the market forces. Competition is becoming increasingly dynamic, while customers are becoming increasingly connected. Consequently, it is the market that essentially calls for a changing paradigm of marketing itself.

When Technology Disrupts Markets

Christensen (1997), a professor from Harvard Business School, in his book *"The Innovator's Dilemma: When Technologies Cause Great Firms to Fail"* introduced the term disruptive technology, which was earlier replaced by him with another moniker — disruptive innovation. Still, the origin of the term disruptive technology is older, first used by Schumpeter (1942). In his book the author described disruptive technology as a technological

Table 3.1: Examples of disruptive technology.

Disruptive Technology	Displaced or Marginalized Product
Digital photography	Analog camera
Mobile phone	Mail, telegram, traditional telephone
Laptops, tablets	Desktops
Music downloads	Compact discs
e-Books	Paper books
Internet	Traditional publishing, newspaper, printed magazine

innovation, product, or service that uses a "disruptive strategy" rather than an "evolutionary" or "sustaining" strategy to overturn the existing dominant technologies or status quo products in a market. Examples of disruptive technology can be seen in Table 3.1.

Faced with these kinds of accelerating disruptions, businesses must act quickly to identify and adjust to these key technological changes, lest they face the risk of being ousted from the market by competition. The almost a century-old postal services industry in Asia may have felt the looming threat from mobile technology. But diversification strategies undertaken over the last few years have led to surprisingly encouraging results. The Global Postal Industry Report 2013 indicates that the total revenue in Asia Pacific grew 10.8 percent during 2011–2012. This positive trend was largely a result of the development of non-mail revenue that realized average growth of 56.4 percent. Thus, during the period when mail volumes fell 3.1 percent, postal services companies were still able to compensate from other revenue sources, especially parcels that increased in volume up to 4 percent (International Post Corporation, 2013).

Although the development of digital and mobile technologies has eroded the popularity of conventional mail services that were once a mainstay of postal services companies, emerging opportunities in line with the technological advancement can be exploited. For instance, the rapid growth in e-commerce transactions in Asia has significantly increased shipment volumes. This bodes well for the parcel business managed by postal service companies. Another diversification is in the form of financial service offerings. The greater connectivity enabled in rural areas through postal services is especially useful as it can be utilised as channels for financial transactions, including payments, in collaboration with the banking sector.

Another way to build a sustainable organization in the connectivity era is through wider adoption of technology. Sticking to older ways of doing business would more likely turn customers away. Today, all players from various industries are expanding the use of digital and mobile technology in doing business, even as the magnitude of this adoption may vary widely: some are simply using social media to interact with customers while others are offering mobile services or apps for additional value or building their own online platforms.

Most major banks in Asia now offer banking services via electronic (e-banking) and mobile (m-banking) channels. Retailers are actively launching online platforms as an alternative means to do business with their customers. Players in the automotive and transportation sectors are offering online and/or mobile apps to provide a digital experience to their customers. Even the public sector is increasingly abuzz with digital-based e-governance services to citizens.

Needless to say that technology poses a massive challenge for most businesses in the form of market disruptions. But under the threat of challenges also lie opportunities for industry players that dare to look at the situation creatively.

The New Face of Competition

Disruptions caused by technology do not only eliminate the boundaries of competition between countries, as mentioned by Harold Sirkin. Digitalization has also rendered the boundaries between industries irrelevant. Competition today can emerge from any industry or sector.

The hospitality industry is another example. Hotels are not only competing with other hotels, but also facing threats from entities such as Airbnb, which simply aggregates lists of lodgings that can be rented in a city. The website, which gives a virtually unlimited range of options to travelers based on price, quality of accommodation, and location, has over 1,500,000 listings in 190 countries and 34,000 cities. Founded in August 2008 and headquartered in San Francisco, California, the company is privately owned and operated (Brennan, 2011).

Conventional transport companies are seemingly panicky in the face of a very real threat. The emergence of online transportation networks such as Uber, as other Asian counterparts — Malaysia's Grab, China's Didi Chuxing (formerly Didi Kuaidi), and Indonesia's GoJek — has triggered a string of negative reactions from conventional transport organizers, especially the taxi operators. The governments concerned are also under pressure. They are facing a unique dilemma since these emerging online transport networks are growing popular among customers, though the question remains whether these should be allowed to thrive at the expense of conventional transport companies, who feel disadvantaged by the convenience and affordability of these alternative transport players and that they may not be subject to the same regulations.

Similar disruptions have long been evident in other industries. Craigslist, a classified advertisment website, puts local buyers and sellers together, making the role of newspapers obsolete. Amazon.com brought disruptions to publishers and bookstores. Google and Baidu have made libraries less relevant. The list goes on. In fact, even conservative sectors such as banking are no longer immune from disruptions. Now banks are dealing with new competitors, from telco operators and fintech companies (Box 3.1).

However, rather than seeing these new players as threats, some banks have found ways to team up with them profitably. The traditional limitations faced by the new players — both legal and technical — have in turn opened up collaboration opportunities with conventional financial institutions. Examples include providing funding for alternative business finance providers or referral arrangements whereby small business customers who do not qualify for a loan can be referred to the bank's associated peer-to-peer (P2P) lenders. The trend is already catching up in the United Kingdom, with encouragement from the government (EY, 2015). Another example is the collaboration between Telenor Pakistan and Tameer Microfinance Bank in offering mobile money for the unbanked sector in Pakistan (see Box 3.2).

In some Asian countries, the regulator acts as the facilitator of collaboration by requiring telecom firms and banks to work together, with banks holding licenses to transaction platforms. In India, the country's largest private sector bank ICICI has teamed up with Vodafone India to

Box 3.1:   The New Competitors in Asia's Banking Industry

Mobile Money

Mobile money, also referred to as mobile payment and mobile wallet, generally refers to payment services operated under financial regulations and performed from or via a mobile device. Instead of paying with cash, cheque, or credit cards, a consumer can use a mobile phone to pay for a wide range of services and products.

According to 2012 data from the World Bank, the countries with the lowest percentage of formal bank accounts in Asia are as follows: Cambodia ranks first with 3.6 percent, Pakistan second with 10 percent, and Indonesia third with 19.5 percent. Vietnam and the Philippines have 21 and 26 percent, respectively. Within South Asia, 33 percent of individuals aged 15 and above were estimated to have an account at a formal financial institution in 2012, the World Bank estimates. That leaves 67 percent of the population unbanked, making the region one of the world's top potential growth areas for the mobile commerce industry.

Sandy Shen, research director at Gartner, said: "For the unbanked sector, banks are not in a leadership role. This area is being driven primarily by telecoms that have wider coverage in terms of distribution network and better customer relationships with people using their mobile services".

Peer-to-Peer Lending

P2P lending is the practice of lending money to individuals or businesses through online services that match lenders directly with borrowers. Since the P2P lending companies offering these services operate entirely online, they can run with lower overheads and provide the service more cheaply than traditional financial institutions. As a result, lenders often earn higher returns compared to savings and investment products offered by banks, while borrowers can borrow money at lower interest rates, even after the P2P lending company has taken a fee for providing the match-making platform and credit checking the borrower.

(Continued)

Box 3.1: (*Continued*)

South Korea and China had the biggest market share in P2P and equity crowd-funding markets in 2013, according to the International Organization of Securities Commissions. Another report from research and advisory firm Celent stated that the P2P lending market in China reached US$940 million in 2012 and was expected to grow in the years ahead.

Online-Only Bank

Chinese technopreneurs became the pioneer of online-only banks in Asia. China's first online-only bank is a joint venture led by gaming and social network group Tencent Holdings. WeBank is one of five institutions to be granted a licence under a government pilot scheme to establish privately operated banks, as part of moves to open up China's banking sector. Banks licensed under the scheme are expected to focus on expanding access to finance for small and micro-businesses, and individuals.

Tencent operates the highly popular mobile messaging and social media app WeChat — one of China's largest social networks, with 549 million monthly active users (as at first quarter 2015). WeChat already offers customers financial services in the form of a bank card linked to their WeChat account and Tencent's wealth management platform, offering customers the opportunity to invest in third-party investment products via their smartphones.

WeBank faces tough competition from online shopping firm Alibaba Group Holding Ltd. and its financial-services affiliate, Ant Financial Services Group. Ant Financial, which operates an online bank called MYbank, had begun its second round of fundraising in 2016. The year before, Ant Financial raised more than 12 billion yuan ($1.82 billion) in its first round of fundraising from outside investors.

The extent to which online players will be able to penetrate and disrupt China's banking sector still depends to some extent on China's regulators. WeBank and MYbank may not be competitive threats to China's bank incumbents for now, but future developments may see the new players start to change China's banking landscape.

Sources: EY (2015), "*Mobile Payment*", Wikipedia; "*Peer-to-Peer Lending*", Wikipedia; Chandran (2014); Li (2014); Carew and Osawa (2016).

Box 3.2:   Easypaisa: Pakistan's Mobile Money

With the goal of financial inclusion for the millions of unbanked people residing in the country, Telenor Pakistan in collaboration with Tameer Microfinance Bank launched Easypaisa in 2009 with the approval of the State Bank of Pakistan. By the end of 2012, it had processed more than 100 million transactions with a throughput of more than US$1.4 billion.

With Easypaisa, a large section of unbanked customers in Pakistan discovered a unique way of money transfer in a safe and convenient manner. Before Easypaisa, customers were to make long commutes, deal with a lot of paperwork, queue up for hours, and could only do financial transactions during limited work hours. With Easypaisa, however, the industry went through a revolution as customers could make financial transactions at local retailers, and that too in a safe and convenient environment. It took only seconds to complete transactions and confirmations received through SMS.

Easypaisa allowed customers to choose from either over-the-counter (OTC) transactions — for which they were to visit the nearest outlet — or simply using their mobile phones by logging into their accounts. Various services are available, including bill payments, sending/receiving money, purchasing airtime, salary disbursements, giving donations, disbursing social cash transfers, insurance, and savings, facilitating a range of financial needs of the customers. The service expansion by Telenor Pakistan continued with additional features such as interbank fund transfers, online payments, handset lending, and health insurance, marking an unparalleled range of services offered to customers.

Easypaisa is not limited to Telenor subscribers only. Anyone with or without a mobile phone can avail many of the services Easypaisa offers. With an increasing footprint of over 70,000 merchants all over the country, Easypaisa also provides numerous employment opportunities for the masses. Since then, Easypaisa has embarked on an extraordinary journey of innovation to achieve financial empowerment for the masses on an individual level.

(Continued)

Box 3.2:   (*Continued*)

Three important mobile money innovations emerge from the Easypaisa story. First, Easypaisa was launched from a unique corporate structure. Telenor Pakistan, an MNO acquired a 51 percent ownership stake in Tameer Bank, a microfinance bank, and then established Easypaisa as a common organization across the two companies. Second, Telenor Pakistan and Tameer Bank introduced OTC mobile money services — an entirely new model that did not require registration for an electronic wallet. And third, Easypaisa achieved rapid national expansion by relying exclusively on its existing Global System for Mobile Communication (GSM) distribution structure.

Sources: "*About Easypaisa*", www.easypaisa.com.pk; Chandran (2014); McCarty and Bjaerum (2014).

---

bring Africa's famed mobile payment service m-pesa to customers. While Indonesia's central bank has invited commercial banks and mobile network operators (MNOs) to introduce hybrid products in certain rural areas (Chandran, 2014).

Market disruptions will inarguably continue to happen in the future, in line with the continuing development of digitalization. This is what the business players should prepare for — to be able to adapt to newer ways to break through. The government, as a regulator, must also act intelligently so as to ensure that there are no policies that could possibly hamper technological innovations in the business world.

The New Customer Path

Technology is not only revolutionizing the way industry players conduct business, but also changing the pattern of customers' decision-making process. In the pre-connectivity era, a customer's journey to buying a product or service was relatively simpler and shorter, which could be described with the 4A process: Aware, Attitude, Act, and Act Again. This funnel-shaped process demarcates the various points in the customer journey where they become aware of a brand, develop an attitude toward it — of like or dislike — based on which they decide to purchase it and also consider if it's worth a repeat purchase. The shape of a funnel represents a decline in the number of customers as they move from one stage to another — people who like the brand would naturally be aware of it; those who buy like it; and those who buy again would have already purchased it once.

Also, the 4A customer path is personal. The customers' decision-making as they move along the path can only be influenced from the companies' touch points, for example, TV advertisements at "Aware" phase, salespersons at "Act" phase, or service centers at "Act Again" phase. The customer journey is seemingly well within companies' control.

Today, in the era of connectivity, the customer journey is no longer a straightforward funnel-like process, and it is not personal. The changes brought about by the technology-driven connected world call for redefining the customer path. The customer path has now transformed into a 5A process: Aware, Appeal, Ask, Act, and Advocate. There are three essential shifts in the new customer path (see Fig. 3.1).

1. In the pre-connectivity era, a customer individually determined his or her own attitude toward a brand. In a connected world, the initial appeal of a brand is influenced by the "community" surrounding the customer, which ultimately shapes the final attitude. Those around the customer, both online and offline — his friends, acquaintances, peers, coworkers, and even interactions on social media, forums, and blogs —, go a long way in influencing their purchase decisions. The observation becomes even more pertinent considering the fact that Asians are characteristically quite communal in nature.

2. In the pre-connectivity era, customer loyalty would typically be characterized by retention and repurchase. In a connected world, loyalty is ultimately defined as willingness to advocate a brand. Even as advocacy puts the customer at a greater risk than simply making repeat purchases of a product or service. When a customer recommends a brand to others, there is a "social risk" he or she potentially faces, which is the possibility of the recipient being disappointed with the quality of the recommended brand. If that happens, it could negatively influence their social relations. Hence, the willingness to give recommendations of a brand indicates that the customer has really high confidence in the brand.

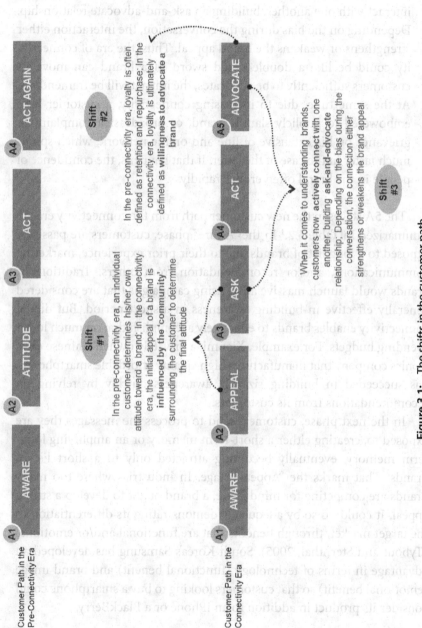

Figure 3.1: The shifts in the customer path.

3. When it comes to understanding brands, customers now actively interact with one another, building an ask-and-advocate relationship. Depending on the bias during the conversation, the interaction either strengthens or weakens the brand appeal. Thus, the era of connectivity could be like a double-edged sword. If a brand can move its customers sufficiently to be advocates, the impact will be tremendous. At the same time, due to increasing connectivity, a customer feels empowered to publicly slam a brand, or broadcast a complaint or grievance on his extensive offline and online network, which spirals much faster in the case of the latter. If that happens, the confidence of people in the brand often erodes rapidly.

The 5A stages in the new customer path from the connectivity era are summarized in Table 3.2.[1] In the "Aware" phase, customers are passively exposed to a long list of brands due to their prior experience, marketing communications, and/or recommendation from others. Traditionally, brands would launch massive advertising campaigns that are considered generally effective in building awareness in a short period. But digital connectivity enables brands to effectively accomplish that on much lower spending budgets. For example, Xiaomi, a privately owned Chinese electronics company that manufactures high-quality affordable smartphones, has succeeded in building sizeable awareness quickly by relying on recommendations from its customers.

In the next phase, customers tend to process the messages they are exposed to, creating either a short-term memory or an amplifying long-term memory, eventually becoming attracted only to a short list of brands. That marks the "Appeal" stage. In industries where too many brands are competing for mind share, a brand ought to develop a strong appeal. It could do so by adequately demonstrating its differentiation to the target market, through benefits that are functional and/or emotional (Tybout and Sternthal, 2005). South Korea's Samsung has developed an advantage in terms of technology (functional benefit) and brand image (emotional benefit) so that customers looking to buy a smartphone could consider its product in addition to an iPhone or a BlackBerry.

---

[1] The shift of customer path in the connectivity era will be part of the topics in our forthcoming book *Marketing 4.0* (Kotler *et al.*, 2017).

Table 3.2: Customer path in the connectivity era.

	Customer Path				
	Aware	**Appeal**	**Ask**	**Act**	**Advocate**
Customer Behavior	Customers are passively exposed to a long-list of brands from past experience, marketing communications, and/or advocacy of others	Customers process the messages they are exposed to — creating short-term memory or amplifying long-term memory — and become attracted only to a short list of brands	Prompted by their curiosity, customers actively search for more information from friends and family, from the media, and/or directly from the brands	Reinforced by more information, customers decide to buy a particular brand and interact deeper through purchase, usage, and/or service processes	Over time, customers may develop a sense of strong loyalty to the brand, which is reflected in retention, repurchase, and ultimately advocacy to others
Possible Touch Points	• Learn about a brand from others • Inadvertently exposed to brand advertising • Recall past experience	• Become attracted to brands • Create a consideration set of brands	• Call friends for advice • Search product review online • Contact call center • Compare prices • Try out product at stores	• Buy in-store or online • Use the product for the first time • Complaint for problems • Get service	• Keep using the brand • Repurchase the brand • Recommend the brand to others

Eventually, prompted by their curiosity, customers actively search for more information on the brands they are attracted to from their friends and family, from the media, and/or directly from the companies. This represents the "Ask" stage. At this stage, the customer path changes from individual to social. Customer decisions are heavily influenced by the takeaway from conservations with others. This acts more like a confirmation on the brand appeal developed earlier by the customer, which helps progress on to the next stage. The emergence of online platforms that facilitate customers to post independent reviews on products and services is a trend businesses must take a close note of. In the hospitality industry, TripAdvisor serves as an example for such an online platform where customers can ask questions and provide comments on various travel-related service providers.

Reinforced by more information, customers decide to "Act". They buy a particular brand and interact deeper with a brand through purchase, usage, and/or service processes. With the development of technology, now a purchase can be made online or through mobile and doesn't necessarily need a face-to-face interaction. According to a survey conducted by GlobalWebIndex in 2014, the population of Asia Pacific that made online purchases using personal computers had reached 51 percent, while purchases on mobile was at 15 percent (IAB Singapore and We Are Social, 2015). This number is expected to increase with improving digital literacy in Asia.

Over time, customers may develop a strong sense of loyalty toward a brand, which is initially reflected from retention, repurchase, and ultimately recommendation to others. This is the "Advocate" stage. In the connectivity era, advocacy is a major attribute of the customer journey that companies should leverage, since positive advocacy and recommendations from personal acqaintances or opinions posted online are emerging to be the most trusted form of information. According to the Nielsen Global Online Survey (2015), the most credible advertising comes straight from the people we know and trust. More than 8 in 10 global respondents (83 percent) said they completely or somewhat trust recommendations from friends and family. But this placement of trust is not confined to those in the inner circle. In fact, two-thirds (66 percent) said they trust consumer opinions posted online — the third most-trusted format.

Advocacy and the WOW Factor

With the new customer path, customer demands in the market have changed as well. Customers are now beginning to shield themselves from over-exposure to brands. They consult with their friends and family members or other close confidants when selecting a brand. They want to make more informed decisions so as to avoid any regrets later.

We could therefore say that more often than not purchasing decisions are turning more social in nature. This calls for the presence of a WOW factor, as anything less may not suffice in generating advocacy — all marketers should strive for that expression from their customers. WOW is an expression of real, sincere praise; it appears when customers are so pleasantly surprised by a brand that they are almost blown away, so much so that they would feel compelled to talk about it. WOW creates an element of surprise, especially when something comes unexpectedly. That is how marketers can beat customer expectations. WOW also signifies a personal expression. Not everyone may feel equally awed by a product or service — it comes when a brand is able to touch a customer personally. And finally, WOW is contagious. It is likely that a WOW story from a customer would be able to trigger similar emotions in others, leading to advocacy.

WOW, in essence, represents the ultimate expression of customer satisfaction. At the other end of the spectrum is "Boo", which is basically an expression of an unhappy customer — who boos a brand or customer to express contempt or grievance, and which most likely triggers negative advocacy. The next expression is that of "Argh", which still comes from an unhappy customer but represents more of a frustration and may not essentially result in a negative review. When a customer feels just satisfied with a brand, the expression will be of an "OK", which describes a neutral attitude. AHA is the next level of expression, characterized by a happy customer who seems impressed with a brand. However, the ultimate expression that marketers should strive to earn from customers is that of WOW (Fig. 3.2).

Creating "WOW!" requires a new, redefined marketing approach. A brand focusing on product and service features will likely get an "OK" approval from customers. But to get to "AHA", the brand must deliver appealing customer experience on top of the product and service features. To get to the ultimate "WOW!", a brand must engage with the

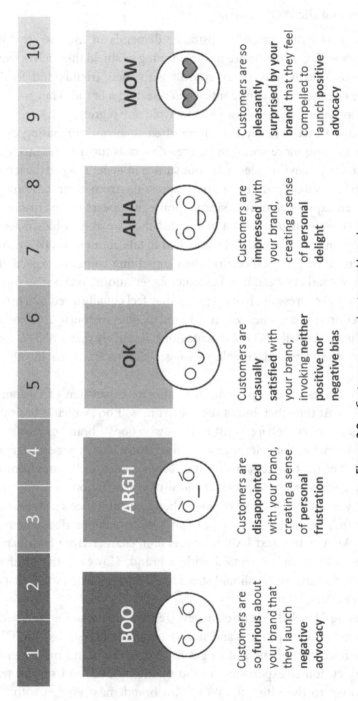

Figure 3.2: Customer expression toward brand.

Table 3.3: Competitiveness level of brands.

Competitiveness Level	Competition Practice	Possible Company Actions	Key Customer Expression
Enjoyment	Developing products and services that meet the needs and wants of customers	• Build superior product and service quality • Communicate unique product and service features	"OK"
Experience	Delivering customer experience on top of products and services that creates positive perceptions beyond expectations	• Improve customer interaction with service blueprint • Design differentiated in-store and digital experience	"AHA"
Engagement	Designing life-transforming personalization on top of customer experience that addresses individual customer's anxieties and desires	• Offer custom product recommendation • Customize customer experience to each individual customer	"WOW"

customer personally. The brand must provide a life-transforming personalization on top of customer experience that addresses the individual customer's anxieties and desires (Table 3.3). In a competitive market, a company will have to aim for "WOW!" and nothing less.

New Market, New Marketing

In view of the greater competition and changes in customer behavior, the market in Asia too has undergone significant transformations. Competition can emerge from anywhere and in any form as customers get exposed to a much bigger pool of information from everywhere. The old rules of the market have changed. And thus the traditional marketing paradigm — as we call it legacy marketing —, which used to be vertical and company centric, must also change. In the midst of such turbulent and chaotic market dynamics, the company needs to revisit and revise its marketing policies and tools. If it fails to do so, the new environment will punish it, perhaps to the point of failure (Kotler and Casoline, 2009).

The approaches in the new paradigm are known as New Wave Marketing. This comprises new strategies and marketing tactics to deliver optimal value to the consumer in the era of digital connectivity. In applying New Wave Marketing, we must revise all conventional paradigms of legacy marketing. In practice, the principles of legacy marketing may still be applied within certain limits, but at the same time, companies need to start redefining their marketing strategies and tactics to become more horizontal in the New Wave era.

In fact, the principles of legacy marketing are still effective in influencing customer behavior to a certain extent, especially the early phases (Aware and Appeal). Mechanical segmentations, targeting, positioning, and conventional communication can still be used to build initial target market awareness. But as the customer path progresses, companies need to add touches of New Wave Marketing in order to create a "WOW", effect which ultimately leads the customers on to the "Advocate" stage, and not just stop at the "Act" stage. It requires a communitization strategy or a New Wave Marketing mix that is more participatory in nature through greater and more in-depth involvement of customers (Fig. 3.3).

In the following chapters, we elaborate more on the changes in the perspective of strategy, tactics, and value of marketing in this era of connectivity.

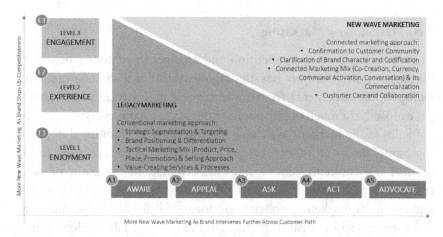

Figure 3.3: The interchanging role of legacy and New Wave Marketing.

References

Brennan, M (September 16, 2011). The Most Amazing and Absurd Places for Rent. *Forbes.*

Carew. R and J Osawa (January 27, 2016). China's Tencent-Backed WeBank Raising Funds at $5.5 Billion Valuation. *Wall Street Journal.* http://www.wsj.com/articles/chinas-tencent-backed-webank-raising-funds-at-5-5-billion-valuation-1453892057 (last accessed April 28, 2016).

Chandran, N (April 16, 2014). How Mobile Money Is Changing Asia. *CNBC.* http://www.cnbc.com/2014/04/16/how-mobile-money-is-changing-asia.html (last accessed April 28, 2016).

Christensen, C (1997). *The Innovator's Dilemma: When New Technologies Cause Great Firms to Fail.* Cambridge: Harvard Business School Press.

Easypaisa (2016). About Easypaisa. https://www.easypaisa.com.pk/about-easypaisa-1, (last accessed July 25, 2016).

EY (2015). *Banking in Asia Pacific: Size Matters and Digital Drives Competition.* Asia Pacific: EYGM Limited.

Friedman, TL (2005). *The World Is Flat.* New York: Farrar, Straus and Giroux.

IAB Singapore & We Are Social (March 10, 2015). *Digital, Social and Mobile in APAC 2015.*

International Post Corporation (2013). IPC Global Portal Industry Report 2013. Brussels: IPC Marketing Department.

Kotler, P and JA Casoline (2009). *Chaotics: The Business of Managing and Marketing in the Age of Turbulence.* New York: AMACOM.

Li, K (March 17, 2014). Hong Kong's First P2P Online Lender to Expand in Asia. *South China Morning Post.* http://www.scmp.com/business/banking-finance/article/1450259/hong-kongs-first-p2p-online-lender-expand-asia (last accessed April 28, 2016).

McCarty, MY and R Bjaerum (2014). *Easypaisa: Mobile Money Innovation in Pakistan.* London: GSMA.

Nielsen (2015). *Global Trust in Advertising.* http://www.nielsen.com/us/en/insights/reports/2015/global-trust-in-advertising-2015.html (last accessed April 27, 2016).

Schumpeter, J (1942). *Capitalism, Socialism and Democracy.* New York: Harper & Row (Reprod. 1950).

Sirkin, HL, JW Hemerling, and AK Bhattacharya (2008). *Globality: Competing with Everyone from Everywhere for Everything.* New York: Business Plus.

Tybout, AM and B Sternthal (2005). *Brand Positioning Kellogg on Branding.* New Jersey: John Wiley.

Wikipedia (2016). Mobile Payment. https://en.wikipedia.org/wiki/Mobile-payment (last accessed July 25, 2016).

Wikipedia (2016). Peer-to-Peer Lending. https://en.wikipedia.org/wiki/Peer-to-peerlending (last accessed July 25, 2016).

Preface

Summary

Chapter 1. Technology as the Primary Driver

- Technology is the primary driver of change because it in turn triggers major changes in other areas, as evident from the Industrial Revolution. Currently, digital technology is acting as the driving force behind major changes in Asia, which is witnessing increasing mobile penetration, currently standing at 93 percent and new user Internet penetration at 40.4 percent.

- The development of digital technology in Asia needs to be supported by a robust digital ecosystem, consisting of infrastructure and support services, network operators, handset manufacturers, distributors and retailers, and content applications and other services.

- The revolution in digital technology creates paradoxes that must be managed smartly by marketers. Paradoxes exist between (i) machine-to-machine versus human-to-human relationships, (ii) substance versus style, and (iii) offline versus online interactions.

Chapter 2. Political-Legal, Economy, and Social Culture as the Main Drivers

- Changes in the political, legal, economic, social, and cultural environments are the main drivers impacting people's lives in a country because they form the basis of the rules and norms that govern interactions between citizens.

- The digital revolution in Asia further casts an impact on other macro factors. Politically, digital technology-enabled governance systems encourage a more open and participatory environment, while economically, digital technology can support economic growth and help ease economic problems.

- The digital revolution has also triggered the emergence of three new subcultures in the world and Asia, namely youth, women, and netizens. In the future, these three are predicted to play greater roles in various fields, including business and marketing.

Chapter 3. Market as the Ultimate Driver

- Digital technology could create market disruptions through innovations that replace the existing dominant technology and products in the market.

- Digital technology could also lead to the emergence of new competitors that traverse the boundaries of traditional industries. For example, banks in Asia are closely monitoring various digital phenomena in the financial services industry, including emergence of online-only banks, mobile money, and peer-to-peer lending.

- Digital technology has also changed the customer path, from the traditional four stages (4A — Aware, Attitude, Act, and Act again) into five stages (5A — Aware, Appeal, Ask, Act, and Advocate).

- These evolving dynamics of competition and customer behavior make it imperative for marketers to adopt a more horizontal approach to marketing, what we term as the New Wave Marketing.

Part I

MARKETING IS TRANSFORMING?
Competitive Landscape: The Dynamic Arena

Over the past several decades, marketing has transformed through three stages that we call Marketing 1.0, 2.0, and 3.0. Long ago, during the industrial age — when the core technology was industrial machinery — marketing was about selling the factory's output of products to all who would buy them. The products were fairly basic and were designed to serve a mass market. This was Marketing 1.0 or the product-centric era.

Marketing 2.0 evolved as a result of today's information age — with information technology at the core of digital revolution. Consumers are now well-informed and can easily compare several similar product offerings. They can choose from a wide range of functional characteristics and alternatives. Today's marketers try to touch the consumer's mind and heart. Unfortunately, the consumer-centric approach implicitly assumes the view that consumers are passive targets of marketing campaigns. This forms the basis of Marketing 2.0 or the customer-centric era.

Now, we are witnessing the rise of Marketing 3.0 or the human-centric era. Instead of treating people simply as consumers, marketers are beginning to approach them as whole human beings with minds, hearts, and spirits. Increasingly, consumers are not only more aware about the many social and environmental concerns but also looking for solutions to their anxieties about making the globalized world a better place. They seek not only functional and emotional fulfillment but also human spirit fulfillment in the products and services they choose. Table A summarizes a comprehensive comparison of Marketings 1.0, 2.0, and 3.0.

Technology continues to play an important role but at the same time customers are becoming more human. Machine-to-machine (M2M) marketing tools are becoming more powerful if a company can utilize them to deliver human-to-human (H2H) interactions. In this transition and adaptation period in the digital economy, a new marketing approach

Table A: Comparison of Marketings 1.0, 2.0, and 3.0.

	Marketing 1.0: Product-Centric Marketing	Marketing 2.0: Customer-Centric Marketing	Marketing 3.0: Human-Centric Marketing
Objective	Sell products	Satisfy and retain the consumers	Make the world a better place
Enabling forces	Industrial revolution	Information technology	New Wave technology
How companies see the market	Mass buyers with physical needs	Smarter consumer with mind and heart	Whole human with mind, heart, and spirit
Key marketing concept	Product development	Differentiation	Values
Company marketing guidelines	Product specification	Corporate and product positioning	Corporate mission, vision, and values
Value propositions	Functional	Functional and emotional	Functional, emotional, and spiritual
Interactions with consumers	One-to-many transaction	One-to-one relationship	Many-to-many collaboration

Source: Kotler *et al.* (2010).

is required to guide marketers in anticipating and leveraging on the disruptive technologies while maintaining the human-centric approach of Marketing 3.0. We call this approach Marketing 4.0.

This marketing transformation — from products to customers to the human spirit — is also reflected in the different ways marketers are approaching, mapping, and analyzing the business landscape. We use three terms to illustrate the shift: (i) Insight (focus on current competitive landscape), (ii) Foresight (focus on future competitive landscape), and (iii) Full sight (focus on both current and future competitive landscapes and how all the factors are connected with each other) (see Fig. A).

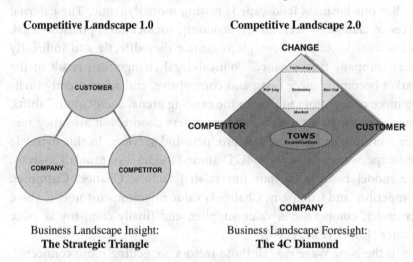

Business Landscape Insight: **The Strategic Triangle**

Business Landscape Foresight: **The 4C Diamond**

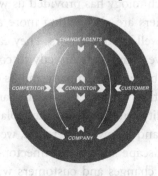

Business Landscape Full Sight: **The 5C Model**

Figure A: The dynamic arena.

Sources: Adapted from Ohmae (1982); Kotler *et al.* (2003); Kartajaya and Darwin (2010).

In the publication, *The Mind of the Strategist*, Ohmae (1982) introduced the three Cs of strategy (The Strategic Triangle). It is a business model that offers business landscape insights on the factors needed for success. It points out that a marketer should focus on three key factors for success. In the construction of a business strategy, three main players must be taken into account: Company, Customer, and Competitors (3Cs). In terms of these three key players, strategy is defined as the way in which a corporation endeavors to differentiate itself positively from its competitors, using its relative corporate strengths to better satisfy customer needs.

But our business landscape is getting more dynamic. The external forces of change — technology, economy, socioculture, political–legal, and market — cannot be neglected since they directly and indirectly affect company performance. Political–legal changes can result in the market becoming more open and competitive, and subsequently inviting more competitors to play in the existing arena. Sociocultural shifts, however, will not only alter how customers choose, but also they way they consume and dispose our products and services. In this dynamic landscape, we need to use the 4C Diamond model as our tool of analysis. The model consists of four interrelated factors: Change, Customer, Competitor, and Company. Change is value migrator, customer is value demander, competitor is value supplier, and finally company is value decider (Kotler *et al.*, 2003).

In the New Wave era, all those factors are getting more connected. Changes in the external environment are easily tracked and monitored by all business players. Technology has provided us with so many practical tools to do so. Customers are also getting more access to information about our company as well as competitors. They can send requests, post questions, and even give complaints directly to companies without any physical and monetary barrier. A company and its competitors will need to compete to discover their customers' anxieties and desires faster. Lack of agility and adaptability will divide business players into two general categories: first-mover and follower. Therefore, we need to put a fifth C to our competitive landscape analysis: Connector. Those who can connect better to external changes and customers will gain a competitive advantage against competitors. In a highly dynamic arena, connectivity will be the new winning formula (Kartajaya and Darwin, 2010).

More than 30 years ago, Kenichi Ohmae stated that a company can choose its strategy among three generic alternatives: corporate-based, customer-based, or competitor-based strategy. According to the previous explanation, we claim that there are three approaches in marketing: product centric, customer centric, and human centric. Despite the trend toward Marketing 3.0, some business players continue to adopt product- and customer-centric perspectives. That is something normal. But, to win the new digital consumers, the old perspective should be equipped with new technology. Chapters 4–6 discuss how different marketing perspectives can be applied successfully in the New Wave era.

References

Kartajaya, H and W Darwin (2010). *Connect: Surfing New Wave Marketing*. Jakarta: Gramedia Pustaka Utama.

Kotler, P, H Kartajaya and I Setiawan (2010). *Marketing 3.0: From Products to Customers to the Human Spirit*. New Jersey: John Wiley.

Kotler, *et al*. (2003). *Rethinking Marketing: Sustainable Market-ing Enterprise in Asia*. Singapore: Prentice Hall.

Ohmae, K (1982). *The Mind of the Strategist: The Art of Japanese Business*. New York: McGraw-Hill.

CHAPTER 4

PRODUCT-CENTRIC PERSPECTIVE: CONNECTIVITY IN PRODUCT DEVELOPMENT

Information technology is revolutionizing products.
Smart, connected products have unleashed a new
era of competition.

Michael Porter and James Heppelmann

Generally, in the early post–World War II years, a mass-marketing and "pure" product-centric strategy prevailed. Henry Ford was famous for his vision of the Model T as a standard product (offered in "any colour you want so long as it's black") and affordable to the broadest market. General Motors, under Alfred Sloan, offered "a car for every purse and purpose" (from Chevrolet to Cadillac) (Quelch and Jocz, 2008). Almost in the same era, Japanese manufacturers started building their industrial empires. Their strategy was based on a mass-market approach incorporating mass production, high volumes, and modest unit profit margins.

Only a limited number of manufacturers emerged from and flourished in Asia, resulting in a not-so-severe competition in the region — certainly not as tight as now. It was also because many countries in Asia had just implemented protectionist economic policies. Businesses in several countries were still monopolized by government- or state-owned companies (such as the Ministry of Transportation and Communications in Taiwan, Pakistan Telecommunication Company Limited in Pakistan, and TELKOM in Indonesia) while regulations served to limit the role of the private sector in some specific industries. Not only the multinational companies, but also the local private companies did not have access to the free space and society as they have now. As a result, customers never really had many options to meet their needs.

In that era, businesses in the world — including Asia — were guided by the product concept suggesting that consumers favored those products that offered the best quality, performance, or innovative features. Managers in these organizations focused on making superior products and improving them over time, assuming that buyers could appreciate quality and performance. Product-centric companies often designed their products with little or no input from potential customers, trusting their engineers to design exceptional products. A General Motors executive once said: "How can the public know what kind of car they want until they see what is available?" (Kotler, 2001).

Centuries have since passed yet business strategy has continued to be driven by the ghost of the Industrial Revolution, long after the factories that used to be the primary sources of competitive advantage have been shuttered and off-shored. Companies are still organized around their products and production management, success is measured in terms of units moved, and organizational hopes are pinned on product pipelines. Production-related activities are honed to maximize throughput and managers who worship efficiency are promoted. Businesses know what it takes to make and move stuff. The problem is, so does everybody else (Dawar, 2013).

This "overconfidence" in a product-centric strategy can lead to *marketing myopia* (Levitt, 1960). Railroad management thought that travelers wanted trains rather than transportation and overlooked the growing competition from airlines, buses, trucks, and automobiles. Colleges, department stores, and post offices all assume that they are offering customers the right product and wonder why their sales slip. These organizations are too often looking into a mirror when they should be looking out of the window.

Gradually, the companies have begun to open up to feedback and criticisms from customers. Even as production processes and product innovations are still major sources of competitive advantage, customers have started to be on the company's radar — everything from what they want to know to how to attract them comes under this. It is no longer just a pursuit of efficiency and productivity. Marketing or customer research has begun to find a place in business organizations, although product-centric companies still put more attention to and investments in product research and development (R&D).

In today's competitive environment, only those companies that develop products that satisfy customer needs better than the products of their competitors will succeed. Therefore, it is necessary that companies conduct thorough research on such needs and generate ideas and solutions that can best satisfy them. The more innovative the new product development (NPD) projects, the greater the need to integrate marketing and R&D functions within the company. However, although the need for integration has been widely recognized, the levels of integration of R&D and marketing in practice vary across companies and industries. It is undeniable that until now there are companies that closely hold the principle that an innovative product will succeed in finding its place in the market. Apple cofounder Steve Jobs once said, "It isn't the consumer's job to know what they want". That was Apple's job.

Product Development and Connectivity

Decades ago, the secret of several Japanese corporations' success was their skill in sequencing improvements in functional competence. In the 1950s and early 1960s, many of them made heavy investments in both money and talent in manufacturing, and together with the advantage in labor cost they enjoyed at that time, it constituted their principal source of strength. At this stage, their investments in R&D and overseas marketing were minor. In the 1980s, they started conducting basic research on improving their functional strengths (Ohmae, 1982).

Kenichi Ohmae, in *The Mind of the Strategist*, gave a classic example about this product-centric perspective. It was the case of Casio, a manufacturer of watches and pocket calculators, against its competitors. Most of its competitors are organized around the traditional functions of engineering, manufacturing and distribution, and have gone in heavily for vertical integration. Casio, in contrast, remained basically an engineering and assembly company with very little investments in production facilities and sales channels. Its strength is flexibility.

Recognizing its competitors' inability to introduce new products rapidly, Casio had adopted a strategy of accelerating and shortening product life cycles. As soon as its 2-mm thick, card-size calculator was introduced to the market, Casio started rapidly bringing down the price, thus discouraging its competitors from following with similar products. Within a few months, Casio introduced another model, which emitted musical notes upon touching the numerical keys.

Casio's internal strength was its ability to integrate design and development into marketing research so that customers' voices were analyzed and quickly converted into tangible products. Because Casio had this function well-developed, it could afford to make its new product obsolete quickly. Its competitors, however, were designing their organization vertically on the assumption of a one- or two-year life cycle, preventing them from achieving shorter product development processes (Ohmae, 1982).

Casio's classic case teaches us that a product-centric company should have the flexibility to make functional improvements and innovations. But it also reveals the importance of connectivity to capture customers' desires faster than competitors. Remember that it is a 35-year-old story, which took place in an industrial era when wireless technology was not developed. Today, connectivity is everywhere. There are many digital and mobile tools that can connect companies with customers at any time and any place. The technology is different, but the main challenge remains the same: how to connect and discover customers' hidden needs and convert them into product innovations. And take a bold note that we should do that faster than competitors or we will just become a me-too player.

New Product Development (NPD) Challenges

As mentioned previously, the key marketing concept for a product-centric company is NPD. Research has shown that new products account for a staggering 28 percent of company sales on average, that is, more than one-fourth of the revenues of corporations are coming from new products. In some dynamic industries, the figure is 100 percent! As might be expected, profits follow closely, with 28.3 percent of company profits derived from new products three years old or newer (Cooper, 2001).

NPD also influences customers' perceptions toward a company's and product's brands. Consumers in Southeast Asia show a strong affinity for brands that invest in NPD and are among the most likely globally to try new product offerings. Approximately three quarters of Southeast Asian consumers (73 percent) say they purchased a new product during their last grocery-shopping trip — 16 percentage points higher than the global average of 57 percent. A further 73 percent like it when manufacturers offer new product options (compared with 62 percent globally), while 56 percent are willing to pay a premium price for innovative new products (compared with 44 percent globally) and 50 percent claim that they are early purchasers of new product innovations (compared with 39 percent globally) (Nielsen, 2015).

Internally, NPD will also keep the "healthiness" of a company's product portfolio. Generally, there are four types of products based on their relative growth and company's relative strength (see Fig. 4.1):

(1) Existential products (commodity products): Must-have products that are needed by customers.
(2) Essential products (foundation or basic products): Primary reasons for customers to be interested in.
(3) Initial products (untested creations): Business opportunities exist but customers' interests are still uncertain.
(4) Potential products (tested innovations): Large potential for growth given appropriate investments in product development and marketing.

Companies must ensure that their product portfolio consists of not only the existential (commodity) but also essential products (foundation).

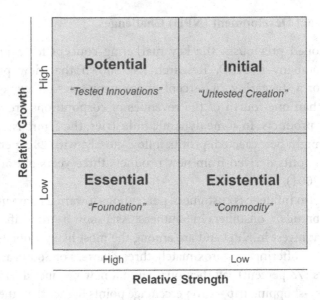

Figure 4.1: Product-portfolio management.

Ideally, a sufficient lead into initial products (untested creations) can be developed through market R&D, enabling the companies to prepare them to become potential products (tested innovations).

Unfortunately, NPD is also one of the riskiest endeavors of a modern corporation. Certainly, the risks are high: many companies have all seen large amounts of money spent on new products wasted. And it is getting riskier today. Customers are more informed and demanding than ever before. Fueled by an unprecedented choice of products and services, customer expectations create serious challenges for business leaders in a marketplace rife with competition. An empirical study on Taiwanese small- and medium-sized enterprises (SMEs) found that keeping close to customers has been a competitive advantage for SMEs, and a present research suggests this is still true. In other words, the managers ought to believe that customer acceptance and customer satisfaction contribute most to the overall success of a new product (see Box 4.1).

At the same time, products and services continue to become increasingly similar — and less differentiated —, making it more difficult to develop and extract real value from a brand. As a result, Asian companies today face a formidable task. Firms must find ways to not only launch new products or services that create meaningful differentiation in the

Box 4.1: NPD in Taiwan: SMEs Case Study

The purpose of this research is to examine the structure of new product success in the Taiwanese SMEs. The authors investigate critical factors affecting the likelihood of new product success for Taiwanese consumer goods manufacturing firms. Several conclusions can be drawn based on the findings. First, using multiple dimensions, the authors have described and classified the new product success performance used by Taiwanese SMEs. The results demonstrate that successful dimensions were financial performance, marketing acceptance, technical-level measure, and customer acceptance.

In contrast with previous research, while these dimensions were correlated, latest findings suggest that the factors measure different aspect of success. In addition, the authors suggest several managerial implications in new product success measure. First, a successful product may need to perform well on all dimensions. Thus, firms should use multiple criteria when measuring the new product performance. The measures that represent various aspects of success seem to be customer satisfaction, profitability, revenue, and product performance. Second, these dimensions are correlated. The implication of the correlation coefficients suggests that the most distinguished components are financial measure (financial performance and market acceptance) and nonfinancial measure (technical-level measure and customer acceptance). Management needs to be aware of the relationships between the factors and select success measures of the new product project at the start.

Moreover, nonfinancial measures such as customer acceptance, customer satisfaction, product performance goal achievement, and quality goal achievement are the most frequently used success criteria considered by Taiwanese SMEs. This suggests Taiwanese SMEs consider the quality and performance of a new product and its market acceptance to be primary measures of new product success, and financial measures seem to be of secondary concern.

(Continued)

Box 4.1: (*Continued*)

Anecdotal evidence suggests that many of the new products develo-ped by SMEs perform well technologically, but not so well financially (Huang *et al.*, 2004). The success measures used by SMEs may explain this phenomenon. The challenges for SMEs are to set financial and nonfinancial goals for their new products, to measure these goals, and to allocate appropriate resources to strategically strengthen their NPD capabilities.

Traditionally, keeping close to customers has been considered a competitive advantage for SMEs. The present research suggests that this is still true. In other words, the managers ought to believe that customer acceptance and customer satisfaction contribute most to the overall success of a new product although the other three factors also contribute to success.

Source: Fu (2010).

---

minds of their customers, but also capture and sustain the value they have created for their different target segments (Ritson, 2009). Such dynamics require companies to use new innovative models if they want to create the necessary conditions for their success. Winston Churchill once said, "Success is walking from failure to failure with no loss of enthusiasm". But, today it seems that the cost of failure is getting more expensive.

But acting extra cautious too comes at a price. If an Asian company is quite considerate about playing safe and avoid risks too often, it will slow down the process of NPD and innovation. As a result, when the final product is launched, customers' needs would have changed or com-petitors — from Asia or other regions — would have already come up with the solutions that customers need. The reducing political and geo-graphical barriers — in view of political changes and development of technology — meant that companies in Asia can no longer take it easy in running a business. Thus, in addition to being able to offer new products that have a meaningful and sustainable differentiation, Asian companies should also be able to accelerate the NPD process, all the way from idea generation, concept development, and market test to new product launch.

Answering the Challenges: The Stage-Gate Model

In a bid to develop new products, companies are often challenged to expedite development while ensuring creation of the right products that are relevant to customers. Speed without accuracy will only lead to products that fail in the market. In contrast, accuracy without speed will put competitors ahead in market introduction. To answer this challenge, Cooper (2001) proposed a stage-gate model as a guide to develop new products effectively and efficiently. This model has two main components: the stage and gate (see Fig. 4.2).

Stages

The stage-gate model consists of several stages that can be clearly distinguished. A process typically has four to six stages. A general model of stage-gate has several stages, which are as follows (Cooper, 2001):

- Discovery: an early-stage remedy aimed at finding and generating business ideas

- Scoping: an initial investigative process on the business ideas or projects that should be completed quickly, mostly through desk research

- Building a Business Case: a more detailed investigation involving primary data collection (both technical data and market), and an explanation about products and projects as well as project planning

- Development: the actual design and development of a more detailed structure of the new products and production processes

- Testing and Validation: testing or experimentation in the market and laboratory to validate and verify the new products developed

- Launch: commercialization of products, including production and marketing execution in full capacity

Gates

In the early stages, gates are devised as checkpoints to ascertain whether the product development process can be continued or not. A gate serves as a point to control the quality. At every gate, there will be an outcome

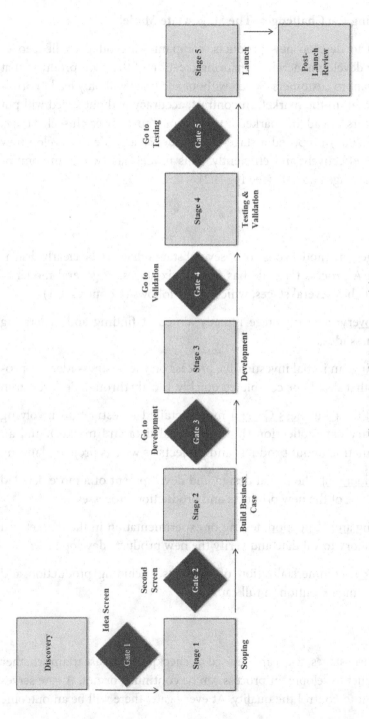

Figure 4.2: Stage-gate model.

Source: Cooper (2001).

of the previous stages (deliverables) that needs to be evaluated as well as the criteria for evaluation. Cooper explains that in general, in a product development process, the gates will be as follows:

- Gate 1 (Idea Screen): The earliest evaluation of the ideas generated, where the criteria commonly used are the project's feasibility, market appeal, product excellence, and compliance with corporate policies

- Gate 2 (Second Screen): At this gate, the evaluations that have been conducted at Gate 1 are generally repeated, but more methodically and using a more rigorous approach based on the new information obtained during the scoping stage

- Gate 3 (Go to Development): The evaluation is based on financial criteria to determine whether a product development project is eligible to receive funding from the company

- Gate 4 (Go to Testing): A revised evaluation using financial analysis based on more accurate data and conducting more detailed studies on operational and marketing plans

- Gate 5 (Go to Launch): The last gate to determine whether a product is eligible to be launched en masse to the market, with the criteria being the degree of financial return as well as the suitability of the product launch plan

Open Innovation and Connectivity

The stage-gate model provides a systematic and effective mix to develop innovations within the organization. But in today's era of hyper connectivity, a product-centric company in Asia cannot rely solely on the internal structure and resources to generate new ideas and develop innovations. In order for the NPD process to run with as much accuracy as speed, the involvement of external parties (customers, suppliers, regulators, etc.) is absolutely necessary. At each stage and gate in the NPD process, the contribution of external parties becomes increasingly important. For example, in the discovery stage, companies cannot just rely on the marketing research team to look for new ideas out there; at this stage, customers should begin to be actively involved to provide inputs. Technological advancements have

Table 4.1:   Characteristics of open and close innovation.

Open Innovation	Close Innovation
To work with expertise inside and outside the company	To work with the best people inside the company
Both external and internal R&D create significant value for company	Finding, developing, marketing, and following up with internal R&D
Obtaining knowledge from external environments to achieve higher profitability than internally focused organizations	Obtaining and utilizing knowledge inside the company for having more advantage than competitors
More flexible and open organizational structure to ensure adaptability	More rigid and close organizational structure to ensure process effectiveness

Sources: Adapted from Chesbrough (2003), Lichtenthaler and Lichtenthaler (2009), and authors' analysis.

greatly improved a company's ability to establish greater connectivity with the customer, thus aiding the process of collaboration on the development of new products. Welcome to the open innovation era.

Open innovation is an expression that was promoted by Chesbrough in 2003. It is defined as the purposive use of knowledge that exists in inputs and outputs of organizations for increasing the speed of internal innovations, and expansion of markets for external use of innovations. Thus, open innovation is a paradigm that promotes the idea of firms using both external and internal ideas. On the other hand, close innovation is a traditional paradigm wherein the innovating firm generates its own ideas and then develops them (Chesbrough, 2003). Table 4.1 shows a list of characteristics on both paradigms of innovation.

Companies from developed countries such as Procter & Gamble, Cisco Systems, Genzyme, General Electric, and Intel are often credited with having attained market leadership through open innovation strategies. That is, by tapping into and exploiting technological knowledge that resided beyond their own R&D structures, these companies outmaneuvered rivals that relied largely on in-house approaches to innovation. But while other organizations — including Asian companies — try to follow the examples set by these trailblazers, research shows that many are failing because they neglect to ensure that the outside ideas reach the people best equipped to exploit them (Whelan *et al.*, 2011).

In order for companies to be able to quickly capture innovative ideas from outside the organization, it is not sufficient to rely solely on the frontline people on the ground. If the idea of discovery is only a side job to them, then surely the results will not be optimal. For that, a greater effort is required to build a more intensive connectivity with external parties, especially customers. Some companies utilise the customer community as a source of new ideas to get feedback. In several Asian countries, the approach works particularly well owing to customers' tendencies to be more communal in their behavior, making the community approach effective enough to build long-term relationships with the customer.

Some Japanese auto companies in Indonesia are quite intensive in their cooperation with the brand communities formed by their own customers. Some popular vehicle brands in Indonesia — both two-wheeler and four-wheeler — such as *Avanza* (Toyota), *Xenia* (Daihatsu), *Ertiga* (Suzuki), and Honda motorcycles boast of a large community of members spread across many cities. Another alternative is to provide a connecting platform that facilitates interactions between companies and customers, both online and offline. One example of such a platform is Fujifilm's the Open Innovation Hub (see Box 4.2).

Another approach proposed by Whelan *et al.* (2011) is through the appointment of an external employee who acts as an idea connector (idea scout) on a special mission to put the organization on the radar of development of external new ideas. An idea scout must have some core characteristics including: (i) a broad network outside the company, (ii) short-to-medium organization tenure, (iii) a higher level degree in specialized technology fields, and (iv) genuine interest in keeping abreast of emerging trends in their field of work. The companies should also support these idea scouts to help them perform their duties effectively, giving them time and opportunities to explore the outside world, encouraging them to attend external networking events, and training them in the effective use of social media technologies.

In order to advance innovation, connectivity to the outside world should be effectively supported by internal connectivity. The company must form an internal task force that is prepared to capture innovative ideas from outside (via an external idea scout or connector) and then process them together with various internal functions (R&D, information

Box 4.2:   Fujifilm's The Open Innovation Hub

Fuji Photo Film Co., Ltd. was established in 1934 with an aim to be the first Japanese producer of photographic films. But today, after more than 80 years, Fujifilm Holding Corporation operates various businesses including document solutions, medical imaging and diagnostics equipment, cosmetics, optical devices, photocopiers, printers, photographic materials, and digital cameras. The company is also behind the development of numerous innovative technologies and products, such as the world's first digital x-ray imaging and diagnostic system "FCR (Fuji Computed Radiography)" and the world's first fully digital camera "DS-1P", introducing completely new values that had never existed before to our society.

As part of its breakthrough initiatives, Fujifilm launched the Open Innovation Hub in 2014, a venue for presenting Fujifilm Group's fundamental and core technologies as well as materials, products, and services based on such technologies to external business partners including companies and research institutes. The company uses this facility to link the business partners' challenges, ideas, and potential needs with its proprietary technologies to create innovative products, technologies, and services, thereby initiating a tide of innovation.

Fujifilm has built its Open Innovation Hubs in Tokyo, Silicon Valley, and the Netherlands. Every hub consists of three areas and two zones:

Introduction Area

This is an area for presenting Fujifilm's corporate profile and corporate social responsibility (CSR) activities to introduce the company to business partners. It is designed to deepen their understanding of Fujifilm's past steps and current business operations as a whole.

Core Technology Area

This is an area for visually presenting the overview of the company's core technologies and history of their application in a wide range of fields. It is designed to showcase the expansive breadth and depth of Fujifilm's technologies.

(Continued)

Box 4.2: (*Continued*)

Touch Zone

This is a zone that allows visitors to physically touch various products, created with the application of the company's core technologies, for first-hand experience of their technological features and superiority, which cannot be fully conveyed with visual presentation alone. The zone helps swiftly match business partners' tasks with Fujifilm Group's knowledge to present solutions.

Ideation Zone

This is a zone adjacent to the Touch Zone for discussions with business partners. An entire wall is made of whiteboard to facilitate free exchange of opinions to encourage fresh inspirations.

Concept Making Area

This is an area for exploring a specific action plan for creating new products and services. The online conferencing system is available for communication between business partners and research laboratory members.

Fujifilm really believes in the power of open innovation in this digital era. Naoto Yanagihara, Fujifilm's General Manager of Innovation & Strategy Planning Division, once gave a message to all the company's stakeholders: "The samurai become(s) stronger by leaving the dojo and sparring with warriors from other traditions".

Sources: fujifilm.com, fujifilm.eu, and others.

---

technology, operations, marketing, etc.). The existence of this internal connector is crucial if the innovative ideas that have been painstakingly obtained are to be transformed into a successful product or service (Whelan *et al.*, 2011). Often, good ideas end up documented into reports and just piled up in the company archives. A mix of internal and external connectivity will help make the process of innovation run quickly and effectively.

Connected Products

In the previous sections, we have discussed how technological revolution has underlined the importance of connectivity in the process of NPD in Asian companies. The ability to perform open innovation — supported by internal and external connectivity — will make a product-centric company develop competitive advantages over other industry players. The company will be better prepared at capturing ideas from outside and swifter at executing them into a product or service compared with its competitors.

But New Wave technology has enabled companies not only in getting smarter at developing new products through open innovation but also in creating smarter and connected products. Connectivity in the product itself is becoming more important as well. According to Porter and Heppelmann (2014), smart-connected products have three core elements: physical components, "smart" components, and connectivity components. Smart components amplify the capabilities and value of the physical components whereas connectivity components amplify the capabilities and value of the smart components and enable some of them to exist outside the physical product itself. If the functional capabilities can be integrated with more emotional touch, then that could help generate not only machine-to-machine (M2M) or machine-to-human (M2H) interactions, but also human-to-human (H2H) engagements.

A physical product is typically made of mechanical and electrical components. They constitute the tangible part of the product — the part responsible for providing a benefit to the customer. However, if the other two — smart and connectivity components — weren't there, a product consisting of only a physical component would be of limited use. For instance, consider a vehicle consisting of an engine, a power train, tires, and batteries. All these physical components would form a very basic product primarily functioning as a means of transport.

But as we add the smart components in a product, think sensors, microprocessors, data storage, controls, software, as well as an embedded operating system and enhanced user interface, it all serves to improve the functionality and user experience. In a vehicle, this would amount to adding smart components such as the engine control unit, antilock braking system, rain-sensing windshields with automated wipers, and touch-screen displays. In some products, software can be used in place of some hardware components or a single physical device could be integrated to perform various functions (Porter and Heppelmann, 2014).

Connectivity components comprise the ports, antennae, and protocols, enabling wired or wireless connections with the product. This component of connectivity takes three forms, which can be present together (Porter and Heppelmann, 2014):

(1) <u>One-to-One</u>: An individual product connects to the user, the manufacturer, or another product through a port or other interface. For example, the smartphone can now be equipped with wireless technology, enabling it to share information with other devices, even with household appliances equipped with digital technology. An example of such connectivity is from Xiaomi, which has developed a smart bracelet to monitor the health of its users and send information to their smartphones (see Box 4.3).

(2) <u>One-to-Many</u>: A central system is continuously or intermittently connected to many products simultaneously. For example, many Tesla automobiles are connected to a single manufacturer system that monitors performance and accomplishes remote service and upgrades.

(3) <u>Many-to-Many</u>: Multiple products are connected to many other types of products and often also to external data sources. This relates to the connectivity between two systems, for example, between all-digital systems in a smart home with sources of external data (weather forecasts, reports on price of goods, public transport schedules, etc.).

In the digital age, connected products will become a source of competitive advantage for product-centric Asian companies. A major advantage of this kind of a product concept is that it's open and opens up opportunities for external parties to contribute in providing inputs. The more the users, the greater will be the opportunities to increase the benefits from adopting connectivity in product development. The result is a virtuous cycle of value improvement.

Box 4.3:   Xiaomi's Smart and Connected Products

Xiaomi Inc. is a privately owned Chinese electronics company headquartered in Beijing. It is one of the world's largest smartphone makers, following Samsung and Apple. Xiaomi designs, develops, and sells smartphones, mobile apps, and related consumer electronics. Since the release of its first smartphone in August 2011, Xiaomi has gained market share in mainland China and expanded into developing a wider range of consumer electronics, including a smart home device ecosystem. The company has over 8,000 employees, mainly in mainland China, Malaysia and Singapore, and is expanding to other countries such as India, Indonesia, the Philippines, and Brazil.

Product innovation and operational excellence have become its competitive strength, supported by Xiaomi's unique business model. Xiaomi says that it listens closely to customer feedback, allows them to test out upcoming features themselves, and builds an extensive online community. Xiaomi's product managers spend a lot of time browsing through the company's user forums. Once a suggestion is picked up, it is quickly transferred to engineers. This is an example of open innovation that we discussed earlier.

Several smart and connected products have been developed by Xiaomi. In August 2014, Xiaomi announced the *Mi Band*. It is a "smart bracelet" that monitors users' activity — tracking their fitness regime — running and walking, monitoring their sleep, sending data and analytics to the Mi Fit app, waking them up with an alarm, and calculating the pulse rate. In doing so, it incorporates both M2H connectivity (between the bracelet and its user) and M2M connectivity (between the bracelet and user's smartphone).

Xiaomi also has a smart home product series. The kit contains a set of smart sensors, including the multifunction gateway, the door/window sensor, the motion detector, and the wireless switch, which can be combined to achieve over 30 different kinds of functions. For example, the motion detector can be paired with the gateway to perform functions such as switching on a light at night when it detects motion and window sensors that can start or stop a connected fan as windows are closed or opened.

Sources: idc.com, Tech in Asia, Boomberg Business, and others.

References

Chesbrough, H (2003). The logic of open innovation: Managing intellectual property. *California Management Review*, 45(3), 33–58.

Cooper, RG (2001). *Winning at New Products: Creating Value through Innovation.* New York: Basic Books.

Dawar, N (December 2013). When Marketing Is Strategy. *Harvard Business Review.* https://hbr.org/2013/12/when-marketing-is-strategy (last accessed July 25, 2016).

Fu, YK (2010). New product success among small and medium enterprises: An empirical study in Taiwan. *Journal of International Management Studies*, 5(1), 147–153.

Huang, X, A Brown and GN Soutar (2004). Measuring new product success: an empirical investigation of Australian SEMs. *Industrial Marketing Management*, 33, 117–123.

Kotler, P (2001). *Marketing Management Millenium Edition*, 10th Ed. New Jersey: Prentice-Hall.

Levitt, T (July–August 1960). Marketing Myopia. *Harvard Business Review*, 45–56.

Lichtenthaler, U., & Lichtenthaler, E (2009). A capability-based framework for open innovation: Complementing absorptive capacity. *Journal of Management Studies*, 46 (8), 1315–1338.

Nielsen (2015). *Nielsen Global New Product Innovation Report*, report summary could be accessed through http://www.nielsen.com/apac/en/insights/news/2015/new-product-development-hits-the-sweet-spot-in-developing-markets.html

Ohmae, K (1982). *The Mind of the Strategist: The Art of Japanese Business.* New York: McGraw-Hill Book Company.

Porter, ME and JE Heppelmann (November 2014). How smart, connected products are transforming competition. *Harvard Business Review*, 1–23.

Quelch, JA and KE Jocz (2008). Milestone in marketing. *Business History Review*, 82, 827–838.

Ritson, M (October 2009). Customers are suddenly hyperconscious of value and new low-promise competitors are nipping at your heels: Should you launch a fighting brand? *Harvard Business Review*, pp. 87–94.

Whelan *et al.* (2011). Creating employee networks that deliver open innovation. *MIT Sloan Management Review*, Fall issue.

CHAPTER 5

CUSTOMER-CENTRIC PERSPECTIVE: CONNECTING WITH THE DIGITAL CONSUMER

Today you are not behind your competition. You are not behind the technology.
You are behind your consumer.

Rishad Tobaccowala, Chief Strategy and Innovation Officer — VivaKi

"Nobody ever got fired for buying from IBM" was a popular "business myth" among computer salespeople in the 1970s and 1980s. Although IBM entered the computer industry later than other big players, it was soon to achieve dominance in the fast-growing market. What was its success formula? Some business people — including executives from IBM competitors — went on to falsely assume that the answer was a superior product. Although IBM's products performed solidly, they usually did not come with the benefit of latest innovations. Some of IBM's competitors have pioneered online operating systems, virtual memory, minicomputers, and most other breakthrough capabilities. IBM was an adopter of these innovations, but not often the leader.

IBM's secret of success was in offering a total solution — rather than just stand-alone products — to its clients. It offered methods of planning new business applications, training development staff, and managing data. It pitched in when a system wasn't working, diagnosing the problem, and getting it back on track. It took care of planning which new machines were needed, which had to be upgraded, and how to integrate the new technology. It also sent clients off for periodic education to deepen their knowledge and broaden their managerial skills (Treacy and Wiersema, 1997).

A similar success story is that of Komatsu — a Japanese multinational corporation that manufactures construction, mining, forestry, agroplantation, and industrial heavy equipment — in Indonesia. Competing with Caterpillar, a top global player in this industry, United Tractors — distributor of Komatsu in Indonesia — sought to build a competitive advantage in the country through proximity developed between business consultants (a term used for the sales team in United Tractors) and its corporate clients. Business consultants have been ostensibly positioned as partners who are ever ready to help the clients solve any problems. Furthermore, they are trained to not only provide technical assistance and consultation in a professional manner, but also add an emotional touch to it. That is how they have succeeded in winning and maintaining customer loyalty.

In these cases, IBM and Komatsu had consequently escaped the *marketing myopia* trap, warned against by Theodore Levitt, a famous American economist and professor at Harvard Business School, many years ago. He once said that many companies were preoccupied with their need to convert products into cash, when the real marketing job was satisfying the needs of the customers by the product and the whole cluster of things associated with creating, delivering, and finally consuming it (Levitt, 1960). Therefore, companies shouldn't always be competing in product leadership. They may choose a different marketing strategy by putting customers at the center of gravity.

This is the main idea of the customer-centric perspective. Asian firms must create value for customers and see the business from the customer's point of view. This perspective differs from the product-centric perspective, which considers product development superior to other marketing activities (Keith, 1960). With this shift in focus, the nature of the buying decision by consumers and business customers came under close scrutiny. Marketing researchers paid closer attention to the psychological and emotional — as opposed to strictly functional — types of "utility" consumers gain from using products or services (Quelch and Jocz, 2008).

The strategic question that drives the customer-centric perspective is not "what else can we make?" but "what else can we do for our customers?" Customers and the market — not the factory or the product — stand at the core of the business. This center of gravity demands a rethink of some long-standing pillars of strategy: first, the sources and locus of the competitive advantage now lie outside the firm. Second, the way company competes changes over time. Downstream, it's no longer about having a better product: its focus is on the needs of customers and its position relative to their purchase criteria. Third, the pace and evolution of markets are driven by customers' shifting purchase criteria rather than by improvements in products or technology (Dawar, 2013).

The Fundamentals of Customer Management

According to the product-centric perspective, a company's competitive advantage is built and developed around upstream activities in the factory and R&D department. Companies compete with each other to achieve a breakthrough and develop innovative products. The health of its product portfolio becomes increasingly important as product life cycles get shorter. "Innovate or die" becomes a common jargon among marketers.

However, customer-centric companies take a different path. Rather than strengthening upstream marketing activities, they choose to go downstream. They learn from the classic experiment in the world of branding where researchers ask what would happen to *Coca-Colás* ability to raise financing and launch operations anew if all its physical assets around the world (factories, distribution channels, authorized outlets, branch offices, etc.) were to go up in flames one night. Most business people conclude that the tragedy would cost *Coca-Cola* time, effort, and money — but the company would have little difficulty raising the funds to get back to the business. The brand would easily attract investors looking for future returns.

However, try this different scenario. What might happen if billions of *Coca-Cola*s consumers around the world could not remember its brand name or any of its associations? In this scenario, most businesspeople agree that even though *Coca-Cola*s physical assets remained intact, the company would find it difficult to raise funds to restart the business. It turns out that the loss of downstream competitive advantage — consumers' connection with the brand — would be a more severe blow than the loss of all upstream assets (Dawar, 2013).

The company–customer connectivity thus calls for industry players' primary attention. As a practical framework for customer management, we have categorized four core activities as follows (see Fig. 5.1):

— **Get:** Gain prospects and acquire new customers
— **Keep:** Focus on loyalty building to keep valuable customers
— **Grow:** Add values for both customers and company
— **Win Back:** Seek opportunities to get back lost customers

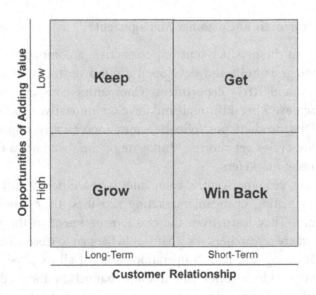

Figure 5.1: Customer value management.

These core activities in customer management cover the full spectrum of interactions with current and future customers. Some variations may exist across different industries. For example, some business-to-consumer (B2C) companies (fast-moving consumer goods, consumer electronics, transportation, property, and health care) will put more attention to "get" and "keep" activities, while business-to-business (B2B) firms (corporate banking, consulting, IT solutions, logistics, media, etc.) may pursue activities to grow existing clients and to win back lost customers.

To get, keep, and grow valuable clients, companies (the first C) cannot just wait passively for customers (the second C) to come to them, because other value suppliers (competitors, the third C) are actively trying to gain their attention. However, the business landscape moves at a faster rate due to another element — which we identify as the fourth C, change. This additional C has brought forth the 4C diamond model — a business model that helps organizations make better projections, or predictions, about future threats, opportunities, weaknesses, and strengths (TOWS) (Kotler *et al.*, 2003). Growing technological connectivity in Asia has created a whole new set of opportunities as well as threats.

Asian countries have been working to narrow the digital divide by improving broadband Internet access. A report by the Asia Pacific Network Information Center (APNIC, 2014) shows phenomenal Internet growth in the last 20 years: from 16 million users in 1995 to 2.8 billion users in 2013 in the world; and from 115 million users in 2000 to 1 billion users in 2013 in Asia alone. The Internet usership is still growing fast: there will be about 3.6 billion Internet users world wide by 2017, accounting for over 47 percent of the world's projected population (7.6 billion). There were over 1.33 billion Internet users in Asia in 2015, a 30 percent increase from 2013.

The impact is crystal clear. Asian consumers are becoming increasingly connected. Digitalization is transforming them from mere consumers into smarter value demanders. Now that company-to-consumer dynamic digital interaction is given, companies without an engaging online presence or an effective mobile strategy or app will suffer in comparison to those who do have them. Therefore, customer management should apply the same logic. The following section discusses how Asian companies can get, keep, grow, and win back their digital consumers.

Getting into Your Digital Consumers' Head

Customers today are smarter and more demanding than before. IT has provided them with abundant information, so much so that sometimes they could be even more knowledgeable than the company's salespersons. Desforger and Anthony (2013) in *The Shopper Marketing Revolution* wrote: "15 years ago we had three key sources of stimulus: TV, PR, word of mouth. And at least two of those were owned by the marketer. What has changed is that customers don't take the marketers' message at face value. They now say, 'Hey, I'm going to take control and responsibility over my product education'.

Customers' decision-making processes are now being shaped long before they enter a grocery store or meet a salesperson. It's a new decision-making moment that plays out a hundred million times a day on mobile phones, laptops, and other wired devices of all kinds. It's a moment where marketing happens, where information happens, and where consumers make choices that affect the success and failure of nearly every brand in the world. Google calls it the Zero Moment of Truth (ZMOT). The ZMOT is that moment when customers grab their laptops, mobile phones, or some other wired devices and start learning about a product or service they're thinking about trying or buying (Lecinski, 2011).

As consumers' behavior evolves, so must the ways in which Asian brands engage with them. In today's forever-connected, mobile-first world, the following four tactics can win the ZMOT (Lecinski, 2014):

(1) Use search to uncover and understand the moments that matter

Digital consumers have long been searching for keywords such as "BB cream", "Greek yogurt", and "Ombre hair" — much before brand managers found out about consumers' interest in these things. It's never easy to figure out what's in the minds of digital consumers. The key is to search for and recognize products, services, moments, and experiences that consumers take note of and incorporate them in their businesses' marketing strategy and tactics.

(2) Be present in the moments that matter

Smartphones are increasingly becoming the go-to devices for consumers for anything they need, whether it's simply browsing Internet, checking social media, or performing more specific tasks such as shopping or booking travel tickets. This also means there are various moments when consumers need products and services and a brand can't be that chosen one if it's not present in the moments when consumers are looking for it.

The company should analyze how many times its products show up in customers' search compared to those of their competitors.

(3) Have something interesting and/or engaging to share

Much is being said about how the overabundance of online information is resulting in shortening attention spans of digital customers. Screen-switching or multiscreen behavior is a common issue brands are tackling with in targeting audiences. It calls for the content that brands put up on the digital channels to be not only informative, but interactive and engaging as well. Simply linking to your products online may not suffice; companies should deliver messages that should make an impression across the devices.

It is also crucial to make it easy for customers to share content through social media and other digital platforms even if it is not designed for digital platforms exclusively. For example, some Thailand-based companies have successfully launched television commercials that became viral on social media and are shared over hundreds and thousands of times (see Box 5.1).

(4) Measure the impact

Finally, a company needs to measure what degree a message wins in advanced business key performance indicators (KPIs) such as awareness, consideration, comment, purchase intent, and recommendation (please refer to the 5A model — Aware, Appeal, Ask, Act, and Advocate — in Chap. 3).

In essence, brands should proactively take advantage of the various digital tools at their disposal — actively perform searches to unravel the moments that matter to consumers, be present at the right places and at the right time, make the content more smartphone-friendly, and evaluate the impact routinely. This would enable brands to score a significant competitive edge as a truly customer-centric organization.

Keeping and Growing Customers in the Digital Era

Online-to-offline (O2O) commerce is a hot topic in Asian retail marketing at the moment, and it is only set to get hotter as new technologies

Box 5.1: Thai "Sadvertising"

In Thailand, creative companies have made millions tugging at the heartstrings of Thai television viewers who tune in for the advertisements during breaks as much as they do for their favorite shows. And these advertisements go viral on social media as viewers share them, each based on a sad theme, about homelessness, poverty, or a sad love story. They are sad, but they're also inspiring. Mostly, they're shareable, which means more people will watch the message and probably buy the product they're selling.

One company in particular, Thai Life Insurance, seems to have mastered the art of so-called "sadvertising". An advertisement titled Unsung Hero, released in April 2014 and made by the creative minds from Ogilvy & Mather – Bangkok, has been viewed more than 26 million times on YouTube. It tells the story of one man's generosity. He feeds stray dogs and gives money to a homeless mother and daughter. He gets nothing in return but at the two-minute mark his reward shows itself.

The Unsung Hero advertisement was the ninth most shared viral video in the world in January 2015, according to Mumbrella Asia. Phawit Chitrakorn, Managing Director of Thai Life Insurance's advertising agency Ogilvy & Mather — Bangkok, explains the secret formula behind the great television advertising:

> The audience crying isn't our main objective. However, we want people to appreciate the "Value of Life", which is a core value of the brand. What people should takeaway is that Thai Life Insurance truly and deeply understands the value of life, and this creates opportunities for us.

Thailand security camera company Vizer made one of the best advertisements of 2015. The extended commercial was viewed more than seven million times on YouTube. In it, a store owner ridicules a homeless man he finds sleeping outside his store. Day after day he kicks him, pours water on him, and tells him to leave. Eventually, when he does leave, the man wonders why. He checks the CCTV footage to discover the homeless man was protecting his store all along.

(Continued)

Box 5.1: (*Continued*)

Sad Sister, a commercial from the National Cancer Institute, is another contender for Thai "sadvertising" of all time. It tells the story of sisters who don't get along until one reveals to the other that she has cancer. The commercial is a call to action for generous Thai women to donate their hair to the institute.

Mr Chitrakorn said it was important for the company never to be "overly melodramatic". "This comes from our belief that a person's life isn't something to be played around with. What we try to do is find a touching human story that we all believe can happen to our neighbours, friends or even family. When we achieve this, life insurance companies begin to have meaning for our lives".

Sources: "Why Thai Life Insurance Ads Are so Consistently, Tear-jerkingly Brilliant" www.mumbrella.asia. January 2015; "Thailand Television Commercials Will Make You Cry, or At Least Get a Bit Sad", www.news.com.au/. September 2015.

and innovations accelerate the opportunities for retailers. O2O commerce is the principle of connecting the online digital world with the offline world through the integration of Internet-connected devices. Contrary to e-commerce, the O2O approach brings customers to shop or obtain a service in offline stores. Customers beginning their journey online are either driven offline through deals and discoveries such as e-coupons and store locators or propelled online through calls for actions in the offline world using quick response (QR) codes and mobile payment systems. The growth of mobile Internet connectivity, speed, and Internet-connected devices such as smartphones, tablets, tablet PCs, netbooks, and terminals has enabled O2O commerce to thrive and "close" the loop. Pizza Hut in Hong Kong — under the Jardine Restaurant Group's management — makes a good example of how O2O implementation can boosts customers' loyalty (see Box 5.2).

While O2O commerce is gaining more popularity among Asian B2C companies, players in the B2B world are dealing with a rather different challenge. The average B2B sale is typically much larger than it is for B2C firms. And for B2B firms, a small number of customers can account for the majority of their revenue. Thus, it pays for B2B companies to go to extra lengths to pay attention to their existing customers. In fact, many devote substantial resources on programs to dissect customer needs, educate prospects on products and services, create personal relationships, and promote their offerings. Seminars, publications, market research, and call centers are among the most important tools in a B2B firm's toolbox. They help them understand, attract, keep, and grow valuable customers.

But in a world of cut-throat competition, increasing technological connectivity, and ever-rising complexity, these activities are no longer enough for many B2B companies. A small but growing number of B2B companies have realized this. While they may not have pulled the plug on existing customer interaction programs, they have adopted a new way of getting inside the minds of buyers on a daily basis: by creating online customer communities. These often take the form of a private website that enables customers to access, create, and collaborate via discussions, content, and information about topics of mutual interest.

Buday and DiMauro (2011), in *Customer Intimacy on Steroids: Why B2B Firms Need Online Communities*, elaborated the following three key elements of online customer communities:

Customers: Online communities of this type focus on achieving the goals of a B2B firm's customers. B2B companies have formed many other types of online communities — internal ones (for virtual support of work teams), communities for suppliers and channel partners, and more. In contrast, the goal of an online customer community is to address the business issues for which customers buy and use a B2B firm's products and/or services.

Collaboration: Online customer communities enable collaborations of two types — between the B2B company hosting the community and its customers, and between those customers. But again, the reason these parties collaborate online is to solve customers' business issues. More attention is required on this aspect because if the community organizer uses the online community to focus on solving its own issues and minimizes customers' issues, customers will check out of the community. In a 2010 study, 95 percent of executives said that the number one reason they use online communities is to be educated on their issues of interest (DiMauro and Bulmer, 2010).

Issues of Mutual Interest: Issues that are not in the best interests of both parties (B2B firm and its customers) are not something to bring to an online customer community. For example, if a B2B company wants to use its customer community for recruiting and direct selling, that may be in its best interests, but, of course, it is not in the customers' best interests. The way to think about the B2B customer community is as follows: It is not about you, it's about them (customers).

Online customer communities have become increasingly important in industries such as IT. Nearly two-thirds (65 percent) of 207 organizations surveyed in 2010 by research firm ITSMA revealed that they are engaged in private online communities hosted by the companies that sell them computer hardware, software, and services (Schwartz *et al.*, 2010). Software companies such as SAP and business information providers such as LexisNexis are some pioneers of this digital company–customer relationship. These online communities help them gain new competitive advantage: the ability to get much closer to customers — rationally and emotionally — and become more connected to customers around the clock.

Winning Back Lost Customers in the Digital Age

Businesses aren't perfect. Sometimes mistakes happen and things fall through the cracks, leading to customers' disappointment and churn. It may not always be the business' shortfall, sometimes customers also make mistakes but can quickly become disappointed with how a situation is handled by servicepersons. Especially in cases of service failures, it is imperative for companies to handle customers' issues with utmost attention and win back lost customers with quick and effective responses. Consequently, developing effective service recovery policies has become integral to many customer retention initiatives. Service recovery policies involve actions taken by service providers to respond to service failures (Johnston and Mehra, 2002).

Both what is done (e.g., restitution and compensation) and how it is done (i.e., employee interaction with the customer) influence customer

Box 5.2: Jardine's Social Customer Relationship Management (CRM) Project

Founded as a trading company in China in 1832, Jardine Matheson is today a diversified business group focused principally on Asia. Its businesses comprise a combination of cash-generating activities and long-term property assets. The Group's interests include Jardine Pacific, Jardine Motors, Jardine Lloyd Thompson, Hong Kong Land, Dairy Farm, Mandarin Oriental, Jardine Cycle & Carriage, and Astra International. These companies are leaders in the fields of engineering and construction, transport services, insurance broking, property investment and development, retailing, restaurants, luxury hotels, motor vehicles and related activities, financial services, heavy equipment, mining, and agribusiness.

Through the Jardine Restaurant Group (JRG), Jardine Pacific, as at the end of 2014, operated over 680 outlets with more than 19,000 employees, making it one of the leading restaurant groups in Asia. The JRG is one of Pizza Hut's largest international franchisees, with operations in Taiwan, Hong Kong, Macau, and Vietnam. In addition, JRG also operates KFC outlets in Hong Kong, Macau, Taiwan, and Vietnam, and provides value pizza delivery through Pizza Hut Delivery (PHD) in Hong Kong.

In 2015, JRG began a digital marketing experiment for its Pizza Hut business in Hong Kong. They called it the Social CRM Project, which they claimed to be the first such social CRM campaign across all Pizza Hut restaurants worldwide. It was a big data project that aimed to activate its most loyal Hong Kong customers.

The agency they appointed had used three-dimensional (3-D) printing technology to create eight mini versions of its most popular Pizza Hut dishes. Data taken from users' ordering habits were used to select the dishes. For any purchase over $250 (in restaurants, pickup, or delivery), Pizza Hut customers would get one of the mini plates and receive that designated dish for free. Each mini plate had a QR code, which was then linked back to its point-of-sale system. Over the weekend, Pizza Hut began touring Hong Kong's hotspots to launch the lucky draw at the street level.

(Continued)

Box 5.2: (Continued)

Rachel Wong, strategic planning director of UM Rally, said early indications had shown that the campaign had already led to sales outperforming pre-Chinese New Year 2015. Ravel Lai, information technology director for JRG, said: "It's really exciting for us to be able to link up our business data, mobile app, restaurant POS and Facebook for this O2O (online-to-offline) campaign". Lai says Pizza Hut customers now expect a level of integration and want to be engaged on a mobile device in intelligent ways. "There's no longer just CRM, it's all social CRM", he says.

He cites one example of letting people use their points in an easier way. This has allowed members to access their points for various purposes, from sharing points with friends or using points for express ticketing to jump long waiting cues. "We're making points a service. Big data analysis shows that when people redeem points they come back to our restaurants more frequently. Points can generate sales. We want people to burn points".

This has had an almost immediate effect. Points redemption in 2015 jumped to 57 percent and sales generated from social CRM and loyalty efforts grew more than 27 percent.

Sources: jardines.com; "Pizza Hut Activates Loyalty Club in Big Data Program", *marketing-interactive.com,* 26 January 2016; "How Jardine Is Revolutionising the Digital World", *marketing-interactive.com,* 19 February 2016.

---

perceptions of service recovery (Andreassen, 2000). Too many Asian organizations don't yet recognize that how they are seen handling and processing complaints matters as much as how successfully the complaints are resolved. That's why a poorly handled call center conversation or chat exchange can spiral viral. The way a customer complains about how a complaint was (mis)handled can prove more dominant and damning than the original issue prompting the complaint.

Dealing well with inquiries and complaints is, of course, an essential customer engagement core competence for Asian companies. Since we live in a digital age, service recovery and complaint handling should utilize effective online methods, without forgetting empathic offline approaches. What's radically different from even 10 years ago is that, for any serious customer-centric organization, transparency and speed around customer handling are as important as the interactions themselves. Several elements of effective and empathic service recovery are available through online–offline integration (Ollila, 2016):

(1) Problem monitoring: Have a system in place

It is critical for companies to formulate a proper plan on the mechanism to address grievances of their customers that are posted online. All the digital channels in use should be routinely monitored, an internal team should be assigned to develop a strategy to identify unhappy customers, and a step-by-step process should be created to execute the redressal strategy.

Digital technology has enabled companies to set up alerts to notify them when their company is mentioned online. There are some digital channels companies need to monitor regularly:

- Social media sites, such as Facebook, Twitter, Google+, LinkedIn, Reddit, and Quora
- Review websites, such as Yelp, Zillow, Google, Amazon, and industry-specific sites (e.g., Tripadvisor for hospitality industry)
- E-mail responses from customers
- Blog and social media influencers

(2) Timing management: Be quick with the response

The more time a company takes in addressing online complaints, the worse is the ripple effect, from a bad review, which could get shared numerous times, or a negative tweet that gets retweeted by hundreds of people. Timely response is absolutely crucial to alleviate disgruntled customers, who might even take time to eventually appreciate the quick response.

Once a company is in personal contact with the customer, it should take a moment to figure out the whole problem. It must identify the issues its customer faces and come up with an effective solution.

(3) Solution delivery: Fix the issue in under 24 hours

As important as it is to quickly recognize a complaint, it's even more important to spring into action to provide a solution to a customer complaint. The sooner you can fix a problem, the better is the possibility of a customer recovering from the bad experience.

If companies properly monitor all related digital channels, then no more than 24 hours should pass before they respond to a customer complaint.

(4) Follow-up: Use personal offline approach

Finally, once the problem is fixed, the company needs to make good on its service promise. The "human-to-human" (H2H) offline approach sometimes works better. Some companies write letters to the customers using personal handwriting and mail to them. In a B2B context, personal face-to-face meeting as a follow-up can make an emotional impact that lasts longer. In short, machine-to-machine (M2M) technology can produce better results when combined with H2H interactions.

References

Andreassen, TW (2000). Antecedents to satisfaction with service recovery. *European Journal of Marketing*, 24(1/2), 156–175.

Asia Pacific Network Information Center (2014). *Internet Infrastructure Development in the Asia Pacific: What's Needed for Sustainable Growth*. https://www.apnic.net/events/apnic-speakers/presentations/other/files2/2014-04-29-apnic-at-adb-itu.pdf (last accessed March 18, 2016).

Buday, R and V DiMauro (2011). *Customer Intimacy on Steroids: Why B2B Firms Need Online Communities*. http://bloomgroup.com/content/part-i-customer-intimacy-steroids (last accessed March 19, 2016).

Dawar, N (December 2013). When Marketing Is Strategy. *Harvard Business Review*.

Desforger, T and M Anthony (2013). *The Shopper Marketing Revolution*. Illinois: PTC Publishing.

DiMauro, V., & Bulmer, D. (2009). *The New Symbiosis of Professional Networks: Social Media's Impact on Business and Decision-Making*. New York: Society for New Communications Research.

DiMauro, V and D Bulmer (2010). *The New Symbiosis of Professional Networks*, SNCR Press.

Jardines.com (2016). Overview. http://www.jardines.com/group-companies.html (last accessed March 19, 2016).

Johnston, R and S Mehra (2002). Best practice complaint management. *Academy of Management Executive*, 16(4), 145–154.

Keith, RJ (January 1960). The marketing revolution. *Journal of Marketing*, 24, 35–38.

Kotler, *et. al.* (2003). *Rethinking Marketing: Sustainable Marketing Enterprise in Asia*. Singapore: Prentice Hall.

Lecinski, J (2011). *Winning the Zero Moment of Truth,* Google.

Lecinski, J (August 2014). *ZMOT: Why It Matters Now More Than Ever.* https://www.thinkwithgoogle.com/articles/zmot-why-it-matters-now-more-than-ever.html.

Levitt, T (July–August 1960). Marketing Myopia. *Harvard Business Review.*

Marketing-interactive.com (2016). Pizza Hut Activates Loyalty Club in Big Data Program. http://www.marketing-interactive.com/pizza-hut-activates-loyalty-club/ (last modified January 26, 2016; last accessed March 20, 2016).

Marketing-interactive.com (2016). How Jardine is Revolutionising the Digital World. http://www.marketing-interactive.com/how-jardine-is-revolutionising-the-digital-world/ (last modified February 19, 2016; last accessed March 20, 2016).

Mumbrella (2015). Why Thai Life Insurance Ads Are So Consistently, Tear-jerkingly Brilliant. http://www.mumbrella.asia/2015/01/thai-life-insurance-ads-consistently-tear-jerkingly-brillant/(last modified January 29, 2015; last accessed March 20, 2016).

News.com.au (2015). Thailand Television Commercials will Make You Cry, or At Least Get a Bit Sad. http://www.news.com.au/entertainment/tv/thailand-television-commercials-will-make-you-cry-or-at-least-get-a-bit-sad/news-story/8640bf2660dbd5c84140dcd7452b3c08 (last modified September 8, 2015; last accessed March 20, 2016).

Ollila, E (2016). *How to Win Back Lost Customers Who Feel Burned.* https://www.nowblitz.com/blog/how-to-win-back-lost-customers-that/ (last accessed March 20, 2016).

Quelch, JA and KE Jocz (Winter 2008). Milestone in Marketing. *Business History Review,* 82, 827–838.

Schwartz, J, K Espinola, and ON Van Tan (2010). *How Customers Choose Solutions Providers: The New Buyer Paradox.* ITSMA 2010 Report. London: ITSMA.

Treacy, M and F Wiersema (1997). *The Discipline of Market Leaders: Choose Your Customers, Narrow Your Focus and Dominate Your Market.* New York: Basic Books.

CHAPTER 6

HUMAN-CENTRIC PERSPECTIVE: DOING GOOD BY DOING WELL IN THE CONNECTED WORLD

*Business is a very beautiful mechanism to solve
problems, but we never use it for that purpose.
We only use it to make money.
It satisfies our selfish interest but not our collective interest.*

Muhammad Yunus — Bangladeshi Social Entrepreneur

Hart (2005), a management professor at the Johnson Graduate School of Management (Cornell University) and founder of the Center for Sustainable Global Enterprise, makes an interesting statement in his book *Capitalism at the Crossroads* (2005). He states that we now bear wit-

101

ness to the onset of a new era in which companies have become one of the most important pillars associated with resolution of the major problems facing mankind today. He identifies companies as the primary driving forces behind creating sustainable products, technologies, and business models that would help solve social and environmental problems, including poverty in the third-world countries, environmental concerns, economic inequality, low levels of education, and health issues.

In the past, all such social problems were seen as the responsibility of state and non-governmental organizations (NGOs). But now, business institutions are evidently being called to take on a greater, more serious role to bring innovations to the world. Some experts argue that business entities (companies) are at a more advantageous position to further the human cause in terms of access to resources, efficiency in carrying out processes, and creativity in solving problems. These advantages are increasingly becoming an authorization for businesses to participate in efforts to achieve a better world for all. In this context, Asia seems to be a prime location to launch such projects, since this is the region that represents a "big house" for the world's developing countries plagued with all sorts of problems.

Some business practitioners are also coming out with initiatives to make the company a "vehicle" in resolving the problems facing the human race. Bill Gates, co-founder of Microsoft and the poster child of the corporate philanthropy movement who made swift inroads in the business world, sparked a new term in this regard: Creative Capitalism (even more appropriately termed Creative Corporation). Creativity, in question, is the company's ability to use its resources in order to find new business opportunities that can, at the same time, contribute to resolving the social problems existing in the community (Kiviat and Gates, 2008).

Another creative approach is offered by Muhammad Yunus through a concept called "social business". A social business is an investment that is aimed at fulfilling some social objectives by creating an enterprise to execute the ideas. A social business-driven enterprise would cover costs and earn profits, but the core objective would be to achieve social objectives, such as housing or health care for the underprivileged, education and nutrition for poor children, and financial services for low-income households. The enterprise is created with the aim to address various social problems.

In the business world, a human-centric perspective emerges as the concept that offers a more systematic integration of social and business objectives. It is a new perspective that aims to deliver not only functional and emotional value but also a "spiritual" value.

Social and Business Objectives Integration

While alluding to the problems of integration between social objectives (such as poverty alleviation, eradication of illiteracy, and health improvement) and business objectives (profit optimization), we may have to go back to the classic argument made by the Nobel laureate economist Milton Friedman. In September 1970, Friedman wrote a ferocious article in *The New York Times Magazine*, flatly stating, "the social responsibility of business is to increase its profits".

The article presented criticism of the concept of corporate social responsibility (CSR) that began to become popular at the time. According to Friedman, when business people (in this case, company executives) indulge in social welfare activities with corporate funds, they become prone to committing the three "sins" of business. The first "sin" is toward shareholders, as the executives would not be entitled to using company's money for something outside their employment contract. According to Friedman, the executive is paid to manage a company, not a foundation. The second "sin" is toward customers, because CSR programs will result in skyrocketing costs for the company, which would further raise the price of products/services. And the third "sin" is toward employees, because the additional costs incurred through CSR would potentially scotch salary increments.

Friedman's above-stated opinion was guided by one basic assumption: business and social objectives are like water and oil — they can never be mixed. Consequently, any company spending on social programs would be perceived as a cost, presumably not contributing to any profits. The opinion seems to be different from that of the strategy expert Michael Porter, who, in a *Harvard Business Review* December 2002 article, asserted that a company could gain competitive advantage from philanthropic activities. A corporate philanthropy program can stimulate the local business environment that is capable of supporting enterprise productivity (competitive context). Porter even concluded, rather boldly, that philanthropy was the most cost-effective to create competitive context (Porter and Kramer, 2002).

That opinion has apparently echoed through the past decade. Many research results indicate that companies concerned with social problems can obtain greater economic benefits. Citing the words of Bill Gates, "they can do good and do well at the same time". This basic idea also underlines the emergence of the concept of human-centric marketing. This concept asserts that we can combine economic objectives with social objectives in "one package", while gaining sustainable competitive advantage.

Human-Centric Marketing in Action

The call for corporations to take a more active role and make greater contributions toward resolving social and environmental problems has long been heard and resonated, although differing in magnitude in various parts of the world. Research conducted in seven countries in Asia (India, Indonesia, Malaysia, the Philippines, Singapore, South Korea, and Thailand) found that awareness of corporations in the region toward CSR still lags behind when compared with that in their counterparts in Europe and North America (Chamber *et al.*, 2003). Nonetheless, companies in Asia can be prepared for the future and provide additional value to the larger community by addressing three major issues in their business model: socio-cultural issues, economic problems, and environmental challenges (Kotler *et al.*, 2010).

Promoters of the social transformation process

The world faces a multitude of social and cultural challenges today. Lack of education, health care problems, and limited access to basic human necessities are some examples. In Asia, school-age children from households in the poorest income quintile are up to five times more likely to be out of primary and secondary school than their peers in the richest quintile; infant mortality rates among the poorest households are 10 times higher than those among the affluent households; and in Central and West Asia, primary and secondary school enrolment levels for girls are 20 percent lower than those for boys. For developing Asia as a whole, 1.7 billion people

(45 percent of the population) lack access to sanitation and 680 million are without access to electricity (Kuroda, 2013).

Here the company's role is to contribute toward the creation of socio-cultural changes in the society. Addressing social challenges should not be viewed only as a tool of public relations or as a way to diffuse criticism of some negative fallout from the company's practices. On the contrary, companies should act as good corporate citizens and address social problems deeply by reviewing their business models and implementing appropriate measures. The key initially is to identify the socio-cultural challenges that exist and the possible consequences thereof.

IBM sets a good example of this approach through its Reinventing Education program. The program helps IBM create a supply of quali-fied human resources while enhancing the quality of education in schools world wide. Pharmaceutical companies, such as Merck, Glaxo-SmithKline, and Novartis, are furthering the cause of disease preven-tion and medication by improving access to specific medicines in certain communities. A similar effort is undertaken by Kimia Farma in Indonesia. One of its noble initiatives is the development of generic drugs that are more readily affordable to lower income households. A generic drug is one for which the patent period has expired, and thus it can be produced by all pharmaceutical companies without having to pay royalties. The quality of generic drugs is no different from that of a patented drug, as the raw material remains the same. Through produc-tion of these affordable generics, Kimia Farma contributes to world's health by providing access to cheap but quality medicines to those at the base of the pyramid.

The poverty problem resolution catalyst

Asia's rapid growth in recent decades has lifted hundreds of millions out of extreme poverty. China's economy has grown at a fast rate, ena-bling it to become a world power. Zakaria (2008) exclaimed that pov-erty alleviation has taken place at a faster rate in China than in any other country. India is also marching ahead on that mission. Extreme poverty in rural India declined greatly from 94 to 61 percent in 20 years, from 1985 to 2005. It is projected to decline further to 26 percent by 2025 (Beinhocker *et al.*, 2007).

Despite all the progress, the region remains home to two-thirds of the world's poor, with more than 800 million Asians still living on less than $1.25 a day and 1.7 billion surviving on less than $2 a day. The gap between Asia's rich and poor has widened alarmingly in the past two decades. In many countries, the richest 1 percent of households account for close to 10 percent of total consumption, and the top 5 percent account for more than 20 percent. The Gini coefficient, a measure of inequality, has increased in much of the region; taking Asia as a single unit, the Gini coefficient has increased from 39 to 46 (Kuroda, 2013). The data show that poverty reduction and income inequality remain daunting tasks in Asia.

A popular saying goes, "give a man a fish, and he'll eat for a day. Teach a man to fish and he'll eat for the rest of his life". The proverb, which puts the ability to create work above handouts, may also be illustrated through the concept of human-centric marketing and how it contributes to resolving economic problems in Asian countries. The jargon is: from aid to entrepreneurship. Businesses work toward accelerating poverty reduction efforts by empowering communities in the lower income segments, rather than merely doling out relief funds for consumption. One example is a program run by Unilever Shakti in India. With a social objective to empower underprivileged rural women, the so-called Shakti entrepreneurs were engaged to sell Unilever products in the village and earn income for themselves. Not only did it help Unilever enter into untapped markets and gain competitive advantage over other fast-moving consumer goods (FMCG) companies, it also helped the rural women community earn extra income through cash rewards and other incentives.

Contributors to resolution of environmental problems

One of the major problems facing humankind today is that of environmental degradation. Notwithstanding its enviable economic growth, urbanization, and much-coveted large, growing population, Asia is battling with several environmental challenges. One of the most visible side effects of Asia's rapid growth is environmental damage in terms of deforestation, global warming, and pollution. The reliance on fossil fuels has degraded air quality and ecosystems, reduced the supply of clean water, and created significant health hazards. Asia has become the world's largest source of greenhouse gas (GHG) emissions, which are linked to global warming and climate change. Its cities are among the most polluted and the most vulnerable to extreme weather conditions (Kuroda, 2013).

Considering the speed and intensity of environmental degradation in today's world, these challenges can be more effectively tackled by tying the business model of the company. Businesses are often involved in environmental issues; big corporations produce industrial waste and regulatory pressures compel them to meet standards and minimize effect on the environment. Some companies may act under pressure to do what is necessary before being exposed and publicly embarrassed by environmentalists. The scandals associated with environmental issues are quite detrimental to any company, negatively impacting its image in the eyes of customers and shareholders. At the other end are the companies that believe they could take advantage of this public interest in environmental causes by aggressively marketing their products and services as "green" (Kotler *et al.*, 2010).

One of the breakthrough approaches is adopted by an American conglomerate by creating a concept of replacing existing products and production processes with more environment-friendly substitutes. DuPont, a chemical company operating for more than two centuries, has dramatically transformed itself from being one of the worst polluters in the United States to one of its greenest corporations today (Varchaver, 2007). From expanding renewable energy usage to self-imposed targets on GHG emissions and zero waste disposals, the company has worked intensively to minimize environmental pollution and build sustainability in business. Another example is PT Pembangunan Perumahan (PT PP), an Indonesian state-owned construction company that has committed to adhering to the concept of green construction and green building development in each of its projects. This business concept has become a solid differentiation of the company, and at the same time, helps it to make a significant contribution to saving energy in Indonesia (see Box 6.1).

Connect and Change the World

In this era of an increasingly connected world, companies find it easier to collaborate with various stakeholders — both online and offline — to achieve business and social objectives. Unilever has set one such example

Box 6.1:   Indonesia's Green Construction Company

PT Pembangunan Perumahan (Persero) Tbk, abbreviated as PT PP, is one of the leading state-owned real estate enterprises in Indonesia, engaged in the planning and construction of buildings. Business activities are classified under four segments, namely construction (including building and infrastructure), engineering procurement construction (EPC), property and realty, and investment.

The construction segment, which contributes the biggest revenue with a growth target of 30 percent, includes construction of multistorey buildings, power plants, bridges, roads, and ports. Under the property and realty segment, PT PP undertakes construction of office buildings, apartments, and shopping malls. The EPC segment provides power plant–related services, meaning electricity to state-owned enterprises (SOEs) and energy companies. Finally, under the investment segment, the company makes capital investments in infrastructure projects and power plants.

Development of environment-friendly buildings or construction practices was not prevalent or popular in Indonesia until 2008. Contractors developing skyscrapers in major cities were not yet concerned about eco-friendly factors. But around that time, PT PP began to see a huge market potential in the green building sector.

The Green Building concept is based on efficiency improvement in energy consumption as well as resource management, including managing costs more effectively: water supply, waste and environmental management costs, as well as operational and maintenance costs. An example of advantages of the green building design is optimal use of natural light, also called daylighting. This enables controlled admission of natural light — direct sunlight and diffuse skylight — into buildings, reducing electric lighting, saving energy, and creating a more stimulating and productive indoor environment.

In addition to daylighting, using renewable solar energy to power outdoor lights in the night is also part of PT PP's green building concept. The efficiency in electricity consumption is further optimized

(Continued)

Box 6.1: (*Continued*)

with the use of motion sensor lighting, which minimizes wastage, along with the use of energy-saving lamps. Use of water in the buildings is also managed more efficiently by utilizing rainwater harvesting, thus saving groundwater.

PT PP's seriousness in applying the concept of green building and green construction is also realized through collaboration with local governments by issuing regulations that support similar initiatives. In recognition of these efforts, PT PP was awarded the Indonesia Green Award 2011 by the Ministry of Environment as well as the ASEAN Outstanding Engineering Award in the Green Construction Development category in the same year by the ASEAN Federation of Engineering Organizations.

---

in Indonesia. Based on its data, an average 80 percent of the global waste (up to 116 million tons per year) that exists is "geared" to be disposed in landfills. With limited landfill capacity in cities in Indonesia, of course this could lead to problems later on. With the initiation of its Green and Clean program, the Unilever Indonesia Foundation is empowering local communities to carry out handling and processing (segregation, recycling, and composting) of garbage in their neighborhood.

But this program is not executed single-handedly. Unilever uses an approach called Cadre network model. The prime movers of this model are the cadres and facilitators responsible for motivating the community around them to participate in the initiative. They are leading volunteers from a local community who have been trained by Unilever's internal team. Training topics include the current waste-related issues, knowledge on the program, interpersonal skills, and environment analysis.

It is the cadres who subsequently become the real change agents in the community. It is they who maintain the program's sustainability by continuing to motivate the members of the community, so that people won't lose spirit in their efforts to do good for the environment. The Cadre network model has proven to be quite successful. At the end of 2010, the number of cadres nurtured by Unilever reached 135,000 people. Compare this with 2001 when there were only 2!

Indeed, the real success of the Green and Clean program is manifested not only through a community approach. A crucial key to its success is collaboration. Through a stakeholder model approach, Unilever encouraged participation from the local government, mass media, and NGOs working on similar causes. No wonder the environmental waste problem became less severe over the years as it was dealt with from many angles.

The progress in digital technology allows companies to establish collaboration with various parties, both customers (downstream collaboration) and suppliers (upstream collaboration). With a human-centric spirit, collaboration is built with an aim to realize transformation that is positive and beyond a mere transactional business relationship. ITC is an example of a company that improves the welfare of the farmers who became its suppliers through the use of communications technology (see Box 6.2).

Even as Asian nations battle various economic, social, cultural, and environment problems, these challenges also present opportunities for creative enterprises to develop novel solutions through their business models. The examples discussed earlier provide a snapshot of how a human-centric perspective can be realized more effectively in this new era by utilizing technology that enables connectivity between various stakeholders. Collaboration among various parties is indispensable to improving the quality of life in the Asian society. Such collaborations should be able to combine an online and offline approach effectively in order to provide optimal impact.

Mobile connectivity indeed is still not evenly distributed among Asian countries. At a time of globalization and regional economic integration, the digital divide that exists between the more developed East Asia countries (Japan, Korea, and China) and some parts of Southeast Asia (Singapore) and other regions in Asia remains a challenge on the whole. In an effort to build greater connectivity in their regions, governments need support from various parties, including from the private sector. Grameenphone, a telecom service provider in Bangladesh, has succeeded in providing almost universal mobile access (99 percent of the population) and improving the quality of life in Bangladesh. The company also provides a wide range of innovative mobile technology to bring more convenience in the economic and social activities of people (see Box 6.3)

Box 6.2: ITC's e-Choupal in India

A business model equipped with a social mission, e-Choupal was designed to empower farmers and create a continuous cycle of higher productivity, higher incomes, enlarged capacity for risk management, and thereby larger investments to enable higher quality and productivity. It is an initiative of ITC Limited, a conglomerate in India, to link directly with rural farmers via the Internet for procurement of agricultural products such as soybeans, wheat, coffee, and prawns. e-Choupal tackles the challenges posed by Indian agriculture, which is characterized by fragmented farms, weak infrastructure, and intervention from intermediaries. The last factor has resulted in unfair pricing for farmers, taking advantage of their limited access to the market (buyer).

e-Choupal presents a good example of how human-centric initiatives can us technology to create connectivity among various stakeholders. The program installs computers with Internet access in rural areas to offer farmers with up-to-date marketing and agricultural information. The company has provided computers and Internet access in rural areas across several agricultural regions of the country, where the farmers can directly negotiate sale of their products with ITC Limited as the buyer. Digital connectivity enables farmers to get information on commodity prices, learn good farming practices, and place orders for agricultural inputs such as seeds and fertilizers. This helps farmers improve the quality of their products and obtain a better price. Intermediaries cannot intervene on pricing anymore.

Each ITC Limited kiosk with Internet access is organized by a *sanchalak* — a trained farmer. The kiosk — along with computer and Internet access — becomes a community hub. Each installation serves an average of 600 farmers in the surrounding 10 villages within about a 5-km radius. The *sanchalak* bears some operating cost but in return earns a service fee for the e-transactions done through his e-Choupal. Abhishek Jain, a soya farmer and e-Choupal sanchalak in Madhya Pradesh district, testifies:

(Continued)

Box 6.2:   (Continued)

Before ITC introduced us to e-Choupal, we were restricted to selling our produce in the local mandi (market). We had to go through middlemen and prices were low. Today we are a community of e-farmers with access to daily prices of a variety of crops in India and abroad — this helps us to get the best price. We can also find out about many other important things — weather forecasts, latest farming techniques, crop insurance, etc. e-Choupal has not only changed the quality of our lives, but our entire outlook.

e-Choupal has triggered a socioeconomic transformation in Indian rural areas. Since its implementation, farmers have seen a rise in their income levels and improvement in quality of output. It also cuts intermediaries, creating less transaction costs for farmers. Farmers can get real-time information despite their physical distance from the market. At the same time, the system also saves procurement costs and provides a more sustainable source of production input for ITC Limited.

These interventions have helped transform village communities into vibrant economic organizations by enhancing incomes and cocreating markets. e-Choupals serve 40,000 villages and four million farmers, making it the world's largest rural digital infrastructure created by a private enterprise.

Source: "Embedding Sustainability in Business", www.itcportal.com.

Box 6.3:   Bangladesh Grameenphone

Grameenphone is the largest mobile provider in Bangladesh with more than 56 million subscribers (as of January 2016). It is a joint venture between Telenor and Grameen Telecom Corporation. Grameenphone was the first company to introduce GSM technology in Bangladesh and built the first cellular network to cover 99 percent of the country. The company was founded as a result of inspiration from the Grameen Bank microcredit model, whereby its founder Iqbal Quadir envisioned

(Continued)

Box 6.3: (*Continued*)

a business model in which a cell phone served as a source of income. The idea is to provide universal mobile phone access throughout Bangladesh, including its rural areas, which could be an accelerator for socioeconomic transformation in the country.

Grameenphone has been a pioneer in bringing innovative mobile-based solutions to Bangladesh. Notable among these is the Healthline, a 24-hour medical call center manned by licensed physicians. Other innovations include Studyline, a call center–based service providing education-related information; Mobi Cash, for electronic purchase of train tickets; Billpay, for paying bills through mobile phones and over 500 community information centers across Bangladesh. These centers bring affordable Internet access and other information-based services to people in rural areas.

Grameenphone also has enabled Mobile Financial Services (MFS) for five partner banks (Dutch-Bangla Bank Ltd., Islamic Bank Bangladesh Ltd., Mercantile Bank Ltd., ONE Bank Ltd., and United Commercial Bank Ltd.). It has opened 61,000 MobiCash outlets, from which customers register for MFS with partner banks, deposit and withdraw cash, and pay utility bills. In Q1 2015, a total of 615,121 deposit and withdrawal transactions and 1.22 million utility bills were processed through MobiCash, amounting to BDT 1.9 billion (US\$244 million) and BDT 1.4 billion (US\$179 million), respectively.

The introduction of MFS to Bangladesh could render a solution for 76 percent of the unbanked population in Bangladesh. The prediction comes from a study conducted by the Boston Consulting Group for Telenor in 2011 on the socioeconomic impact of MFS. The Bangladeshi economy stands to gain as well with the introduction of MFS, which resulted in a 2 percent increase to the total gross domestic product by 2020. The economical and societal contributions of the new business activity include creating 500,000 new jobs and improving health care access.

As part of corporate social responsibility, Grameenphone has also initiated the Online School in Bangladesh. The idea of the Online

(*Continued*)

Box 6.3: (*Continued*)

School is that a teacher conducts class from a distant location using video conferencing technology with the aid of moderators in the actual class. These moderators, who are from the local community, have no teaching background but can help the teacher in operational issues. The main objective of the Online School is to ensure quality education for underprivileged and secluded children living in urban slums and remote areas. It also helps develop teachers who can deliver quality education.

The Online School is a unique idea through which quality education, similar to that available in major cities, may be provided to the disadvantaged population living in slums and remote areas. Children having such access find it very interesting to study this way and find learning to be fun. Initiatives such as this educate people on the benefits of the Internet and the amazing things that can be done through it.

Sources: Telenor.com; grameenphone.com.

References

Beinhocker, ED, D Farrell and AS Zainulbhai (August 2007). Tracking the Growth of India's Middle Class. *The McKinsey Quarterly*.

Chamber, *et al.* (2003). *CSR in Asia: A Seven Country Study of CSR Website Reporting. ICCSR Research Paper Series*. Nottingham: International Centre for Corporate Social Responsibility.

Friedman, M (13 September 1970). The Social Responsibility of Business Is to Increase Its Profits. *The New York Times Magazine*.

Grameenphone (2016). Company Profile. http://grameenphone.com/about/investor-relations/corporate-factssheet/company-profile (last accessed July 26, 2016).

Hart, SL (2005). *Capitalism at the Crossroad: Next Generation Business Strategies for a Post-Crisis World*. New Jersey: FT Press.

ITC Limited (2016). Embedding Sustainability in Business. http://www.itcportal.com/sustainability/embedding-sustainability-in-business.aspx (last accessed July 26, 2016).

Kiviat, B and B Gates (July 31, 2008). Making Capitalism More Creative. *Time Magazine*.

Kotler, P, H Kartajaya and I Setiawan (2010). *Marketing 3.0: From Products to Customers to the Human Spirit*. New Jersey: John Wiley.

Kuroda, H (2013). Asia's Challenge. http://www.oecd.org/forum/asia-challenge.htm (last accessed July 26, 2016).

Porter, ME and MR Kramer (December 2002). The Competitive Advantage of Corporate Philanthropy. *Harvard Business Review*.

Telenor Group (2016). Grameenphone Bangladesh. https://www.telenor.com/about-us/global-presence/bangladesh/ (last accessed July 26, 2016).

Varchaver, N (22 March 2007). Chemical Reaction. *Fortune*.

Zakaria, F (2008). *Post-American World*. New York: W.W. Norton.

Part I

SUMMARY

Chapter 4. Product-Centric Perspective: Connectivity in Product Development

- Companies that adopt a product-centric perspective believe that the key to success in business is to develop the most appropriate products to satisfy customer needs.

- Companies need to pay attention to the "health" of its product portfolio. On the basis of their relative growth and the company's relative strength, there are four types of products a company should consider — (i) existential products (commodity products), (ii) essential products (foundation or basic products), (iii) initial products (untested creations), and (iv) potential products (tested innovations).

- In the digital era, a product-centric competitive advantage is built through new product development supported by strong connectivity with customers (open innovation), "smart" products that can be connected with customers, as well as the various related products (Internet of Things).

Chapter 5. Customer-Centric Perspective: Connecting with the Digital Consumer

- Companies that implement a customer-centric perspective believe that the key to success in business is to provide value based on the customer's point of view. The marketer is paying greater attention to the psychological and emotional aspects — as opposed to strictly functional benefits — for customers using their products or services.

- There are four core activities in customer management: get (acquire new customers), keep (focus on loyalty building to keep valuable customers), grow (add value for both customers and company), and win back (seek opportunities to get back lost customers).

- The digitalization era is transforming Asian consumers into demanders of smarter value from the products and services they purchase. Therefore, companies that do not have an engaging online presence or effective mobile strategy will now pale in comparison with those who do. Customer management should hence apply the same logic to get, keep, grow, and win back their digital consumers.

Chapter 6. Human-Centric Perspective: Doing Good by Doing Well in the Connected World

- Companies that implement a human-centric perspective nurture a vision to integrate social and business objectives. In addition to functional and emotional benefits, they also offer societal benefits to consumers using their products or services.

- Companies in Asia can adopt a human-centric perspective and provide additional value to the larger community by addressing three major challenges in their business model: sociocultural, economic, and environmental.

- The digital age has made it easier for companies to connect and collaborate, both online or offline, with various other stakeholders (governments, customers, non-government organizations, and others) so that it can create a greater impact on the community.

Part II

MARKETING IS MOVING?
Competitive Position: The Core Essence

Every business organization operating in a free market must deal with the competitive situation. Therefore, solid integration between marketing strategy and tactic is a must to win the customers' mind and heart. This involves the analysis of internal competitive advantages and the external environment in order to position the organization's brand, products, and services in the minds of its stakeholders. Positioning is about the promise of delivering value to the organization's customers. It is the core of a company's marketing strategy.

Using positioning as the "umbrella", the organization then must perform the actual delivery of value by carefully choosing the tactics on how its products and services can be received by the customers. Successful marketing tactics will differentiate an organization from its competitors in terms of content (what to offer), context (how to offer), and infrastructure (the enabler of content and context, i.e., technology, people, and facilities). Differentiation is about how an organization applies the understanding of its customers' needs to satisfy their desires. It's the core of marketing tactic.

Formulation of a clear positioning and differentiation will help to define the brand identity, integrity, and image. Therefore, companies must realize that a brand is more than just a name. Branding is not just about advertising and public communications. It is more about an organization's overall efforts to win the customers' trust, loyalty and conviction in its brand, and to avoid presenting its products and services like commodities.

The positioning statement defines a promise, and a company develops its positioning by communicating a marketing message (the brand promise) that is meant to create a certain perception in customers' mind. In order for companies to have brand integrity, it must support this promise with a solid and concrete differentiation. These three core elements of the strategic business triangle (positioning–differentiation–brand [PDB]) are interlinked and work seamlessly as one self-reinforcing mechanism. Without this relationship, an organization will be drifting directionless battled out by competitors, or simply become irrelevant amid rapid environmental changes.

The PDB triangle is one of the most important marketing tools that becomes the core essence of marketing. Many companies have successfully used the PDB triangle as their winning formula. When applied consistently in an organization's day-to-day marketing activities, the strategic business triangle can create a strong foundation to build competitive advantages and strong brand values (Kotler *et al.*, 2014).

But the world of marketing as it is today would no longer be the same in the future. The business landscape in the future will be characterized by three major changes: inclusivity, horizontalization, and socialization. Inclusivity is going to be witnessed in the world of science and technology, characterized by the fading of barriers between different scientific

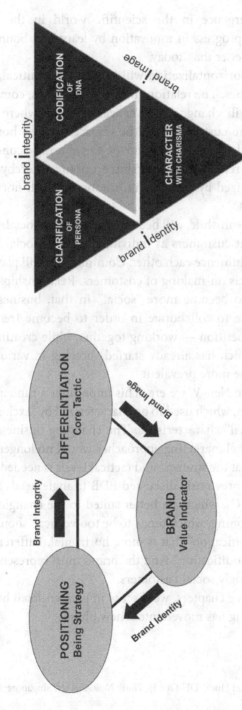

Legacy Marketing

The PDB Triangle:
Positioning-Differentiation-Brand

New Wave Marketing

The Triple Cs:
Clarification-Codification-Character

Figure A: From PDB triangle to triple Cs.

disciplines. Convergence in the scientific world in the future will eventually lead to progress in innovation by leaps and bounds, making human life much better than today.

The wave of horizontalization will impact the political, economic, and social landscapes. The relations between countries, companies, and also individuals will change. The vertical era, one where companies could dominate the customers, will be replaced with a horizontal era that puts them side by side. The era of the sharing economy would gradually begin to replace the ownership economy, whereby the ownership will be optimized by resource utilization and will not rotate only within a few hands.

The market, meanwhile, will become increasingly social. Companies will no longer treat customers as individuals, but as social beings who interact with and influence each other. Communities will play an important role in the decision-making of customers. Relationships with competitors would also become more "social", in that, businesses will be required to be able to collaborate in order to become trendsetters in any industry. Coopetition — working together while creating a healthy competition — which has already started showing in various business sectors, will become more prevalent.

Welcome to the New Wave era. This underlines a fundamental shift from the Legacy era, which used to be characterized by "exclusive", "vertical", and "individual" characteristics. The changing business landscape means the traditional marketing approaches would no longer be entirely relevant. A change at the strategic and tactical levels is needed. Therefore, the concept of the previously discussed PDB triangle needs to be transformed into triple Cs, which are better suited to the changing demands (see Fig. A). Positioning, which tends to be too vertical, should be transformed into a "clarification" that is more horizontal. Differentiation has been changed to "codification". And the brand must represent a "character" to the increasingly social customers.

In the next three chapters, we discuss in greater detail how the core essence of marketing has moved into a new phase.

Reference

Kotler, P, H Kartajaya and Hooi, DH (2014). *Think New ASEAN*. Singapore: McGraw-Hill.

CHAPTER 7

BEING STRATEGY: FROM POSITIONING TO CONFIRMATION

Identifying one brand position, communicating it in a repetitive manner is old-fashioned, out of date, out of touch.
(This is) The end of brand positioning as we know it

Larry Light — Former McDonald's Chief Marketing Officer

In the legacy era, the concept of positioning remains at the core of marketing strategy. It is a product's or service's "being strategy". It articulates the goals that a consumer will achieve by using a brand and explains why it is superior to other means of accomplishing this goal. Al Ries and Jack Trout (1981), in their legendary book *Positioning: The Battle of Your Mind*, said that marketing war unfolds not in the market, but in the minds of customers. It is a war fought to snatch away a piece of land (space) in the minds of customers. In the book, the authors define

123

positioning as what you do to the mind of the prospect and not what you do to a product. Each successful product, brand, and company has managed to gain a strong and unique position in the minds of customers.

For example, HSBC Bank has a global positioning as a financial services institution adept at understanding the anxieties and desires of the local community it serves. Jollibee Foods Corporation, which operates fast-food restaurants, wants to be perceived as the number one family restaurant chain in the Philippines. Honda's One Heart campaign in Indonesia seeks to show how the motorcycle manufacturer wants to build emotional intimacy with its customers. Vietravel strategically positions itself as a higher end tourism company offering unique trips and exclusive experiences (see Box 7.1). While to its global customers, Samsung wants to be known as one of the leading companies inherently focused on technological innovation.

Box 7.1:   Vietravel: Vietnam's Premium Travel Agency

Becoming "a professional travel organizer" has been the principle and mission of Vietravel company throughout its more than 20 years of constant development and renovation. In the initial days after Vietravel was established in 1995, it faced many difficulties in the tourism market, lacking employees, funds, and facilities. But with a determination to overcome difficulties and an effective business strategy, the company has gradually grown. It has continuously expanded operations and footprint, from just being known domestically to becoming a renowned international player in the travel industry, especially popular within the Southeast Asia region.

The company also uses technology effectively to keep up with the changing purchasing behavior of its consumers. In 2007, Vietravel launched the first online tour booking website in Vietnam, helping to create a link between the company and its customers all the time and everywhere, and followed them up adequately by mobile phone applications. These online platforms have expanded their reach among customers who can easily browse through various tour packages and get detailed

(Continued)

Box 7.1:   (*Continued*)

information about tourist destinations anywhere, anytime. The application also helps visitors in Vietnam plan their trip, featuring highlights on events happening in Vietnam.

As part of its product management, Vietravel routinely launches packages covering new destinations and tour itineraries. In 2012, it launched a tour package to Mauritius bringing visitors to the capital city as well as the Mauritius National Park. Other exotic destinations include Russia and Tibet. Customers can also choose from tours classified into various types: trekking tours for the adventurous ones, culinary tours for foodies, or off-the-beaten-track tours for those who want something different. There are even more unique types of tours for those who are "Empty Nesters", "Responsible" travelers, or visiting destinations with families. Most recently, in February 2016, the tour operator has launched two new luxury package tours: a five-star cruise package and a five-star holiday package.

Beyond doing business as usual, Vietravel is able to expand its presence on a global front and gain a reputation as an event and activity organizer and not just as a tour operator. It has attempted to gain international recognition by organizing a variety of international events, including the Asia Pacific Economic Cooperation (APEC) meeting in 2006 and the Southeast Asia Undergraduate Sports Festival of 2008. It also launched a "Go Green in Tourism" campaign in 2012 to raise awareness about environment- and sustainability-related issues, and utilized the platform to promote its own set of eco-friendly tour packages.

Due to its reputation in the tourism industry, Vietravel has been listed among the top 16 travel companies in Asia and was given the Asia's Leading Travel Agency 2015 award by the World Travel Awards. As a company that has received numerous awards and recognitions, it is encouraging to see how Vietravel is still striving to be the best in its customers' hearts and minds. Its strategic positioning as a higher end tourism company offering unique trips and exclusive experiences has helped expand its appeal to a growing middle class in the region.

(*Continued*)

Box 7.1: *(Continued)*

According to Nguyen Minh Man, deputy director of Vietravel Marketing and Media Department, the long-term development orientation of the company for 2015–2020 is to have 1,000,000 customers in 2020 and to become one of the top 10 tourist companies in Asia.

Sources: Kotler *et al.* (2014); "Vietravel — A Professional Travel Organiser", July 20, 2014, www.vietnam.vnanet.vn/; "Vietravel Launches Luxury Package Tours", February 19, 2016, www.talkvietnam.com.

The process of determining its positioning forms a fundamental part of any company's marketing strategy. There are many examples of companies that became successful as a result of the strength of their positioning. Southwest Airlines was once the most profitable airline in the United States because it meticulously positioned itself apart from other air transport companies. At a time when competitors sought to improve customer service, expand their global flight network, and race ahead to be the largest, Southwest Airlines actually went the opposite way, by concentrating on short-distance flights and high frequency. With a fleet of short-to-medium-range airplanes, no-frills service — not even reserved seats or luggage transfer — the airline focused exclusively on providing timely service and low airfares. It well positioned itself as the "on-time", "low-fare", and "friendly service" airline.

A similar story emerged from Asia when Tony Fernandez turned around AirAsia, an ailing and heavily indebted company he bought from the Malaysian government. Adopting the slogan "Now Everyone Can Fly", AirAsia together with its subsidiaries operating in South Asia (India) and Southeast Asia (Thailand, Indonesia, and the Philippines) as well as a long-haul airline AirAsia X positioned itself as the first low-cost air transportation services provider, especially in the fast-developing South-east Asian region.

Also, positioning represents a "frame of reference" by claiming membership in a product category. The goal is to avoid customer comparisons of a brand with competitors from a different class. When AirAsia emerged as a low-cost carrier, rivals in the region including Singapore

Airlines and Indonesia flag carrier Garuda Indonesia sought to maintain their customer base by offering a unique service experience. Both the airlines did not want to compete by lowering prices, as that would have damaged their existing positioning. By providing additional value in the form of functional and emotional experience during travel (pre, during, and postflight), these airlines have succeeded in their category of "full-service airline", a clear positioning that is different from the "low-cost carrier" class.

Positioning Development in the Legacy Era

Kotler (2001) states that positioning includes every effort made toward designing products and brands in such a way that they occupy a unique position in the minds of customers. The end result of positioning is creation of the right value proposition, which becomes the reason for customers to buy a product or service. To have a unique and strong position in the customer's mind, traditional wisdom suggests that companies should develop a powerful but simple tagline. The slogan is then usually campaigned repetitively to create a lasting memory in the minds of customers.

Actually, a tagline is just a summary of the company's positioning statement. Managers develop formal positioning statements to ensure a shared vision for the brand throughout the organization and to guide tactical actions. Although formats for presenting a brand's positioning may vary by companies, the following five common elements have been identified as critical (Kotler *et al.*, 2003; Tybout and Sternthal, 2005):

(1) **Target market:** reflection of the customer profile to which the products or services are being offered. The profiles are typically selected on the basis of geography, demography, psychography, or customer behavior.

(2) **Brand name:** reflection of a proposed value offered to the customer. A brand name should be easy to remember and shouldn't create negative associations.

(3) **Frame of reference:** an idea, condition, or assumption that determines how something should be achieved, accepted, or understood. These frames of reference fall into two general categories: (i) frames that are

depicted in terms of product features and (ii) frames that are represented by more abstract consumers' goals.

(4) **Point of differentiation:** the reasons why a customer should choose the company's product rather than the competitor's. We will discuss further on differentiation tactics in Chap. 8.

(5) **Reasons to believe:** the proof(s) that the brand delivers what it promises to customers. This final element is more important when the differentiation claims are relatively abstract.

The brand's final positioning statement may be distributed widely within the firm but may need some adjustments before being communicated externally to customers. To create a powerful and memorable impact, companies need to summarize the positioning statement into a short and "sexy" slogan. That is called a tagline (see Fig. 7.1). For example, Nissan creates a comprehensive positioning statement for its SUV as follows:

> For contemporary and value-oriented people (*target market*) Nissan X-Trail (*brand*) is an SUV (*frame of reference*) with perfect balance of cool exterior/interior design, enjoyable handling, and excellent engine performance (*points of differentiation*) available in wide range of variants, most reliable customer support and high resale value (*reasons to believe*).

The above statement will sufficiently act as a practical guidance internally. But externally — via advertising, brochures, websites, and so on — Nissan would need to highlight a simpler and shorter tagline: **The Real SUV.**

The Fall of Positioning, the Rise of Clarification

In the short discussion on positioning, we reckoned how brand positioning formed a core part of the marketing strategy and was fundamentally important for marketers in the legacy era. Of course, in the changing world — from legacy to the New Wave era today — the brand positioning, as we have known it, is no longer entirely relevant. That is because the act of a company-driven positioning is one way and more dominated by the company — no longer in accordance with the character of the new customer who

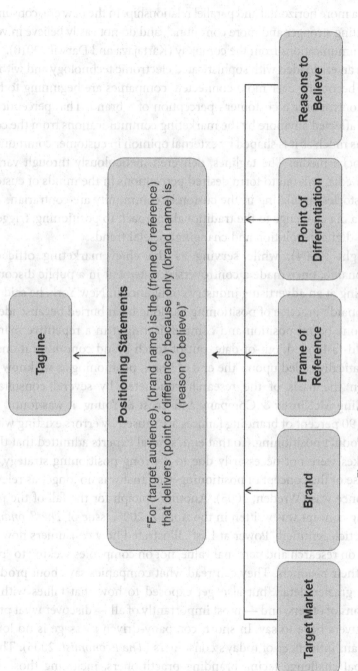

Figure 7.1: Positioning statement development.

wants a more horizontal and parallel relationship. In the new era, consumers are getting stronger and more communal, and do not easily believe in vertical communications from the company (Kartajaya and Darwin, 2010).

In an era loaded with sophisticated electronic technology and with the world becoming ever more connected, companies are beginning to have little control over a customer's perception of a brand. That perception is not as affected anymore by the marketing communications from the company as much as it is shaped by external opinion in customer communities and social media. The taglines, delivered meticulously through various paid media, will fail to form desired perceptions in the minds of customers if stories circulating in the customer community are contrarian. This poses a big challenge to the traditional approach to positioning, triggered by the digital revolution and changing societal trends.

Light (2004), while serving as the chief marketing officer at McDonald's, once made a controversial statement in a public discourse. Speaking at an advertising industry conference in New York, he said that McDonald's practice of positioning has long been buried because identifying one brand position and communicating it in a repetitive manner was old-fashioned, out-of-date, out-of-touch brand communication. He emphatically called upon, "the end of brand positioning as we know it".

On the basis of the research conducted by several consultants, including McKinsey & Company and Ernst & Young, it was found that about 90 percent of branding failures are caused by errors existing within the product positioning. To that end, several experts admitted that those mistakes were not necessarily due to a wrong positioning strategy, but because of the concept of positioning itself that was no longer as relevant as it once was (Wreden, 2005). Another epitaph for the fall of the positioning concept was written in the April 2, 2005, issue of *The Economist*. The article, entitled "Power at Last", illustrated how consumers now buy based on research and personal value, not on companies seeking to "position" their products. They can read what companies say about products in far greater detail, but also get exposed to how that tallies with the opinions of others, and — most importantly of all — discover what previous buyers have to say. In short, company-driven message is no longer the main influencer of today's consumers (*The Economist*, 2005). This is a global challenge facing branding practitioners, including those who market their products to and from Asia.

Clarification Anatomy

If a company such as McDonald's — a symbol of globalization in the fast-food market serving more than 100 countries — believed positioning was dead and abandoned the concept, what they replaced it with is what comes to be known as Brand Journalism. The concept was built around the basic assumption that no single message could tell the whole multidimensional story of a mega-brand like McDonald's, which means different things in different regions to different people in different situations with different needs. A brand's story cannot be a simple-minded, oversimplification of a complex brand idea. While it kept its "I'm lovin' it" tagline alive, McDonald's radically changed the way it was communicated externally.

With the new campaign, McDonald's rejected the traditional marketing and advertising approaches that focused on a single and repetitive message. Instead, it adopted a multidimensional approach of sending messages via multiple channels to multiple audiences. It was the same way an editor approaches the creation of a magazine, with its array of different contents and stories aimed at a variety of interests but with a coherent editorial framework (Light, 2014). In the changing world of marketing, what McDonald's did could well be compared with the content marketing trends embraced by start-up companies today. It involves a strategic marketing approach focused on creating and distributing valuable, relevant, and consistent content to attract and retain a clearly defined audience — and, ultimately, to drive profitable customer action (Content Marketing Institute, 2016).

The concept of clarification bears some fundamental similarities with the new practices discussed earlier. This is actually an evolution of the concept of positioning in a new form, which is more horizontal, inclusive, and social. There are three fundamental differences between the positioning and clarification strategies (see also Table 7.1).

Table 7.1: Comparison of positioning and clarification.

Positioning	Clarification
Focus on a penetrating single message	Involving multidimensional messages
Company-oriented content	Customer-oriented content
One-way communication	Multiple-way communication

Single message versus multidimensional message

In positioning, the tagline becomes the main message and is spread across through advertising, events, sponsorships, publicity activities, and other marketing campaigns. The purpose is to help form a strong perception of a product. Ries (2012) even stressed on the importance of developing a "visual hammer" — an emotionally powerful image — to nail a company's brand into customers' minds. The objective is to subconsciously communicate the emotional power of your brand while also driving a verbal idea into the mind. She disagreed with her father's legacy concept but at the same time agreed with the basics of positioning that focus only on delivering a single message.

In clarification, the tagline does not consist only of a message that is delivered repeatedly across media, but rather serves as a "cover story" that gets translated in various forms of content. While McDonald's continues to use the "I'm lovin' it" tagline in a variety of media promotion activities for over 10 years, the company has not imposed a single meaning through its use, on its customers. The campaign has appeared in over 100 countries in more than 20 languages, even changing the language but the underlying emotion is love. In Azerbaijan, for example, the tagline literally translates to "See, this is the love".

The intent is basically for customers to have their own reasons and ways of "loving the brand". McDonald's marketing communication aims to illustrate how the love emotion is expressed across different cultures, segments, and situations. Customers can so choose to have their own definition of love and review of their own emotional expression.

Company-oriented versus customer-oriented content

In positioning, the focus of its content is all about the product or service of a company. The main objective is to effectively convey the functional and emotional benefits that can be obtained by customers using a particular product/service. Car manufacturers, for instance, rave about their elegant design and superior engine. Banks will talk about the returns customers get, or their excellent, personalized services. Telco providers will swear by their vast wide-reaching network quality. The focus is entirely on their own interests. But this approach may not be relevant anymore. In an era when customers are highly aware and exposed virtually all the time to a variety of information, they will ultimately hear and see what they want to and what really matters to them.

The approach that the process of clarification advocates is using content that is more tailored to customer needs. Often, the content is not even directly related to the products on offer, but it could provide real benefits to customers. Car manufacturers could produce how-to videos explaining practical tips on engine maintenance. Banks may create free e-books on personal financial planning. And telco providers may launch free applications for subscribers to provide entertainment through music or other viral content. Clarification could use a variety of other forms of providing users with useful information: pictures, articles, movies, music, e-books, apps, and other downloadable content. Despite the many forms, the principle remains the same: it is all about customers, not the company. A good example is from Unilever's *Paddle Pop*, which the company has been successfully practicing since 2011 (see Box 7.2).

One-way versus multiple-way communication

In the past, positioning was formed through communication controlled by the company while the customer acted as just a passive receiver of the messages. But with advancements in technology, the interactions have grown not only into a two-way communication (between company and customers) but also into a multiple-way communication (customers among themselves). Mobile and digital technologies have made it easier for customers to share information with the people around them (friends, families, and also followers). Online reviews, social media, and online forum postings have begun to play an increasingly important role as a reference point for customers to make crucial purchasing decisions.

To that end, it is vital for Asian companies to produce customer-oriented content, which is deemed exciting, entertaining enough by customers to be shareable in their networks. Companies cannot force them to give testimonies or positive recommendations. Instead, companies should follow a twofold approach: (i) create useful content that is functional or appeals emotionally so as to prompt customers to share it with others voluntarily, and (ii) provide a mechanism that will allow customers to

Box 7.2:   Paddle Pop Adventure: Creating Customer-Oriented Content

Kids aged between 8 and 12 years certainly love ice cream. But maintaining its position as a top-of-mind choice amid an increasing number of snacks was a big challenge for Unilever's *Paddle Pop* ice cream. Instead of using marketing campaigns focused on single taglines, *Paddle Pop* launched a variety of entertaining content to clarify "who they are".

In 2011, *Paddle Pop* engaged agency Lowe and Partners to create a unique marketing approach to differentiate it from competitors who would focus only on product innovation and consumer promotion. *Paddle Pop* used its flagship mascot, Paddle Pop Lion, as the core character in their 360-degree entertainment content. The goal was to create a story that would enliven a livelier brand essence through the mascot's adventures. Moreover, the lion mascot of the *Paddle Pop* became an icon loved by children.

In 2012, *Paddle Pop* launched a campaign in the form of a digital entertainment portal featuring 11 adventure video series, each a duration of 22 minutes and titled Paddle Pop Adventures. In the video series, it introduced other characters, namely Leena, a female lion and Paddle Pop's friend, and together they jointly fought against the malicious Shadow Master.

Paddle Pop Adventures was released online on YouTube, as well as through television advertising in 30 countries; and a big screen 90-minute movie *Paddle Pop Begins* was screened in cinemas and made available on DVD. A series of two-dimensional platforming games were also developed on the themes surrounding the lion's adventure.

In addition, *Paddle Pop* performed offline clarification in the form of Paddle Pop Adventures theme parks, public relation activities, sponsorships, competitions (ice-cream sticks promotion), and other such offline activation events. All these promotional efforts aptly supported the *Paddle Pop* ice-cream parlors in around one million ice-cream outlets globally.

(Continued)

Box 7.2: (Continued)

In markets where *Paddle Pop* already existed, customer loyalty reached new heights. In Indonesia, brand loyalty reached 71 percent, from 65 percent previously. In markets where *Paddle Pop* was newly launched, brand awareness hit 90 percent.

In the markets of Indonesia, Australia, Mexico, and India, the television program was created to attract the attention of children who had been exposed to a variety of popular programs, such as SpongeBob, High School Musical, Phineas & Ferb, and Harry Potter. In Turkey, where the content was introduced in cinema, *Paddle Pop* managed to emerge as the third most watched movie in the country, ahead of several Hollywood films.

In India, more than 1.2 million children joined the Paddle Pop Gaming League, and more than 5 million DVDs were redeemed via promotions across Southeast Asia. In terms of sales, the program managed to increase *Paddle Pop* sales globally by 26 percent in 2011. Meanwhile, in the new markets, *Paddle Pop* sales grew even more strongly, by 43 percent.

Source: marketeers.com.

---

create and share content, for example, by providing sharing buttons in the social media so that with one click, the content could be easily shared with the audience customers desire to.

References

Al Ries and Trout, J (1981). *Positioning: The Battle of Your Mind*. New York: McGraw Hill.

Content Marketing Institute (2016). *What Is Content Marketing*. http://contentmarketing-institute.com/what-is-content-marketing (last accessed March 26, 2016).

Kartajaya, H and W Darwin (2010). *Connect: Surfing New Wave Marketing*. Jakarta: Gramedia Pustaka Utama.

Kotler, P (2001). *Marketing Management Millenium Edition*, 10th Ed. New Jersey: Prentice Hall.

Kotler, *et al.* (2003). *Rethinking Marketing: Sustainable Marketing Enterprise in Asia*. Singapore: Prentice Hall.

Kotler, P, H Kartajaya, and Hooi, DH (2014). *Think New ASEAN*. Singapore: McGraw Hill.

Light, L (2004). The End of Brand Positioning as We Know It Conference Speech presented at the ANA Annual Conference, cited in *The Ramsey Report: The State of the Online Advertising Industry*, November 8, 2004.

Light, L (July 2014). Brand Journalism Is a Modern Marketing Imperative. *Advertising Age*. http://adage.com/article/guest-columnists/brand-journalism-a-modern-marketing-imperative/294206 (last accessed March 26, 2016).

Marketeers Editor (2016). Content Marketing: Paddle Pop Kembali Rilis Film Animasi Terbarunya. http://wwwmarketeers.com/peduli-content-marketing-paddle-pop-kembali-rilis-film-animasi-terbarunya/ (last modified January 12, 2016; last accessed July 30, 2016).

Ries, L (2012). *Visual Hammer: Nail Your Brand into the Mind with the Emotional Power of a Visual*. Georgia: Laura Ries.

Talk Vietnam. (2016). Vietravel Launches Luxury Package Tours. https://www.talkvietnam.com/2016/02/vietravel-launches-luxury-package-tours/ (last modified February 19, 2016; last accessed July 30, 2016).

The Economist (March 31, 2005). Power at Last. *The Economist*.

Tybout, AM and B Sternthal (2005). *Brand Positioning Kellogg on Branding*. New Jersey: John Wiley.

Vietnam Pictorial (2014). Vietravel — A Professional Travel Organiser. http://vietnam.vnanet.vn/english/vietravel-a-professional-travel-organiser/58823.html (last modified July 30, 2014, last accessed July 30, 2016).

Wreden, N (June 2005). The Demise of Positioning. *Asia Pacific Management Forum*. http://www.apmforum.com/drops/000319.php (last accessed March 26, 2016).

CHAPTER 8

CORE TACTIC: FROM DIFFERENTIATION TO CODIFICATION

I think airlines have been very much like parrots.
They will just follow what everyone else is doing.
And it takes someone like myself or Richard Branson
who comes from outside the industry to say,
"Hey, let's try something new".

Tony Fernandez — Group CEO of AirAsia

As discussed earlier, positioning essentially is a promise delivered by a company to customers. For the company not to lose customers' trust, the promise must be fulfilled. Therefore, positioning must be supported by strong differentiation. If a company fails at creating a strong differentiation, it results in an overpromise but underdelivery situation. Ultimately, the company's brand reputation is endangered. Conversely, when differentiation is implemented in line with the positioning that is communicated, then it will naturally help to build a solid brand integrity.

In the legacy era, positioning, supported by strong differentiation, becomes a crucial factor for a company's success. In a classic article published in the *Harvard Business Review*, strategist Porter (1996) concluded that choosing a strategy is essentially about creating a unique and valuable position, which involves a set of different activities. The essence of this differentiation is in choosing activities that make a company stand apart from competitors. Thus, a company's sustainable competitive advantage will awaken through the "strategic fit" between a wide selection of these activities. In the book *Rethinking Marketing: Sustainable Market-ing Enterprise in Asia* (2003), we assert that the "strategic fit" can be harnessed if the positioning is consistent with the differentiation that is executed, because positioning is at the core of marketing strategy and differentiation is the essence of tactics.

In addition to shaping the brand integrity, differentiation is also necessary for any company considering the many choices facing a customer. Jack Trout and Steve Rivkin named this phenomenon "the tyranny of choice". Those who do not stand out will get lost in the pack. In their book, *Differentiate or Die*, they provide some important notes related to differentiation (Trout and Rivkin, 2001):

(1) If companies ignore their uniqueness and try to make everything for everybody, they quickly undermine what makes them different
(2) If companies ignore changes in the market, their differentiation can become less important
(3) If companies stay in the shadow of their larger competitors and never establish their differentiation, they will always be weak.

How can companies find their differentiation and shape it is as important as differentiation. According to Kotler and Armstrong (2008), it is actually about differentiating a company's market offering to create superior customer value. More elaborately, it is described as "integrating the content, context and infrastructure of our offers to customers" (Kotler *et al.*, 2003). To create a differentiation, a company can either focus on one of these aspects or, better still, combine all three to form a more solid differentiation (see Fig. 8.1).

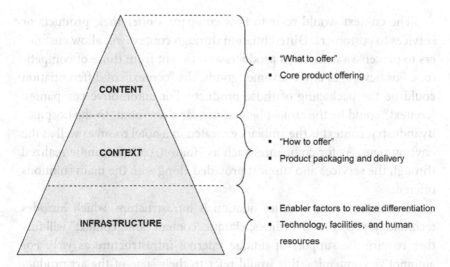

Figure 8.1: Elements of differentiation.

As shown in the figure, there are three elements of differentiation that need to be considered by a company: content ("what to offer"), context ("how to offer"), and infrastructure ("enablers"). Content is a dimension of differentiation that refers to the core value offered to customers. For some companies, this could be tangible. For beverage companies such as Thai Beverage and Philippines' San Miguel, content would refer to the taste and freshness of their drinks. For automakers Honda, Toyota, Hyundai, and so on, the content could be about the performance of their vehicle, represented by their engine — how fast it can go or how fuel efficient it is.

In the services industry, according to Christopher Lovelock's and Jochen Wirtz's flower of service models, content is the core product offered by the company (Lovelock and Wirtz, 2011). For hotel businesses — Singapore's Banyan Tree, India's Oberoi Hotel, and Sri Lanka's JKH Hotels — content is the rooms they offer. As for technology companies such as Huawei, content differentiation lies in providing a comprehensive end-to-end networked solution. The Huawei's B2B client can get all kinds of hubs, switches, wireless access devices, and equipment through one door and need not engage with many vendors. The concept of a one-stop shop from Huawei cuts costs and makes business processes more efficient.

The context would refer to how companies offer their products or services to customers. Differentiation through context will allow customers to perceive a company's products as different from those of competitors. For beverages and consumer goods, the "context" of differentiation could be the packaging of those products. For automotive companies, "context" could be the atmosphere of the car showroom. In the hospitality industry, context is the ambiance created in a hotel room as well as the environment. As for companies such as Huawei, context can be realized through the services and support provided along with the main solutions offered.

The third aspect of differentiation is infrastructure, which includes technology, people, and facilities. Unique "content" and "context" will further require the support of unique internal infrastructure as well. For automotive companies, this would refer to their state-of-the-art production facilities and skilled labor in order to produce quality products in accordance with the target segment. Beverage companies such as Thai Beverage and San Miguel are racing to expand their market through strong distribution channels. To realize differentiation for a hotel with unique characteristics, such as W Hotel, a luxury hotel chain owned by Starwood Hotels & Resorts Worldwide and, typically catering to a younger crowd, may require appropriate technological support, facilities, and personnel.

Differentiation of infrastructure is often necessary to combine the sophistication of technology (high-tech facilities and machine-to-machine [M2M] mechanisms) and the personal touch of frontline companies (human-to-human [H2H] approach). An example of companies that have successfully achieved it is Bank Rakyat Indonesia (BRI) in Indonesia, which targets the microfinance segment. To deal with the competition from other banks in the segment, BRI's strategy is that of fast expansion of its network. The way it is done is a key factor of the differentiation of its infrastructure.

BRI has a unique channel called Teras BRI. This is an operational office, designed to be an informal unit located in wet markets. The channel has proven to be quite effective in touching base with the small and medium enterprise (SME) segment, which continues to be somewhat resistant toward formal banking products and may feel unease in approaching modern offices. As for reaching remote areas in Indonesia, an extension of the Teras BRI Mobile concept accomplishes that. Quite literally, it refers to a special van — a bank on wheels — moving around to serve customers in remote areas. Not just on the road, BRI Teras Mobile also includes boats made into "floating banks" to reach areas inaccessible by land.

Even in building this infrastructure, BRI gives special attention to the importance of personal touch for its customers. In terms of human resources, the strategy is to multiply the sales force that specifically deals with microcredit, known as the Mantri BRI. This agent is recruited from the local population for understanding the potential of a region as well as the character of local customers. The approach is similar to how Grameen Bank in Bangladesh reaches out to its customers — mostly women with economic disadvantages. The Nobel Peace Prize–winning community development bank prepares a team of business consultants to reach out to customers in a very informal environment. The emotional value of the interaction between the sales team and customers becomes the determining factor of differentiation that distinguishes it from the competitors.

To be able to win over rivals in the supercompetitive Asian banking industry, businesses inevitably need a strong differentiation. Although banking products and services are often considered commodities, banks can still build their uniqueness by focusing on some critical aspects. CIMB Group — a universal bank headquartered in Kuala Lumpur — sets an example of how proper differentiation tactics helped support its business expansion to countries in Association of Southeast Asian Nations (ASEAN) and even Asia (see Box 8.1).

From Differentiation to Codification

Long ago, it was common for Asian companies to bombard their messages through advertisements in various media. Some companies even concoct a not-so-authentic differentiation in order to be able to stand out from the crowd and support their brand image (Dawar, 2013). Technology has, however, transformed the company–customer relationship in Asia and the world, making it increasingly inclusive and horizontal. The positions of the two have become increasingly aligned. Customers can easily access information about the company from various sources, so what's right can be easily identified by customers as differentiation.

In today's New Wave era, a company should be able to cultivate an authentic uniqueness — one that cannot be easily copied by its competitors.

Box 8.1:   Malaysia's CIMB Group

CIMB Group is an indigenous ASEAN investment bank, the largest Asia Pacific (ex-Japan)-based investment bank and one of the world's largest Islamic banks. It operates under several entities, which include CIMB Investment Bank, CIMB Bank, CIMB Islamic, CIMB Niaga, CIMB Securities International, and CIMB Thai. The business activities are primarily in the areas of Consumer Banking, Wholesale Banking, comprising Investment Banking and Corporate Banking, Treasury and Markets, and Group Strategy and Strategic Investments.

CIMB recognizes the tough competition in the banking industry in ASEAN and Asia, from local banks as well as other regional banks. Even as a number of global banks withdrew in the wake of the global financial crisis, this did not discourage regional players from competing in Asia, which remains attractive in view of relatively stable economic growth. Two regional banks that are the main competitors of CIMB include Maybank and United Overseas Bank (UOB).

Maybank (Malayan Banking Berhad) is CIMB's strongest competitor in the domestic market, aggressively pursuing its strategy of expansion in the Consumer and Commercial Banking markets. By positioning itself as a leading financial services provider that gives a touch of personal service, Maybank has tried to create its differentiation. This includes enhancing client relationships and actively expanding regionally. In fact, Maybank also has plans to expand to all countries in the Middle East, as well as in China and India.

Meanwhile, UOB, a Singapore regional bank, is also focusing its business activities on the Consumer and Commercial Banking markets. UOB has positioned itself as a premier bank in the Asia Pacific region committed to delivering quality products and exceptional customer service. Its differentiation strategy includes advancing technological innovation, strengthening fee-based activities, and targeting organic growth and M&A in ASEAN.

(Continued)

Box 8.1: (*Continued*)

Amid such a stiff competition, CIMB decided to differentiate itself by focusing on its strengths. It strengthened the internal resources of the bank with the release of "CIMB 2.0" — a movement of internal changes to create internal synergies and strengthen competitive advantage. The first change that was made through "CIMB 2.0" was to consolidate all corporate lending, deposit taking, transaction banking, treasury markets, and other such activities into one division called Corporate Banking, Treasury and Markets (CBTM). The implication? CIMB found it was easier to undertake cross-selling, product bundling, and a reduction in duplication processes.

CIMB strongly believes that the future of the banking industry is online. Recognizing the digital era, CIMB offered products to optimize value creation in the realm of digital banking, such as the "Mobile Account" product, which was initiated in Indonesia. These products allowed customers and even noncustomers of the bank to transfer funds free of charge to all mobile numbers, buy credits, make bill payments, and withdraw cash at ATMs without using a card. This product was then adopted in other ASEAN countries, such as "OctoSend" in Malaysia. Another innovative product is a Kwik Account, which was launched first in Malaysia, enabling accounts to be opened online without having to come to a CIMB branch.

In terms of differentiation in infrastructure, CIMB operates a core banking system named 1Platform, which allows the bank to perform product roll outs quickly and transfer products across markets. With 1Platform, CIMB can improve collaborations between the frontline and back office, thereby improving productivity, strengthening governance and risk management products, and reducing IT costs.

Armed with such differentiation, CIMB has since expanded aggressively by entering new markets such as Cambodia (2010), and expanding operations in Sydney, Melbourne, Hong Kong, Seoul, Taipei, and London (2011). The bank expanded to Taiwan, India, and Korea in 2013, and began operations in Laos PDR in 2014.

Gilmore and Pine (2007) proposed three key drivers behind the demand for authenticity. First, they acknowledge the growing supply of commercial experiences, from birthday parties given at local restaurants to extreme adventures such as exploring the world's hidden places. When consuming experiences, consumers are sensitive to whether the experience is "real" or not. A "fake" experience would likely be remembered as a waste of time while a truly authentic experience would be treasured for life. Second, Pine and Gilmour argued that the industry is becoming increasingly impersonal as people are replaced by machines. As the age of technological revolution progresses, people will look, more and more, for something genuine and authentic. This is the paradox of our time: high-tech (M2M) mechanism creating the demand for high-touch (H2H) interaction. Third, deceit from major corporations has resulted in many consumers losing faith in institutions. Consequently, consumers look up to organizations that come across genuinely as socially responsible entities; the ones who are what they say they are!

To create an authentic uniqueness, a company should be able to extend the brand internalization of its DNA beyond the marketing department. Brand DNA constitutes the unique components of a brand that should be a common language for all employees of the company, not only those on the frontline who deal directly with customers. In fact, brand DNA should animate all the important processes in the company, ranging from leadership, recruitment, performance appraisal, to culture building (Barlow and Stewart, 2004). This is what we call codification. To better understand the difference between differentiation and codification, refer to the comparison between both in Table 8.1.

What has been done by BRI in Indonesia, Grameen Bank in Bangladesh, and CIMB in Asia is not merely differentiation. They have been able to achieve a codification of the brand DNA into their human resource management processes as well as the company's internal systems. The authentic uniqueness that is built as a result of that would be difficult to be imitated by competitors.

Codification of the Brand DNA

A uniqueness that has been coded will certainly be difficult to be imitated by competitors. That said, it also poses a challenge as codification is a

Table 8.1: Comparison of differentiation versus codification.

Differentiation	Codification
Brand differentiation has only become the marketing department's concern	Brand DNA has penetrated the whole organizational culture
The brand differentiation is considered to be a domain of marketers	The brand DNA is understood and valued and provides meaning to all employees
The brand differentiation is developed in isolation from the service and organizational culture	The brand DNA provides guidelines and context for all service deliveries and employee behavior
There are some contradictions between leadership practice and brand differentiation	Leaders at all levels understand the brand DNA and reflect it in their own behavior
Recruitment is driven primarily by knowledge, skills, and experience without considering the candidate-brand fit	Recruitment is conducted based on the candidate's capacity to behave in line with the brand DNA
Performance management doesn't incorporate measurement of brand-aligned behavior	Performance management clearly measures congruence of employee behavior and the brand DNA

long process and requires serious commitment from all stakeholders in the company, not just the marketing department or division. At the core of codification is the process to internalize the brand DNA as an inherent component in the product or services as well as understood, practiced, and propagated by every employee of the company. The brand DNA would no longer be just a guide in formulating marketing activation programs but also a guide on employee behavior. If codification of the brand DNA can be successfully achieved, then every employee will stand for a representation of the company's brand in each of his or her interactions with a customer. And it is precisely this level of commitment to create a uniqueness that is hard to be duplicated by competitors.

According to Berry and Seltman (2008), reputation and brand equity of an organization are affected by two factors: brand awareness and brand meaning. Brand awareness means the extent to which people know or are familiar with a company or brand. While the brand meaning is the customers' perception of an institution or brand; it could be positive or negative. Of these two factors, what affects brand equity more dominantly is brand meaning. This means that a customer could have been aware of a company as well as its brand but not yet sure on whether he or she carries a positive perception (meaning) for it. In fact, it is this meaning that is more important for the brand.

An organization's presented brand (advertising, publicity, etc.) has a direct effect only on the brand awareness. That means advertisements will only make people familiar with your company or brand, but cannot guarantee that they would like the company or your brand. For customers to fall in love with a company or brand, the key is a meaningful customer experience with your organization. This is why in a company, every employee should ideally animate the brand DNA in their behavior. Every officer in the front office and back office will affect the touchpoints traversed by the customer. If, at every touchpoint, the customer can feel a certain unique experience, then this would result in a truly unique codification, which cannot be imitated by competitors.

The Onion Model of Codification

The codification of the brand DNA in a company is done through implementation of three interconnected layers (see Fig. 8.2). The first layer is

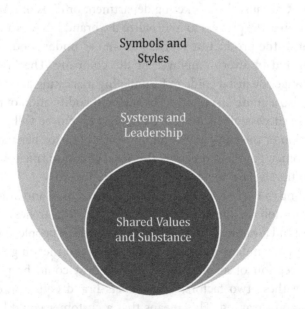

Figure 8.2: The onion model of codification.

the most tangible aspect and most easily executed. The next two layers, while somewhat intangible and requiring longer time and more efforts, have an increasingly fundamental role. Here we present an explanation of the three layers from the onion model of codification.

Layer 1: Symbols and styles

In the concept of differentiation, if we know context as a way to package a product or service to the customer, then Layer 1 would be about the way a company "packages" its look outside the organization and the employees with symbols and styles that reflect the brand DNA. If a brand aims to be considered as young and energetic, the symbols installed as artifacts within the company (office room, office branches, service center, lobby, channels of distribution, etc.) should reflect the same young, vibrant spirit. All aspects appealing to the human senses of perception also need to support this: background music and jingles (audio aspect), working space layout and color (visual aspect), and even scent (smell aspect). Through the placement of symbols and styles that are in tune with the brand DNA, employees would be able to better understand and practice the expected behavior.

Google makes a case in point in that; its offices and campuses around the globe reflect the overarching philosophy of the company, which is nothing but "to create the happiest, most creative workplace in the world". Google allows many of its hundreds of software engineers — its core intellectual capital — to design their own desks or workstations out of what resembles oversized Tinkertoys. Some of them work standing on their desks, a few even have treadmills attached so they can workout while working. Employees are free to express themselves by scribbling on walls. The result may look a little chaotic, perhaps similar to some kind of a high-tech refugee camp, but Google says that's how its engineers like it (Stewart, 2013). Those symbols and styles are meant to codify creativity and innovation as Google's brand DNA.

Layer 2: Systems and leadership

Codification would not yield desired results if it stops at the surface; it should inject the characteristics of the brand DNA deep into organizational processes/systems as well as into the leaders' decision-making. By systems, we also mean systems encompassing the process of hiring a new employee, employee training, performance appraisal, and promotion. Asian companies must incorporate elements of their brand DNA in this process, so as to acquire and develop relevant skills and attitude among its employees. The role of leaders at all levels is also important in order to execute and evaluate each process. In addition, they serve as role models who are looked up by their subordinates.

One concrete example in the effort to build codification throughout the system is Starbucks. There are four things Starbucks does to this effect:

(1) On-brand recruitment

At the time of recruitment, the interview follows a guide consisting of screening techniques that can help determine whether a prospective employee has the right "on-brand" attitude and behavior in accordance with the character of the Starbucks brand.

(2) Employee immersion

New employees must attend a full-day paid course on "first impression" while it is mandatory for new retail managers to take part in a brand-focused management training for 10 weeks.

(3) Employee communications

The entire line of communication (including blogs, newsletters, and daily meetings) is active to the fullest possible extent to create and maintain openness of dialogue, from the chairman to local managers worldwide.

(4) Employee incentives

The employees who work more than 20 hours are entitled to a "Starbucks Total Pay Package" consisting of medical benefits, retirement savings, insurance options, and a number of other interesting perks.

By applying the four practices mentioned previously, it helps in the creation of a character of Starbucks brand DNA among its employees. Evidently, the formation of this character begins right at the time of the recruitment process by filtering candidates who possess "by default" attitudes and show behaviors aligned with Starbucks brand DNA. But, of course, it must be followed with the development of competence in the following stages.

Layer 3: Shared values and substance

The shared values and basic assumptions existing within an organization may appear as intangible yet have a deep impact on the conduct and interactions of its members. Through a continuous codification process applied through the first and second layers, the long periods of shared values would become a sort of "soft control" on the behavior of employees in general. If the system in an organization acts as a "hard control" that provides a reward for behavior consistent with the brand DNA and punishment for the deviants, then the shared values and substance would provide a "soft control" through social pressure among members of the organization.

Examples of companies that have succeeded in instilling strong shared values include Mayo Clinic, one of the best hospitals in the world that is also well known as "A big brand from a little town". Located in Rochester, indeed a small town in the United States, the hospital receives patients from all over the world. Known for its "patient-first" philosophy, this is adopted as a shared value by every hospital personnel, thus resulting in a natural urge to be deeply empathetic toward patients. At Mayo Clinic, if a nurse was faced with two choices: return to work desk on time or face a 10-minute delay in order to fetch a wheelchair for a patient, they would pick the second choice without a thought, even not having to consult with a head nurse first. This is what an expert on service, Leonnard Berry, calls values-based authority (Berry and Seltman, 2008).

In essence, these are the three ways a company can develop codification of its brand DNA. The cases of Western companies discussed previously — Google, Starbucks, and Mayo Clinic — can hopefully serve as practical examples of implementation of the codification concept for Asian companies. Building a truly authentic differentiation is not an easy process. But most importantly, it cannot be built instantly, it may even take years — therefore consistency would be a key. Garuda Indonesia, an airline in Indonesia, has taken substantial time to internalize its brand DNA in its entire service process (see Box 8.2). But the hard work has

**Box 8.2:   The Garuda Indonesia Experience:
A Case of Brand DNA Codification**

Indonesia's flag carrier Garuda Indonesia is a state-owned enterprise that serves domestic and international routes, covering Southeast Asia, the Middle East, China, South Korea, Australia, and the Netherlands. As of January 2015, Garuda operates 134 aircraft consisting of a mix of Boeings and Airbuses, including 15 CRJ1000 NextGen aircraft. Its budget carrier affiliate Citilink operates 30 aircraft consisting of 24 Airbuses, and 6 Boeings.

Needless to say, competition in the region that Garuda serves has intensified in recent years. Domestically, with the growth of low-cost carriers (LCCs), Garuda, being a full-service carrier, must still compete with the likes of Lion Air and AirAsia despite different target segments. Lion Air is aggressively expanding operations over new routes, supported by an increasing aircraft fleet and is the airline with the highest passenger growth. The launch of its full-service airline, Batik Air, has further intensified the competition.

At a regional level, Garuda Indonesia faces many competent rivals. For full-service flights, a number of commercial heavyweights operate in the region including Singapore Airlines, Cathay Pacific, Thai Airways, and Malaysia Airlines. In the LCC segment, several players are providing tough competition including AirAsia, Jetstar Airways, and ValueAir. Most of these players are aggressively expanding operations in the region, for both short- and long-haul service, by purchasing new aircraft or refurbishing their old fleets.

A new economic policy called ASEAN Open Skies Policy — which took effect under the ASEAN Economic Community (AEC) at the end of 2015 — further changes the competitive situation in the region. It allows carriers from all 10 member nations to fly freely within the region. This liberalization policy is aimed at encouraging competition, resulting in more traffic and better fares and services — ultimately posing as either a threat or an opportunity for airlines, including Garuda Indonesia. Lately, Garuda Indonesia has been expanding flights to Indonesia by doing promotions abroad, with a dual purpose to improve its brand awareness and traffic and to attract more international tourists to come to Indonesia.

(Continued)

Box 8.2: (*Continued*)

Garuda Indonesia, well aware of the increasing competition, launched a revitalization program back in 2010, in order to create a unique authentic Indonesian hospitality. The airline designed its customer experience blueprint, starting at the ticket counter, from arrival at the airport, waiting in the boarding room, getting into the plane, sitting through the flight, getting out of the place, to receiving the baggage and exiting the airport. The concept of customer experience is delivered under the motto, "Garuda Indonesia Experience".

The "Garuda Indonesia Experience", which is Garuda's brand DNA, relies on the Indonesian friendliness to provide a unique and the best customer experience at every touchpoint. This dimension of service quality integrates all five senses — sight, sound, taste, scent, and touch. It is not only the cabin crew that is well trained in delivering this service experience but also all personnel including ground staff. This is done to ensure consistency in the overall customer experience when traveling by Garuda Indonesia. This Indonesian style codification will be quite difficult for other regional and international competitors to incorporate.

In order to realize the development of a strong brand DNA, Garuda Indonesia focuses not only on marketing communications to the outside world but also on the establishment of a system of shared values internally. The airline seeks to create formal and non-formal values that focus on the style of service with typical Indonesian character. This is a part of the corporate culture that is associated with human resource systems that organize training programs, recruitment, and all the way through performance appraisal.

Consequently, Garuda Indonesia's investment in human capital is highly important, including revamping the education and training systems, and developing career paths as well as leadership at various levels of management. At the time of recruitment of pilots and flight attendants, it is not only the skills and experience of candidates that are looked into but also their attitude that should be in accordance with the company's brand DNA. Through these efforts, Garuda Indonesia has been able to create a unique character of its service quality, in line with the authentic traditional Indonesian hospitality.

yielded tangible results, with several prestigious awards coming its way, including the "The World's Best Economy Class" by airlines service quality reviewer, SKYTRAX, during the Paris Airshow in 2013. Another famed honor for Garuda Indonesia was receiving the Passenger Choice Awards 2013 as best in Asia and Australia regions. The uniqueness of such exemplary service is certainly not easy to build but will be more sustainable because it is supported by a solid internal foundation, which would be difficult for competitors to mirror.

References

Barlow, J and P Stewart (2004). *Branded Customer Service: The New Competitive Advantage*. San Francisco: Berrett-Koehler Publishers.

Berry, LL and KD Seltman (2008). *Management Lessons from Mayo Clinic: Inside One of the World's Most Admired Service Organization*. New York: McGraw-Hill.

Dawar, N (December 2013). When Marketing Is Strategy. *Harvard Business Review*.

Gilmore, JH and IBJ Pine (2007). *Authenticity: What Consumers Really Want*. Boston: Harvard Business Review Press.

Kotler, P and G Amstrong (2008). *Principles of Marketing*, 12th Ed. New Jersey: Prentice Hall.

Kotler, *et al.* (2003). *Rethinking Marketing: Sustainable Marketing Enterprise in Asia*. Singapore: Prentice Hall.

Lovelock, C and J Wirtz (2011). *Services Marketing: People, Technology, Strategy*, 7th Ed. New York: Prentice Hall.

Porter, M (November–December 1996). What Is Strategy. *Harvard Business Review*.

Trout, J and S Rivkin (2001). *Differentiate or Die: Survival in Our Era of Killer Competition*. New Jersey: Wiley.

Stewart, J (15 March 2013). Looking for a Lesson in Google's Perks. *The New York Times*. http://www.nytimes.com/2013/03/16/business/at-google-a-place-to-work-and-play. html (last accessed March 31, 2016).

CHAPTER 9

VALUE INDICATOR: FROM BRAND TO CHARACTER

Every brand is human, and every human is a brand.
Chris Malone — Branding Consultant and Author

From our discussions on the PDB triangle model, namely positioning–differentiation–brand in the previous chapters, we establish how PDB is at the core of marketing. The relationship between positioning and brand is defined by "identity", meaning it is positioning that gives identity to the brand so that it is more than just a name or logo without meaning. If a brand succeeds in developing a clear positioning, the next step is to develop a concrete differentiation to support it.

Without differentiation, brand and positioning will only be in the form of an unrealized promise to customers. It will instead backfire as long-time customers, aware of the positioning of a brand but failing to see any differentiation, will consider the brand to be just making empty

153

promises. Conversely, if an Asian company can consistently build upon its differentiation in accordance with its positioning, it will develop a strong brand perception in the minds of customers.

It is therefore said that the brand is the value indicator in the classic marketing era. Aaker and Joachimsthaler (2000) stated that the brand is an asset that could be the basis of competitive advantage and long-term profitability and thus needs to be monitored closely by the top management. This is the goal of brand leadership, according to them.

Aaker (1996) asserted that a strong brand is like an asset that could provide additional value to the company and customers. The concept, known as brand equity, lays down five major asset categories to build a strong brand: (i) brand awareness, (ii) brand loyalty, (iii) perceived quality, (iv) brand associations, and (v) other proprietary brand assets.

A brand's strength as an asset can be measured through research exploring customers' opinion on certain attributes. For example, Nikkei BP Consulting, a consulting and research company based in Japan conducts Brand Asia surveys every year. These surveys are part of a brand evaluation project that covers 12 regions across Asia. The survey aims to evaluate the image equity of reputable brands in various Asian regions by measuring attributes, such as their friendliness, usefulness, and perceived quality, as well as investigating regional differences and image trends and evaluating the cross-regional overall strength of major brands. On the basis of the Brand Asia 2014 results, smartphone-related brands such as *Apple*, *Samsung*, and *Google* received high ratings throughout Asia. They emerged as the strongest global brands in Asia.

With a strong brand, the company will be able to free itself from the supply–demand curve. And as it manages to do so, the price offered no longer depends on the equilibrium point in the market. This allows the company to be a price maker, not a price follower. This is what is described as the ability of a brand or a company to escape the commodity trap (Kotler *et al.*, 2003). A strong brand is not just a name or logo — it is an "umbrella" that represents all the company's products or services while reflecting the value offered to customers. Dawar (2013) has argued that the brand is a more critical source of competitive advantage than the production technology itself.

The ability to establish such a competitive advantage through brands has been recognized well by companies in Asia, both local and multinationals operating in the region. Several local firms that have managed to amass a huge customer base try to build an emotional bond between the brand and its customers. The pride of being a local brand becomes one of the main campaign themes commonly used to fight giant competitors from outside. Therefore, some multinational companies subsequently decide to acquire local brands to enter a market and then develop their own brand. One such example is the acquisition of Laser by Colgate-Palmolive in Myanmar (see Box 9.1), demonstrating how a strong brand can have a high financial value.

Box 9.1:   Colgate-Palmolive Co. in Myanmar

The Colgate-Palmolive Company is an American multinational consumer products company focused on production, distribution, and provision of household, health care, and personal products, such as soaps, detergents, and oral hygiene products (including toothpaste and toothbrushes). Colgate (subbrand of Colgate-Palmolive) is an oral hygiene product line of toothpastes, toothbrushes, mouthwashes, and dental floss. Colgate toothpaste was first sold by the company in 1873. It has been in Singapore since the 1920s. In 1992, Colgate established its first factory in India to produce toothpaste for the domestic market.

In 2014, *The Wall Street Journal* reported that Colgate-Palmolive acquired a toothpaste brand Laser from local Myanmar-based firm Shwe Ayar Nadi Co. Ltd. for about $100 million. This turned out to be one of the largest investments ever made by an American company in Myanmar since the easing of some of the economic sanctions against the country in 2012.

According to Colgate, the investment reflected its commitment to growing business in what it said was an important emerging Southeast Asian country. As per the deal, the company acquired Laser's manufacturing and tube-manufacturing facilities, and the company decided to produce the Laser brand of toothpaste, along with importing Colgate-branded goods from Thailand. Colgate also announced plans to eventually shift domestic production of the Colgate brand toothpaste from Thailand to Myanmar.

(Continued)

Box 9.1: (*Continued*)

Colgate is not the first multinational company to re-enter Myanmar since the easing of restrictions. Others including General Electric, Coca-Cola, and Gap have also restarted operations in Myanmar since 2012; the soft drink giant even promised more than $200 million in investment there over the next five years. The gradual lifting of the economic and diplomatic sanctions against Myanmar by Western nations has turned the country into an attractive market and put it into the spotlight. It has various advantages such as its natural resources, youthful low-cost workforce, and strategic location in Asia. The foreign investments, consumption, and exports have helped Myanmar to achieve a record economic growth, averaging about 8 percent over 2013–2014.

No wonder, Myanmar is particularly lucrative for multinationals dealing in consumer goods, given the rising disposable income of Myanmar's 51 million population. The beauty and personal care market in the country, growing at a rate of 14 percent since 2009, reached a market value of $318 million in 2014, according to the research firm Euromonitor International. Myanmar has also been identified as one of the 20 markets that will offer most opportunities for consumer goods companies globally (Euromonitor, 2014).

Sources: Venkat and Mahtani (2014) and Euromonitor (2014).

Brand as Human

As stated earlier, in the new world, marketing has become more horizontal. The relationship between brand and customers has become increasingly aligned. The customer himself is becoming more social. At a time when information technology (IT) was still limited, customer purchasing decisions were driven more individually and hardly influenced by other customers, save for a close-knit group of family or friends. The customer path, therefore, went through a process of 4A's: Aware, Attitude, Act, and Act again. But in the New Wave era, the customer path has been transformed into 5A's: Aware, Appeal, Ask, Act, and Advocate.

The stages "Ask" and "Advocate" manifest how customers are not isolated anymore when making decisions. Not only do they actively ask other customers, but they also advocate products and services — and not only to their close ones anymore, but to a larger group of customers — enabled by the Internet and social media. Clearly, it casts an influence on customers' decision making. IT has made it so easy to share information. Without having to spend a cent or make too much effort, customers today can interact with a global audience around the world. Just creating massive advertising campaigns to establish awareness among customers is no longer as efficacious as it used to be. A mere negative review that goes on to become viral can easily make customers reject outright the messages spread through massive advertising campaigns.

According to Nielsen's "Trust in Advertising" report 2013, "earned" advertising in the form of word-of-mouth recommendations from family and friends continues to be the most influential source of advertising among Southeast Asian consumers. The Nielsen study polled more than 29,000 Internet respondents in 58 countries to measure consumer sentiment on 19 forms of advertising. Across Southeast Asia, consumers placed the highest level of trust in word-of-mouth endorsements, with the Philippines leading the way (up 3 percentage points from 2007 to 89 percent and five points above the global average of 84 percent), followed by Malaysia (up eight points to 86 percent), Singapore (up seven points to 85 percent), and Indonesia (down four points to 85 percent). Thailand (down two points to 79 percent) and Vietnam (up two points to 81 percent) were the only Southeast Asian countries to fall below the global average.

On the flip side, other research studies conducted by Hill Holiday and Lippincott (2013) asserted that trust in institutions has eroded drastically in the past few years. This is hailed as the end of the institutional era and the beginning of what they call the human era. They believe this trend has been spurring companies' desire to behave more like people. The article outlines a number of key traits that the so-called "human" companies possess, such as having customer empathy, talking and acting like people, not being boring, and empowering individuals to be the brand.

In 2013, the American low-cost airliner JetBlue announced the launch of a new campaign called "Air on the Side of Humanity", which focused on the qualities that make JetBlue a carrier that cares about people. The idea was to establish how JetBlue offers a more respectful, humane way to fly for its customers — by offering the most legroom in coach class, free unlimited snacks, and friendly service at every point along the journey. Global insurance company Liberty Mutual too has tried to distance itself from being seen as an impersonal institution by devoting more airtime to campaigns around "human and humanity" as part of strengthening its brand platforms. To drive home the message, Liberty Mutual goes so far as to adopt the song "Human" by the band Human League in its advertisements (Parekh, 2013).

All these are efforts undertaken by several brands to be seen not as big corporate behemoths, but as companies that value their customers as individuals. They want to be seen as brands that care about human in general and value the relationships they form with their customers. While traditional branding techniques are still popular, the latest trend for brands is to be simply human — talk like a human, have a human-like personality, and are not afraid to show their human side. The "brand is human" concept is increasingly being recognized as a new and essential way of approaching business in this connected age.

Branding with Character: New Formula of Brand Leadership

The classical literature on branding explains that in order to build a strong brand, it is necessary to determine the right direction, purpose, and meaning for the brand. This is called brand identity (Aaker, 1996). Brand identity helps to establish a relationship between the brand and its customers by generating a value proposition involving functional and emotional benefits. Furthermore, Aaker (1996) explained that a brand identity can be shaped around four perspectives: (i) the brand as product (product attributes, quality, value, user, use, and country of origin), (ii) the brand as symbol (visual imagery and heritage), (iii) brand as institution (organizational attributes), and (iv) brand as person (brand personality, brand–customer relationship).

In view of the declining customer confidence in institutions, the company would need to emphasize more on the identity of brand as person. This approach would position brands like human beings, not as an organization or institution "amid" its customers. This is the era of the human brand as mentioned earlier. With this kind of a philosophy, companies can build brand leadership in this new era.

In management and psychology, leadership is defined as the ability to influence behavior of other people who would want to be a leader's voluntary followers (Jennings, 1960; Wren, 1995). The keyword here is "influence". Even John Maxwell said that leadership is influence, nothing more, nothing less. This idea of leadership can apparently be applied to the modern science of branding, where a company is in a position parallel to the customer and cannot force them to buy its products or services. What it can do is to influence customers to make them want to choose their products and services.

In order to be able to build such a horizontal leadership, it is clear that Asian leaders cannot rely on titles or positions that would still represent an old style of leadership in the erstwhile vertical world. What would need to be done is to build an internal charisma that will make others want to follow without being forced (Sampson, 2011). In order to create this charisma that casts a strong influence, a leader must have character. The same principle applies to brands too. In order to establish brand leadership, Asian companies must implement a branding concept with character.

How can companies nurture a brand with character? Taking inspiration from the concept of leadership, a company that wants to build a brand with character must consider six aspects. These six aspects have been adapted from the WOW Leadership model (Kartajaya and Ridwansyah, 2014) and combined with the three winning keys in the New Wave era, as discussed in Part I. The six aspects of WOW Leadership to build the internal charisma of a leader include physicality, intellectuality, emotionality, sociability, personability, and moral ability. And the three winning keys are: (i) combining online and offline approaches, (ii) creating style with substance, and (iii) using machine-to-machine (M2M) mechanism to gain human-to-human (H2H) emotional relationship.

The combination of these two concepts yields the "branding with character" model, which can be seen in Fig. 9.1. The model represents a new branding philosophy to build a brand character like a leader who can spread influence among its influencers in a horizontal world. With such a "branding with character" approach, Asian customers would act more like followers, following a brand, choosing it over the competitors,

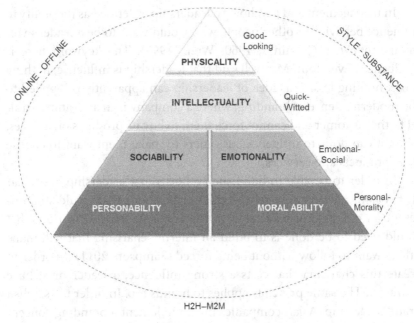

Figure 9.1: Branding with character.

and even defending it — and voluntarily because of the brand's charisma. As for the six aspects of "branding with character", they are:

1. **Physicality**
   The physical aspect (something that can be felt by the five senses) will help form the first impression of anything, including that of a brand. Therefore, a brand must be designed to be good-looking. At the same time, the physical appearance of a brand should be able to represent its character. This is what we describe as style with substance. For example, a brand with a youth character should bear an appearance of being fashionable and cheerful. But that character of the brand must not be reflected only from its symbol or logo, but also through its entire physical evidence: product packaging, promotion materials, visual merchandising, service center's layout, and so on.

2. **Intellectuality**
   In a dynamic industry environment, a brand should be allowed to grow with respect to the changing trends, and not remain static with its messages. When a new feature is introduced in the product

category the brand caters to, the company must be able to adopt or adapt. This is the intellectual aspect that helps establish a brand leadership with strong character. The key is the ability to capture new opportunities from outside and quickly adopt them into the product or service. A company must be able to undertake rapid innovation in order to develop this aspect.

3. Emotionality

A brand with character should be able to provide a personal and emotional touch to its customers. This can be done by giving special attention to the emotional benefits that a product or service provides. These benefits can be communicated to the customers in a way that helps create an H2H touch. One way could be through storytelling associated with the brand. Storytelling, if done rightly, is a powerful way to move customers to connect with your brand more effectively than with the mere use of data and rational facts (McKee, 2003).

4. Sociability

The next aspect to build a brand with character is sociability. It is the ability of a brand to facilitate relationships among customers. Technology has made it much easier to enable interactions among people, especially with the social media becoming a favorite hangout place online. The social media do not only enable Asian brands to interact with their customers, but also facilitate interactions among its customers. This can be used by the brand to encourage establishment of online and offline communities. These communities provide platforms for both brands and customers to create and connect. They are also evidently instrumental in driving brand advocacy as messages get reinforced by like-minded followers.

5. Personability

Like a human being, a brand is also born into the world with a mission. Personability refers to that characteristic of a brand which identifies it as not being born only for the pursuit of profit alone, but also to extend care for people and the planet. An example is Body Shop, which, in addition to being business-oriented, also pursues a noble mission to promote self-esteem, protect the planet, support community trade, and is against animal testing. Brands with such strong personality will usually be able to generate a customer base with high loyalty.

6. **Moral ability**

The last aspect is the moral ability. This is related to a brand's responsibility to protect the rights owned by customers as well as maintain its integrity. Customer's trust is a highly valued element in the New Wave era because once customers feel betrayed by a brand, they could spread that disappointment everywhere. In order for brands to build long-term trust, it should be able to put the interest of customers as a matter of priority. If at any time, an issue that could potentially pose a risk to customers arises, the company must intervene immediately. This was done by Toyota when it issued a massive worldwide product recall in 2014. Although the implications of such actions may be huge such as in terms of monetary loss, these steps need to be taken as a moral responsibility to the customer.

An Asian brand that can build upon its character based on these six aspects can exert a strong influence like a charismatic leader. Customers will voluntarily buy and recommend such brands to people in their vicinity. In fact, if a situation of negative commentaries against the brand emerges, customers will defend the brand without expecting anything in return. One example of such a brand is Tesla Motors, Inc., an American automotive and energy storage company

---

Box 9.2: Tesla Motor Goes to Asia

Tesla Motors, Inc. is an American automotive and energy storage company that designs, manufactures, and sells luxury electric cars, electric vehicle powertrain components, and battery products. Tesla first gained widespread attention following the production of their *Tesla Roadster*, the first fully electric sports car, back in 2008 (Tesla Motors, 2016). The company's second vehicle is the *Model S*, a fully electric luxury sedan, which was followed by the *Model X*, a crossover.

Having launched its premium electric cars in the United States and Europe, Tesla Motors naturally eyed the Asian market. Tesla opened its

(Continued)

Box 9.2: (*Continued*)

first Japanese showroom in Aoyama in November 2010 and a branch in Singapore in July 2010. However, in the latter market, the company eventually ceased operations due to a lack of tax exemptions. Tesla continued its business expansion in Asia by establishing a Hong Kong branch and showroom in 2011. The Hong Kong showroom consists of a "Design Studio" where prospective buyers can design their own vehicle on a large touchscreen by selecting from a range of options including battery, drive, and other equipment. Tesla's Chinese website was launched in December 2013 to sell the *Model S* and *Model X*. The launch followed the opening of a Tesla showroom in Beijing in November 2013. Apart from showrooms and physical stores, Tesla is now available for in-person customer demonstrations and test drives in several Asian countries.

Although still relatively a new brand in America as well as in other places in the world, Tesla Motors has managed to amass a base of "fanatic followers" everywhere, including those who do not even come from the target market. The company has been able to build such a powerful brand from scratch that among industry observers Tesla is seen as a disruptive force of innovation and among customers, a brand with a higher purpose. Here we interpret how Tesla has managed to adopt the six aspects of branding with character:

Physicality: Premium Electric Vehicles with a Gorgeous Design

The aspect of physicality is readily noticeable with Tesla as we look at its product range. Tesla premium electric cars are highly praised for their design, pleasing to the eyes, and widely recognized as one of the main attributes that attracts customers toward the brand. Tesla has been aware of how important the physical aspect is, and hence each vehicle is designed to have an attractive exterior appearance. Right from *Tesla Roadster*, which looked like an exotic sports car and not an electric vehicle, to *Model S* and *Model X* and the latest *Model 3* — aimed to be a mass market electric car — Tesla has always been highly mindful of the physical aspect.

(*Continued*)

Box 9.2:   (*Continued*)

Tesla not only makes electric cars, but in order to provide a premium dashboard experience to its users, it launched *EVEs For Tesla* app, which seeks to provide a connected car experience. Basically, the application connects Tesla cars with other devices (M2M). With this application, drivers can adjust the lighting, control the locks in the house and garage, turn off the lights, turn on the air conditioner — all from their vehicle dashboard. This application can also be used to obtain various types of information such as the weather and e-mail access, and be used as a navigational tool.

Intellectuality: Endless Innovation without Compromise

Tesla was named after the famous inventor Nikola Tesla. Right from the beginning, the company has been relentlessly pursuing innovation. A recent innovation is the development of an autopilot system, which was available to drivers through a software update. This feature helps the driver to automatically control the steering, speed, change lanes, and park without actually driving the vehicle. Equipped with a combination of cameras, radar, and ultrasonic sensors, the autopilot system works to make it more convenient and safe to drive its cars and reduce the driver's workload. With this feature, Tesla took a step further to bring intelligent vehicles to its customers.

Sociability: "Informal-Loyalty Program" for Each Customer

Tesla is well known as a brand with a highly loyal customer base. For example, based on a survey conducted by Jefferies, a global investment banking firm, 85 percent of users said they would buy a Tesla product again in the future and 83 percent of them would recommend Tesla to their community (Zacks Equity Research, 2015).

One way Tesla has managed to garner such loyal support from its customers is through its constant endeavor to learn about various customer activities. Interestingly, this approach is done informally. When customers buy a vehicle, Tesla tries to gather information about them, such as their location and common routes, owner's driving style, and most frequently used features. Armed with this

Box 9.2:   (*Continued*)

information, Tesla can provide the most appropriate solutions to address the anxieties and desires of customers.

Besides, Tesla also encourages interactions among fellow owners. One example can be found in the Tesla website. Tesla presents a special platform for car owners to share their experiences while using the vehicle. Because it comes from the customers themselves, Tesla manages to get personal stories from many of these customers. In Asia, such an online forum approach can be highly useful to be able to trigger the emergence of offline community activities that are initiated by customers.

Emotionality: The World-Changing Technology Experience

When buying a car, customers in Asia typically pay close attention to the features offered in the vehicle. Apart from features, they also consider how the vehicle would symbolize prestige in the community. However, in the case of Tesla, the owners are not only made to take note of the technological sophistication and prestige, but also consider how Tesla, as a pollution-free electric car, contributes to the movement to make the world a better place. Tesla is using a means of environment-friendly transportation. Thus, each Tesla owner takes pride in the fact he has done something to make the world better.

Personability: Accelerating the World's Transition to Sustainable Transport

Since its inception, Tesla has had a clear intention, which is to make the present and future of this world better. This mission of the company is quite clearly articulated, as its electric cars help accelerate the transition in the automotive world toward a more sustainable means of transportation. By owning a Tesla, it could be the first step in the way customers switch to a more eco-friendly transportation and the effect may spread to their other daily activities to promote a more sustainable lifestyle. The growing public awareness of the importance of environment-friendly products in Asia is in line with the mission of Tesla.

(*Continued*)

Box 9.2:   (*Continued*)

Moral Ability: Maximum 5-Star Safety Standard

As noted earlier, Tesla is working hard to realize its mission of accelerating the world's transition to sustainable energy, beginning with transportation. But in doing so, Tesla has not neglected other important aspects of its vehicle, namely safety and comfort. In designing each model, Tesla has adhered strictly to guidelines by the National Highway Traffic and Safety Administration (NHTSA) in the United States. The goal is to ensure the safety of each driver. No wonder its *Model S* set a new NHTSA safety score record in the United States by gaining a 5-star score in every subcategory. Tesla also did not hesitate to issue a massive recall of over 90,000 cars to ensure the safety of passengers as a preventive measure.

---

that designs, manufactures, and sells luxury electric cars, electric vehicle powertrain components, and battery products. In Box 9.2, how Tesla has succeeded in adopting "branding with character", mainly associated with its plans to strengthen its market position in Asia, has been described.

References

Aaker, DA (1996). Building Strong Brand. New York: The Free Press.

Aaker, DA and R Joachimsthaler (2000). *Brand Leadership*. New York: The Free Press.

Dawar, N (December 2013). When Marketing Is Strategy. *Harvard Business Review*.

Euromonitor (June 2014). *Markets of the Future in Myanmar: Executive Summary*. http://www.euromonitor.com/markets-of-the-future-in-myanmar/report (last accessed April 4, 2016).

Hill Holiday and Lippincott (2013). *Welcome to the Human Era*. New York: Hill Holiday & Lippincott.

Jennings, EE (1960). *An Anatomy of Leadership: Princess, Heroes, and Supermen*, p. 30. New York: McGraw Hill.

Kartajaya, H and A Ridwansyah (2014). *WOW Leadership*. Jakarta: Gramedia Pustaka Utama.

Kotler, *et al.* (2003). *Rethinking Marketing: Sustainable Market-ing Enterprise in Asia*. Singapore: Prentice Hall.

McKee, R (June 2003). Story Telling That Moves People. *Harvard Business Review*, pp. 51–55.

Nielsen (2013). *Global Trust in Advertising and Brand Messages.* http://www.nielsen.com/us/en/insights/reports/2013/global-trust-in-advertising-and-brand-messages.html (last accessed April 3, 2016).

Parekh, R (September 20, 2013). The Newest Marketing Buzzword? Human. *Advertising Age.*

Sampson, SJ (2011). *Leaders without Titles: The Six Powerful Attributes of Those Who Influence without Authority.* Amherst: HRD Press.

Tesla Motors (2016). About Tesla. http://www.tesla.com/about/press/releases/tesla-unveils-roadster-25-newest-stores-europe-and-north-america (last accessed July 30, 2016).

Venkat, PR and S Mahtani (28 October 2014). Colgate Buys Myanmar Toothpaste Brand. *Wall Street Journal.* http://www.wsj.com/articles/colgate-buys-myanmar-toothpaste-brand-1414510599 (last accessed April 3, 2016).

Wren, JT (1995). *The Leader's Companion: Insights on Leadership through the Ages.* New York: Free Press.

Zacks Equity Research (2015). Tesla Scores High on Brand Loyalty. http://www.zacks.com/stock/news/179793/tesla-scores-high-on-brand-loyalty-85-owners-to-buy-again (last accessed April 1, 2016).

Part II

SUMMARY

Chapter 7. Being Strategy: From Positioning to Confirmation

- Positioning is referred to as a company's efforts to put the product and its brand into the minds of customers. In the Legacy era, each successful product, brand, and/or company is recognized by its strong and unique position in the minds of customers.

- Since the practice of positioning is company driven — it is one way and more dominated by the company — it no longer fits with the character of the digital consumer who wants a horizontal and parallel relationship.

It calls for the companies to now begin applying what we call "clarification", instead of traditional positioning.

- Clarification has several characteristics that distinguish it from positioning. Most importantly, clarification involves multidimensional messages, using customer-oriented content and utilizing multiple-way communication.

Chapter 8. Core Tactic: From Differentiation to Codification

- In the Legacy era, differentiation used to be a core tactic for companies to support their positioning that is formed in the minds of their customers. Differentiation was aimed to create a unique and superior customer value by integrating the content, context, and infrastructure of the company's offering to the customers.

- In the New Wave era, companies must be able to nurture a truly authentic uniqueness, which cannot be easily copied by competitors. For that, a company must be able to internalize its brand DNA into all the processes and functions, and not just the marketing team. This is called "codification".

- Codification of the brand DNA can be applied by the company through three interconnected layers: (i) symbols and styles (artifact), (ii) systems and leadership, and (iii) shared values and substance.

Chapter 9. Value Indicator: From Brand to Character

- Brand was considered a value indicator in the classic marketing era. A strong brand would be like an asset that could provide additional value to the company and customers.

- In this New Wave era, marketing has become more horizontal and the relationship between the brand and customers has become increasingly aligned. In view of this, the brand must transform into more of a human-like entity — one with character.

- To enable the brand to develop a strong character like a human or a leader, there are six aspects to imbibe: physicality, intellectuality, emotionality, sociability, personality, and moral ability.

Part III

MARKETING IS CREATING?
Competitive Marketing: The Whole Set

Marketing is about creating, enhancing, communicating, and delivering value to all companies' stakeholders. To develop a consistent value, strategic marketing concepts must be used. This involves the analysis of internal competitive conditions and the external environment in order to formulate a strategy to position an organization's brand, products, and services in the minds of its stakeholders. Next, the strategy needs to be translated into a set of tactics, which are more down-to-earth and practical.

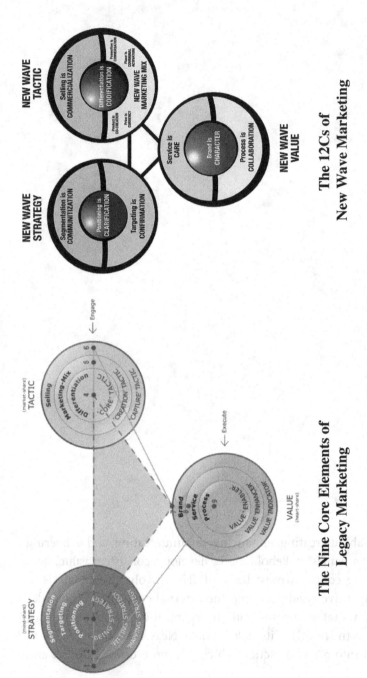

NEW WAVE TACTIC

NEW WAVE STRATEGY

NEW WAVE VALUE

The 12Cs of New Wave Marketing

Selling is COMMERCIALIZATION

Differentiation is CODIFICATION

NEW WAVE MARKETING MIX

Promotion is CONVERSATION

Place is COMMUNAL ACTIVATION

Product is CO-CREATION

Price is CURRENCY

Service is CARE

Brand is CHARACTER

Process is COLLABORATION

Segmentation is COMMUNITIZATION

Positioning is CLARIFICATION

Targeting is CONFIRMATION

The Nine Core Elements of Legacy Marketing

TACTIC (market-share)

Selling

Marketing-Mix

Differentiation

CORE TACTIC

CREATION TACTIC

CAPTURE TACTIC

Engage

VALUE (heart-share)

Brand

Service

Process

VALUE ENABLER

VALUE ENHANCER

VALUE INDICATOR

Execute

STRATEGY (mind-share)

Segmentation

Targeting

Positioning

BEING STRATEGY

FITTING STRATEGY

MAPPING STRATEGY

Explore

Figure A: From Legacy Marketing to New Wave Marketing.

In short, there are three dimensions of marketing architecture: strategy, tactic, and value. First, you must explore the market by performing segmentation. You then need to target certain segments. You can target one, two, several, or all segments within the market, depending on your competitive advantage and the competitive situation. Then you must position your company in the customer's mind: what exactly are your offerings?

However, positioning needs to be supported by solid differentiation. Afterwards, differentiation can be translated into your marketing mix (product, price, place, and promotion). Finally, the selling tactics, the only element that "captures the value" back from the market, is the transaction-oriented element. Brand should be created as the *value indicator*, and the value of the brand should be enhanced continuously through the service strategy. Last but not least comes process, the *value enabler*. No matter how strong you are in the other eight elements, they will be ineffectual unless you have a good process.

All of the above refer to the practices used in Legacy Marketing — a concept developed when connectivity between various stakeholders involved in the process of value creation was not as strong as today. However, a lot has changed over the past two decades. The digital technology revolution that is fast unwrapping in the world, and especially in Asia, makes the vertical Legacy Marketing approaches not entirely relevant anymore. This is why the marketers of today need to understand how the entire concept of marketing has undergone a fundamental transformation, in view of a world that has become more connected and horizontal. This has led to the birth of what we call New Wave Marketing (see Fig. A). In the chapters compiled in this part, we discuss in more detail how digital technology has made marketing strategy, tactic, and value more horizontal.

CHAPTER 10

MARKETING STRATEGY FOR VALUE EXPLORATION

*We forget that the world looks to us the way it does
because we have become used to seeing it that way
through a particular set of lenses. Today, however, we need
new lenses. And we need to throw the old ones away.*

Kenichi Ohmae

If compared with a building, then the marketing architecture would consist of three main pillars, namely strategy, tactic, and value. In the legacy era, marketing strategy has been known to consist of three main elements: segmentation, targeting, and positioning. All three constitute the foundation for a company to win mind share (Kotler *et al.*, 2003).

Segmentation can be defined as the way companies look to market their products and services creatively. We call segmentation a "mapping strategy" as it primarily deals with mapping the market in order to determine segments. Having mapped the market and segmented into groups of potential customers with similar characteristics and behaviors, companies can then choose which segment(s) to target more effectively. This is called targeting. Targeting is defined as a means of allocating corporate resources effectively by choosing the right target market(s). We term targeting as a "fitting strategy" because it entails adjusting the company's resources with the needs of the target market.

The last element of the marketing strategy is positioning. Positioning is the way by which the company occupies a position in the minds of customers. As it helps establish an identity among customers, positioning is also described as a "being strategy". Once a market has been mapped for segments and the company has adjusted its resources in line with the target segment, it must define the image it wants to build to achieve credibility in its target market.

That's how the company would typically develop a marketing strategy in an era when the world had not yet been hit by the wave of horizontalization as a result of the progress in information technology. However, technological advancements have dramatically changed customer behavior, thus demanding a new approach in business. As already discussed in Part II, positioning — which is the core of marketing strategy — has transformed into clarification. This chapter explains how the other two elements of marketing strategy — targeting and segmentation — have also undergone a fundamental shift. Segmentation has turned into communitization and targeting has become confirmation, thus forming the basis of New Wave Marketing strategy (Fig. 10.1).

From Segmentation to Communitization

In traditional marketing concepts marked by a vertical approach — where a company positions itself to its customers — segmentation would be the process by which it would explore business opportunities to divide a market into segments or clusters. Market mapping would be based on certain predetermined characteristics/variables, so as to help companies identify more clearly which segments to enter. In his article, Smith (1956) suggested that segmentation might be an effective way for an organization to manage diversity within a market.

In doing segmentation, there are several options to select variables whereby each variable bears a different level of effectiveness in predicting

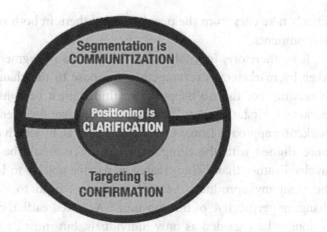

Figure 10.1: New Wave Marketing strategy.

customers' buying behavior (Goyat, 2011). In general, marketers usually develop market segmentation strategies based on attributes that are either static or dynamic.

Static attributes would determine variables that demonstrate a specific profile of the consumer but would not always reflect his or her buying behavior. Examples include a type of segmentation based on geographic and demographic variables. This type of segmentation is easier to define, but unfortunately often not quite effective as it does not provide a clear picture of how consumers choose and buy a product. Unlike segmentations based on dynamic attributes (psychographic and behavioral variables), which can be highly instrumental in mapping the real characteristics of consumers (Kotler *et al.*, 2003).

Segmentation is a "vertical" marketing practice because it is done as a top-down initiative from companies to differentiate among its customers. The criteria/attributes used are determined by the company and are not based on the initiatives from the customers. In the new marketing world of today, Web 2.0 technologies have brought us to the horizontal era, where the consumer wants to be considered as a person, not just as a hotbed of the company.

Further, technology has also spawned a sharing culture that has ostensibly evolved into a sharing economy. Consumers have become increasingly social and less individualistic. The decisions they take in selecting products and services do not rely only on themselves; they actively take cues from the people around them in both real and virtual environments.

It is, therefore, inevitable that the process of segmentation under-taken by marketers is revamped in response to the changing world of marketing. For that to happen, two things must be considered by the marketers. First, they should be able to recognize the need to change the marketing approach from vertical to horizontal, by which consumers are more aligned with the company. Consumers should be more actively involved rather than being treated as passive objects to be loaded with the company's products. Second, marketers need to understand the changing perspective of the consumer. As noted earlier, consumers can no longer be regarded as only individuals, but must be understood as social beings who relate to each other and have a greater community sense. Nicholas Christakis, a Sociology professor at the Department of Sociology in the Harvard Faculty of Arts and Sciences, stated that the key to understanding people is understanding the ties between them; there-fore it is these ties that we should turn our focus to (Christakis and Fowler, 2011).

In today's New Wave era, instead of traditional segmentation, what companies need to do is communitization — seeing consumers as a group of people who care for each other, have common purposes, and share values and identity. Communities can be formed by the company (by design) or as a result of customers' own initiatives (by default). What's important for marketers is to ensure and formulate a plan to make customers an active part of the company's business strategy, and not just a passive entity at the receiving end of their public relations activities or sponsorship. That's why we put communitization as part of the marketing strategy, not just a tactic.

Fournier and Lee (2009), in their article in the *Harvard Business Review* titled "Getting Brand Communities Right", wrote: "For a brand community to yield maximum benefit, it must be framed as a high-level strategy supporting businesswide goals". Harley-Davidson is an example of companies that have succeeded in implementing this paradigm. Following the 1985 leveraged buyback that saved the company, the management com-pletely reformulated their competitive strategy and business model around a "community" brand philosophy. Other than changing its marketing pro-grams, Harley-Davidson retooled every aspect of its organization — from its culture to its operating procedures — to support its community strategy. Another example is the communitization strategy undertaken by Hindustan Unilever in India. Through a strategic program called Project Shakti, the company has successfully expanded into the rural market by cooperating with local communities (see Box 10.1).

Box 10.1:   Hindustan Unilever's Project Shakti

Hindustan Unilever Limited (HUL) is an Indian consumer goods company based in Mumbai, Maharashtra. It is owned by Anglo-Dutch company Unilever, which owned a 67 percent controlling share in HUL as of 2015. HUL's products include foods, beverages, cleaning agents, personal care products, and water purifiers. Its distribution covers over two million retail outlets across India directly and its products are available in over 6.4 million outlets in the country.

The company generates around half its business from India's towns and cities and half from rural areas. By the end of the 1990s, however, the company realized that to increase its market share it had to expand the market. Almost 67 percent of India lives in villages. The challenge was how to reach the 500,000 villages with smaller populations in more remote parts of the country where there are millions of potential consumers but no retail distribution network, no advertising coverage, and no proper roads and transport.

HUL's solution, called Project Shakti (which means "strength" or "empowerment" in Sanskrit), was born in December 2000, in a district called Nalgonda in the southern Indian state of Andhra Pradesh. Its business objectives were to extend HUL's reach into untapped markets and to develop its brands through local influencers. Its social objective was to provide sustainable livelihood opportunities for underprivileged rural women.

The company decided to tap into the growing number of women's self-help communities that had been springing up around the country. These communities, about one million of which now exist across India, are usually formed to help women save money and borrow from each other to avoid the excessive demands of unscrupulous moneylenders.

(Continued)

Box 10.1: (*Continued*)

HUL made presentations at rural self-help community meetings, initially in Andhra Pradesh, and invited women to become direct-to-consumer sales distributors.

The company provides self-help communities with training in selling, commercial knowledge, and bookkeeping, teaching them to become fully fledged micro-entrepreneurs. The women who are trained can then choose to set up their own businesses or to become Project Shakti distributors — or Shakti Ammas ("mothers") as they have become known. Each woman who becomes a distributor invests 10,000–15,000 rupees (US$220–330) in stock at the outset. Each aims to have around 500 customers, mainly drawn from her village's self-help communities and from nearby smaller villages. In 2010, Project Shakti was extended to include "Shaktimaans" who are typically the husbands or brothers of the Shakti Ammas.

The project has proved to be a great success for both HUL and the rural community in India. Two years after its establishment, Project Shakti expanded to two states, and by the end of 2004, it had grown to over 13,000 Shakti women entrepreneurs covering 50,000 villages in 12 states. In 2016, Project Shakti provides livelihood-enhancing opportunities to over 70,000 Shakti entrepreneurs who distribute HUL's products in more than 165,000 villages and reach over four million rural households.

HUL's Project Shakti has become the model to reach out to rural markets by empowering local customer communities. The project has been customized and adapted in several emerging Asian markets such as Bangladesh, Sri Lanka, Pakistan, and Vietnam. In Bangladesh, it is being promoted as project Joyeeta. In Pakistan, the Shakti Amma is called "Guddi Baji" (Urdu for "doll sister"). Guddi Bajis, who are trained to provide beauty care services, sell brands such as Lux and Fair & Lovely. During visits to rural customers' homes or communities, they also teach them the importance of handwashing, educating girls, and registering births and deaths. In Sri Lanka, they are called "Saubhagya", which means good luck. There are nearly 2,000 Saubhagya entrepreneurs in Sri Lanka and 1,100 Guddi Bajis in Pakistan.

Sources: Rangan and Rajan (2007); Shashidhar (2013); "Project Shakti: Creating Rural Entrepreneur in India", *unilever.com*, 2005; "Enhancing Livelihoods through Project Shakti", *hul.co.in*, 2016.

Table 10.1: Segmentation versus communitization.

	Segmentation	Communitization
Paradigm	Customer as individual	Customer as social creature
Factors/variables	Geography, demography, psychography, behavior	Purpose, values, identity
Company–customer relationship	Vertical: customer as passive target segment	Horizontal: customer as active community member
Objective	Customers mapping based on similarity	Community potential identification based on cohesivity and influence

Segmentation versus Communitization: Some Core Differences

Segmentation and communitization could be deceptively similar because in practice, both processes focus on companies that are dealing with a group of customers with certain characteristics. But there are some fundamental differences between the two (Table 10.1).

The first distinction has been mentioned earlier. Segmentation focuses on individual characteristics of the customer, while communitization tries to see the customer in his or her position as a social being who has interactions with other people around him or her. In a segment, there are common geographic, demographic, psychographic, and behavioral characteristics, but there is not necessarily a continuous interaction between them. A segment is merely a collection of individuals grouped by certain criteria, whereas a community has a purpose, values, and identity (PVI) for members in it. The second difference of segmentation and communitization is the variable or factors used by companies in the analysis or identification of the group.

The third difference between segmentation and communitization is the approach used. The mindset used by marketers when segmenting the market is how to make the brand as the center of gravity. The customer just being a passive object is categorized as such and targeted by the company. While in communitization, marketers treat consumers in a horizontal position. This is because basically communitization is the involvement of community members to participate and interact more deeply with the company.

The fourth difference is that they are different in terms of objectives and indicators used. In segmentation, the company's goal is to map the consumers into groups with similar characteristics so that each group can be given a particular offering that is more striking. The indicator used is the similarity of each "residents" segment in terms of preference and needs. While in communitization, the objective of the company is to work together with a group of consumers who have a PVI with the same company. The indicators used are not only the homogeneity among consumers in a segment/group, but more than that, the extent of the attachment between the group members and the company as well as the influence of the group/community on the behavior of each of its members.

Community Modeling

In communitization, a marketer must understand the general model of the community that may be formed. According to marketing professor Susan Fournier, there are three forms of community affiliation: pools, hubs, and webs (see Fig. 10.2).

Pools

A pool is the most organic and natural form of community. Pools are formed by shared values and/or interest among its members, or by virtue of the same activity. The relationships between them, however, tend to be weak. The *Apple Mac* user community is an example of a pool, because the pooling factor is clear: it is united against Microsoft. Companies that can identify the presence of such pools would usually try to nurture such communities in order to be able to transform them into hubs or webs models.

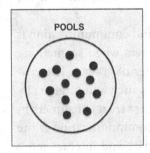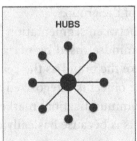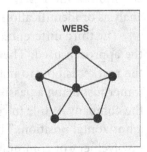

Figure 10.2: Community affiliation.

Source: Fournier and Lee (2009).

Hubs

The second type is a hub community. Such communities are usually formed as a result of admiration among its members toward a particular individual or group. As an example, a community of fans for a music band or a celebrity would be a type of hub community. The weakness of such communities lies in its reliance on a certain central figure as a magnet or icon, which unites its members. This would mean that the level of association among its members would greatly depend on the aura or attractiveness of the icons, which makes it somewhat temporary in nature. If the popularity and influence of its icon dim or no longer exist, such communities can be easily dissolved.

Examples of hubs are that of fan communities of football clubs such as Manchester United, Real Madrid, or A.C. Milan. Fans clearly share the same interest and love for the game, but could also demonstrate a sense of bigotry against other clubs. To maintain the strength of such communities, the appeal of the icons must be maintained. In the case of a football club community, the management's primary task is to ensure the team continues to boast of star players who have huge individual fan bases.

Webs

Webs would represent the most powerful and stable form of community because its members are able to develop a fairly close relationship or engage in intensive interactions with one another. Communities such as these can be formed both online and offline. The emergence of social media platforms such as Facebook and LinkedIn is an example of online communities shaped as webs. SAP, a multinational software company, has successfully created an online community that facilitates interactions between its users in different regions, including China (see Box. 10.2). Webs are equally effective in offline structures. Examples would be movements with certain social missions for which members voluntarily join and contribute toward their activities.

In communitization, companies must identify the forms of community that they are looking to create affiliation with (pools, hubs, or webs) and their special characteristics (PVI). This would set the stage for the next step, which is confirmation.

Box 10.2:   SAP Community Network China

SAP, started in 1972 by five entrepreneurs in Germany, is a multinational software corporation that makes enterprise software to manage business operations and customer relations. Headquartered in Walldorf, Baden-Württemberg, Germany, it operates regional offices in 130 countries and has over 293,500 customers in 190 countries. On the basis of market capitalization, it is the world's third largest independent software manufacturer.

As part of its strategy to provide the best solutions for clients, the company formed the SAP Community Network (SCN). SAP software users, developers, consultants, mentors, and students use SCN to get help, share ideas, learn, innovate, and connect with others. An average of two million unique visitors go to SCN each month, using the wealth of information shared on the site. SCN has over 430 spaces (subgroups) dedicated to SAP products, topics, technologies, industries, programming languages, and more. Almost all spaces contain related discussion threads (forums), blogs, documents, e-learning, and polls.

Reinforcing its commitment to the Asia-Pacific region and to online community network collaborations, SAP AG announced significant new offerings for its China-based community in 2009. They include publicly available content relevant for the Chinese market. The company has built new online discussion areas, forums, wikis, and blogs for its SCN China, enabling members to share knowledge and experiences on numerous solution areas and industry topics.

Recent updates to SCN China include:

- Relevant new discussion areas, including the topics of product life-cycle management (PLM), customer relationship management (CRM), and areas addressing the automotive, manufacturing, and consumer products industries.
- Fourteen discussion forums covering various hot topics important to the Chinese market, such as the enterprise resource planning (ERP) application, process integration, master data management, business intelligence, automotive solutions, and governance, risk,

(Continued)

Box 10.2: (*Continued*)

and compliance — all in the Chinese language to serve the local technologists and business process experts.

• Five new wikis now available in Chinese, addressing the areas of CRM, product after-sales service, and a best practice guide.

Mark Yolton, senior vice president, SCN, SAP AG, explained the background to this strategic initiative:

China is a rapidly growing region with a community eager to share knowledge. Our goal is to build efficient and expedient methods for sharing information — in that audience's native tongue, as well as in English throughout the larger global SAP Community Network — to accelerate innovation and promote knowledge exchange.

Sources: SAP official website, http://go.sap.com; SAP Social Network, http://scn.sap.com; "SAP Fosters Co-Innovation in China through New Online Collaboration Tools for the Local Community Network", http://global.sap.com, November 2009.

From Targeting to Confirmation

As discussed earlier, in the "legacy era", marketers would generally undertake segmentation in an attempt to map the potential market segments in accordance with certain traits or characteristics. As the segments are mapped, the next step would be to evaluate and determine which segments are to be targeted. That is targeting — the process of choosing the right target market for your products and services.

Targeting is usually seen as a strategy to allocate the company's resources effectively, so as to ensure optimal utilization. It draws upon considerations on how companies "fit" into a chosen segment. In practice, there are three criteria used by companies when evaluating the segments they look to target. The first is to ensure that the chosen market segment is sufficiently large and profitable for the company. This is termed as the market size. The second is that the growth potential of the market should also be considered. A segment could be small in size, but if it carries a potential to experience high growth in the future, it would be deemed fit for targeting.

The third criterion would be based on a competitive advantage that a company may possess. It is a way to measure whether the company has sufficient strength and expertise to serve and dominate a segment. Companies must consider the competitive situation to analyze this aspect, which may directly or indirectly affect its profitability.

By using a mix of these criteria, companies look to hone their targeting capabilities in order to find a fit in a market segment or evaluate how a market segment fits its business goals. This would generally summarize the process of targeting in legacy marketing.

As noted previously, in a world that is becoming increasingly horizontal, consumers and marketers are more aligned. Consumers are no longer willing to be treated as targets or recipients of passive marketing. They now want to be positioned as a community with a more active role. This calls for segmentation to be turned into communitization. And consequently, targeting should also become confirmation.

Confirmation Is Beyond Permission

Long ago, it was already predicted by the noted marketing author and blogger Godin (1999) that "interruption marketing" would eventually die. According to him, the world is changing rapidly and is much different from decades ago when consumers still enjoyed being plagued by various forms of interruptions from marketers. There was a time when consumers were happy to see commercials on television. With the emergence of television, consumers were almost fascinated with all these forms of advertising interruptions, offering various products and services through a visual medium. Of course, the world has changed much since then. Today, marketers fight tooth and nail to leverage all the creativity they can just so that their marketing communications are not considered interference (clutter) by the customer.

Godin stated that on an average, a consumer is targeted by about one million messages that reeked of marketing, meaning about 3,000 messages a day. Certainly, no one could pay attention to all these messages every day. And considering these estimates, it is no wonder that more and more people are getting accustomed to ignoring various forms of promotion they meet. It is no surprise that customers are increasingly tuning out mass-market advertisements; in a 2015 Marketo (a marketing automation firm) poll comprising more than 2,200 consumers worldwide, almost two-thirds (63 percent) of respondents said how it annoyed them to see brands continuing blasting generic advertising messages at them.

Godin also said that the biggest problem of mass advertising is the way it treated customers as "strangers" rather than "friends". Marketers fight to get the attention of people by interfering with their time, in any form, anywhere, and at any time. And all that is done without caring about the feelings of consumers who are targeted.

Godin offered an alternative model that, he said, was more powerful and friendly in the new era. He called it "permission-based" marketing. With this approach, he advises marketers to first seek permission before they went out to interrupting the consumer. Permission marketing, as he puts it, was the privilege (not the right) of delivering anticipated, personal, and relevant messages to people who actually want to get them. Subscription to a service is one such form of permission. If a company wants to convey an advertising message to a specific consumer, then the consumer must give permission or prior approval. The bottom line is that for any communication made by marketers to consumers, the permission of the consumer becomes a necessity.

But asking for permission may not guarantee that the existence of the marketer is automatically accepted by the consumers. Through permission, marketers can basically request for attention, which can be either approved or ignored. That's why we prefer to use the word "confirmation" and not "permission". Confirmation reflects a more horizontal mindset, wherein the company and the customer are aligned. In "permission-based" marketing, the enterprise can only wait for the customers passively until the request is accepted. But when horizontally aligned, the company may be able to more actively indicate to the customer community the commonalities that exist between them, so that the existence of the company can be accepted. This is called confirmation.

Successful Community Confirmation

As with targeting, when marketers can commonly use four criteria as described previously (market size, market growth, competitive advantage,

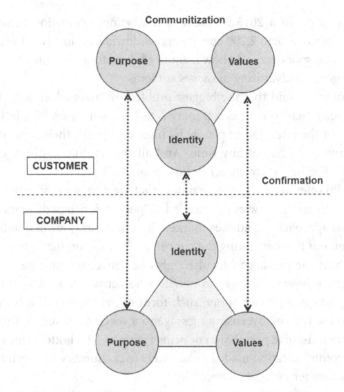

Figure 10.3: Communitization and confirmation of PVI.

and competitive situation), for confirmation, there are three additional criteria that need to be considered: relevance, level of activity, and the number of community networks (NCNs).

Relevance would refer to the similarity of the PVI between a community and a brand. For a community of Harley-Davidson owners, the purpose for its members to come together and form a community is to find partnership for activities. The values that unite them are brotherhood and freedom. Members have their specific costumes designed, which brings them a sense of shared identity. If a brand is able to achieve the alignment with these three elements, it helps the process of confirmation (see Fig. 10.3).

As the name suggests, the activity level would determine how actively community members engage with each other. Does a community have members who discuss and participate in a variety of activities, or is it only there for namesake — with only a list of names? If it's the latter, it is simply not a community, but just a database. In communities shaped as hubs and webs, there is usually a higher level of activity compared with pools.

Finally, the last criterion is that of NCNs. It essentially refers to the reach of a community, meaning the number of networks owned by a community or those with a potential to engage with the community. NCN, therefore, is not limited to the members within the community but also their external reach across other networks.

Among the three criteria, the relevance of PVI for a company/brand that is in line with the PVI for customers is a more mainstream consideration in conducting a successful community confirmation. But that is not to say that level of activity and community-level network are not important. They indeed are, but may not be as instrumental as the relevance of PVI in ascertaining the very existence of a community. If it turns out, a community has many active members and also has an expanding network of other communities, but what the community lacks is relevance of PVI for a brand, then the confirmation process will be difficult to attain.

The three criteria are basically the steps taken by the company in exploring a community that has existed as a result of initiatives by the consumers themselves. In the absence of such relevant communities, the company may eventually be able to form its own community. Indeed, such "by-design" communities could be better directed from the outset to reflect the PVI of the company.

References

Christakis, NA and JH Fowler (2011). *Connected: The Surprising Power of Our Social Networks and How They Shape Our Lives*. New York: Back Bay Books.

Fournier, S and L Lee (April 2009). Getting Brand Community Right. *Harvard Business Review*.

Godin, S (1999). *Permission Marketing: Turning Strangers into Friends and Friends into Customers*. New York: Simon & Schuster.

Goyat, S (2011). The basis of market segmentation: A critical review of literature. *European Journal of Business and Management*, 3, 45–54.

Hindustan Unilever Limited (2016). Enhancing Livelihoods through Project Shakti. https://www.hul.co.in/sustainable-living/case-studies/enhancing-livelihoods-through-project-shakti.html (last accessed August 1, 2016).

Kotler, et al. (2003). Rethinking Marketing: Sustainable Market-ing Enterprise in Asia. Singapore: Prentice Hall.

Marketo (June 22, 2015). Consumers to Brands: The Louder You Scream, the Less We Care. http://investors.marketo.com/releasedetail.cfm?releaseid=918797 (last accessed May 21, 2016).

Rangan, VK and R Rajan (June 2007). Unilever in India: Hindustan Lever's Project Shakti — Marketing FMCG to the Rural Consumer. Harvard Business School Case.

SAP AG (2009). SAP Fosters Co-Innovation in China through New Online Collaboration Tools for The Local Community Network. http://global1.sap.com/chile/press.epx?pressid=12203 (last modified November 11, 2009, last accessed August 1, 2016).

SAP (2016). About SAP SE. http://go.sap.com/corporate/en.html (last accessed August 1, 2016).

SAP (2016). SAP Community Network. http://scn.sap.com/welcome (last accessed August 1, 2016).

Shashidhar, A (July 7, 2013). Empowering Women-and Men. businesstoday.com.

Smith, W (1956). Product differentiation and market segmentation as alternative marketing strategies. Journal of Marketing, 21, 3–8.

Unilever (2005). Project Shakti: Creating Rural Entrepreneur in India. https://www.google.com/search?q=Project+Shakti%3A+Creating+Rural+Entrepreneur+in+India&ie=utf-8&oe=utf-8&aq=t&rls=org.mozilla:id:official&client=firefox-a&channel=fflb (last modified February 28, 2005, last accessed August 1, 2016).

CHAPTER 11

MARKETING TACTIC FOR VALUE ENGAGEMENT

*People just don't listen to ads, salespeople,
or important messages anymore. They don't care what you
have to say, sell, or even give away. The number one reason
that people don't listen to you is because they are too
busy listening to their friends.*

Tara Hunt in "The Whuffie Factor"

The previous chapter covered the three components of marketing architecture, namely strategy, tactics, and value. Tactics, the second component of the architecture, in the Legacy era, would consist of three main elements: differentiation, marketing mix, and selling. Differentiation is the core tactic of the company, describing the uniqueness that it offers to the target market. This uniqueness is then created through the 4Ps—product, price, place, and promotion (marketing mix). Further, to build

Figure 11.1:   New Wave marketing tactic.

and maintain long-term relationships based on mutual benefits with the customer, selling is an effective tactic (Kotler *et al.*, 2003).

Part III covers the shift from differentiation to codification. This chapter deals with the transformation of the elements of marketing mix: from product to co-creation, price to currency, place to communal activation, and promotion to conversation.

From Product to Co-creation

The process of new product development (NPD) always makes for interesting study. Akin to the birth of a baby, the process consists of various stages that are full of challenges and high risks. It will inevitably be of huge concern to any company when developing a new product as to whether or not it will be well-received by its potential customers.

In the Legacy era marked by a vertical marketing approach, companies play the most dominant role in the NPD process. All stages of development are duly controlled by the company, while consumers are to be treated as passive recipients whose role is limited to having an opinion on the product. This could be termed traditional, company-centric NPD.

In the New Wave era, the development process takes a more "horizontal" route. The companies keenly provide several opportunities for customers to be actively involved in various product development stages. This effectively means that the final product could be the result of collaborations between the company and its customers. Prahalad and Ramaswamy (2004) argued that if a company can execute such a process of co-creation well, the value of the resulting product will be higher.

Developments in information technology (IT), particularly the Internet, have led to a growing momentum to the process of co-creation. The Internet provides a platform for enhanced interactions between companies and consumers, making the desired collaboration much easier to achieve. It provides a vast resource of information to customers, which further helps sharpen their creative inputs. And the flag-bearers of the co-creation movement indeed are technology-driven companies such as Firefox, Fiat, Boeing, and Electrolux.

Lately, other industrial sectors are also widely embracing the concept of co-creation; for example, Lego, which is considered a pioneer in encouraging co-creation among its fans and customers to produce a wide variety of new game designs. Starbucks also uses an online platform called My Starbucks Idea to accommodate the aspirations of consumers related to improvements in Starbucks' products and services. Another example is from Nike, which gives consumers a chance to design their own shoes and T-shirts online, through NIKEiD.com. In fact, it is not only businesses that are experimenting with co-creation, the concept has even been adopted by governments. The Singapore government is one such example (see Box 11.1).

Of course not all consumers — or in the case of Singapore, citizens — can be engaged productively in the process of co-creation. Companies or organizations must select the right customers who can be involved as co-creators. In an article published in *Research World* in October 2009, Needham and Zohhadi (2009) confirmed that a company's foremost challenge in the process of co-creation is to find "adfluentials", which are typically about 1 percent. Adfluentials are consumers with the following characteristics: (i) they have the passion and the brand connection to work with the company, (ii) they have the skills to do so, and (iii) they have the networks to offer the greatest potential to involve their peers and friends in the activity. The use of online platforms — as done by Starbucks and the Singapore government — is one way to conduct a preliminary selection in order to find co-creators with brilliant ideas.

194 · *Marketing for Competitiveness: Asia to the World*

Box 11.1:   Singapore eGov2015: Co-creating for Greater Value

The Singapore e-governance journey began in the early 80s with the goal of transforming the government into a world-class user of information technology. The late 90s saw the convergence of information technology with telecommunications, which revolutionized the concept of service delivery. This paved the way for the launch of the e-Government Action Plan (2000–2003) and the e-Government Action Plan II (2003–2006). The key objective of the first plan was to roll out as many public services online as possible, while the emphasis of the second plan was on further enhancing the service experience of customers.

iGov2010 Masterplan (2006–2010) was developed on the basis of this strong Information and Communication Technology (ICT) foundation. It focused primarily on creating an Integrated Government that operates seamlessly behind the scene to serve customers better. During this period, mobile services were also introduced to ride on the wave of the high mobile phone penetration rate, in order to offer customers an additional channel for accessing public services.

Building on the success of the earlier e-Government masterplans, eGov2015 aims to connect government agencies to its citizens using a variety of social media and crowdsourcing platforms. The ultimate goal is for Singapore to end up with "a Collaborative government that co-creates and connects with the people". The plan will serve as a five-year guideline for the implementation of new ICT programs among all government agencies.

eGov2015 focuses on three strategies in attempting to achieve the e-government vision: co-creating for greater value, connecting for active participation, and catalyzing a whole-of-government transformation.

The government will take advantage of a variety of technologies in order to improve the delivery of services to the public. eGov2015 also makes allowances for co-creation between the public and private sectors. The plan kicks off with the launch of a new website and mobile app. Data.gov.sg is aimed at providing easy access to government data from more than 50 agencies. The mobile app, mGov@SG, allows users to easily search for, and use, government services.

(Continued)

Box 11.1: (*Continued*)

In an effort to increase participation, the government will send out alerts on its actions through various mobile applications and social media platforms. Several government agencies have already launched their own social media platforms in order to educate the public on their ongoing projects.

With the rising popularity of social networking, the government can more easily tap on the collective intelligence of the crowd. As such, the government can go beyond its traditional role as a service provider, to also serve as a platform provider to encourage greater co-creation of new e-services. For instance, members of the public will be able to readily look for and download publicly available government data from data.gov.sg, which can be used for research purposes as well as to encourage the development of innovative and impactful applications.

Sources: *"eGov Master Plan"*, http://www.egov.gov.sg/egov-masterplans/; *"Singapore Moves Towards a Collaborative Government"*, http://dailycrowd-source.com/content/open-innovation/573-singapore-moves-towards-a-collaborative-government

---

Although the selection of right co-creators is highly important, the more crucial aspect is the establishment of appropriate internal teams within the organization. Without the right team, the creative ideas developed through collaboration with customers will not be able to be integrated into real products. David Cousino, Global Consumer Marketing Insight Director for Unilever's skin care products, once said: *"Consumers want to be engaged with brands more closely and we as marketers must do that. The challenge lies less in finding passionate consumers than in hiring the right team to lead them. Marketers must be prepared to relinquish creative control rather than steer participants towards favored, often predictable, outcomes* (Wong, 2010)."

As companies and consumers are able to engage in direct interactions, the process of customer research undergoes significant changes. In traditional NPD, the market research techniques most often used include conventional methods such as focus group discussions (FGDs) or surveys. FGDs are usually conducted for brainstorming and exploration of new ideas and for product testing, while surveys help determine market opportunities and the level of consumer acceptance toward upcoming products.

Such research methods consider consumers to be passive participants who are simply waiting for the questions to be asked by the manufacturer. It is certainly antithetic to the spirit of co-creation if consumers adopt a more active role. Since it is marketing research, the researcher must change the original paradigm of that of an "interrogator" to become a "facilitator" who listens more and facilitates the interactions between businesses and consumers.

In order for the process of co-creation to run effectively and efficiently, Prahalad and Ramaswamy (2004) emphasized the importance for companies to pay attention to the following four building blocks:

Dialogue

In the process of co-creation, a dialogue between the company and the customer is absolutely necessary. A dialogue symbolizes a horizontal process in which both parties are more or less on an equal standing. It is much more than just listening to customers: it implies shared learning and communication between two equal problem-solvers. There are several things that must be considered to ensure that the dialogue facilitates the purpose of co-creation. These are: (i) focus on the mutual interest between company and customer, (ii) need of forum in which the dialogue can occur, and (iii) requirement of rules that allow a productive interaction.

Access

With the emergence of a "sharing economy", the goal of a large section of consumers is gaining access to desirable experiences, and not necessarily ownership of a product. Access begins with information and tools. When customers have access to the company's information and resources, they will be able to make greater contributions to support the process of co-creation. Ease of access is also proven to improve loyalty among customers, as it happened in the case of the Taiwan Semiconductor Manufacturing Company (TSMC) (see Box 11.2).

Box 11.2: Taiwan Semiconductor Manufacturing Company

Taiwan has replaced South Korea as the country with the biggest fab production capacity of integrated circuit (IC) wafers in the world. As of December 2015, wafer capacity in Taiwan accounted for 21.7 percent of the world's total, higher than the 20.5 percent in South Korea. Analysts said the increase in Taiwan's IC wafer production capacity resulted largely from expansions in capacity by TSMC. TSMC is the world's first dedicated semiconductor foundry, with its headquarters and main operations located in the Hsinchu Science and Industrial Park in Hsinchu, Taiwan. In addition to semiconductors, the company has also begun investing in lighting and solar energy-related industries.

When the company was formed in 1987, it manufactured chips on a contract basis for established players like Philips. But the top management of TSMC soon noticed that top engineers were leaving old-guard firms to start their own chip businesses. It made them foresee the need for a dedicated manufacturer to expand its designs. In 2002, these "fabless" firms represented more than two-thirds of TSMC's revenue. As part of its co-creation initiative, TSMC has given them online access to data on its engineering processes, design, fabrication libraries, and supply-chain and quality processes.

TSMC wants its fabless customers to feel that they have their own fab. These numerous customers, with limited resources, could now take advantage of the abundant data in TSMC's virtual lab. It puts in place an online system that allows them to get up-to-date information. Customers can even access sensitive information such as technology roadmaps, yield analysis, and process reliability data. This exclusive access has allowed TSMC's customers to minimize their investment in the semiconductor business.

Through this kind of co-creation, TSMC can provide greater value to its customers. The booking process, design, and delivery can be done more efficiently by more transparent information exchange between the two parties. And not to forget, increasing customer loyalty. This kind of

(Continued)

> ## Box 11.2: (*Continued*)
>
> customer base provides a solid foundation to TSMC's semiconductor business, as was evident during the early 2000s, in the aftermath of the Asian financial crisis. When some other global players witnessed downfall, TSMC continued to expand its business.
>
> *Sources*: "*About TSMC*", www.tsmc.com; "*Taiwan Semiconductor*", www. wired.com; "*Taiwan Overtakes South Korea as Top Chip-maker in Integrated Circuit Wafer Fab Capacity with 3.55 Mil Units*", www.chinapost.com.

Risk Assessment

Risk refers to the probability of harm caused to customers. In general, the company has more mature capabilities in conducting risk assessment and management, so what is of greater concern is the risk associated with customers. Along with the growing trend of co-creation, consumers will expect businesses to share complete information with them about the risks, providing not just data but appropriate methodologies for assessing the personal and societal risks associated with products and services.

Transparency

Information asymmetry between firms and customers is disappearing fast. IT has dramatically improved customer access to information about products, price, all the way down to the company's business model. In view of such transparency, customers are becoming more aware of the importance of openness in other aspects. In the process of co-creation that puts a customer as an active partner in product development, providing transparent information related to the company helps evaluate business and social impact of the products that are to be developed jointly.

From Price to Currency

The next element in the marketing mix is price. The impact of changes in price is seen not only on a business' sales volumes, but also on its bottom line (profit). On the basis of research cited in *The Pricing Advantage* by

Baker *et al.* (2010), it can be said that if the product price increased by 1 percent, with unchanged fixed costs and variable costs, operating profit could rise by 11 percent.

The price effect is much larger when compared with other aspects. For example, if the variable cost is lowered by 1 percent, the increase in operating profit would be limited to only 7.3 percent. And if fixed costs are lowered by 1 percent, its impact on the operating profit is only 3.2 percent. In another scenario, if the volume is multiplied by 1 percent, the effect on profit increase is only 3.7 percent.

A price drop is acceptable by marketers, provided there is high elasticity, so that the decline in margins per product can be compensated by the increase in sales volumes. Another prerequisite is that the reduction in price should not negatively affect the brand image. If pricing tactic can be used appropriately, marketers will be able to successfully penetrate a market or build a specific brand image. Conversely, if they can't get the pricing right, it usually results in a disaster.

In the Legacy era, pricing would be based on a mechanism. First, the price is determined in consideration of market volatility (market-based pricing). In this case, marketers would just be price-takers, not price-makers. Pricing is based on the balance that is governed by the law of supply and demand in the market. If demand increases while the quantity of product remains the same or declines, it would push the prices up. Vice versa, if the supply of goods is abound in the market while demand from customers is constant, then the price will go down. If marketers are stuck in such a pricing mechanism, it would mean that their products are viewed by consumers as commodities bearing minimal differentiation.

The second mechanism is cost-based pricing. The formula is already commonly used across industries. Prices are calculated based on the costs incurred plus the expected target margin. In plain language, marketers must calculate the costs and how much profit is targeted from each product, and based on this information the price can be formulated. This is an example of a company-centric approach.

The third is competitor-based pricing. The company already collects data on similar products from existing competitors in the market. On the basis of these data, the company establishes whether to fix the price above, below, or at the average price at which competitor products are available in the market.

The fourth approach is more focused on customer expectations and perceptions. Here the company sets the price based on the value of the product in the eyes of the customers. Prices are determined after thorough research on how much would the customers be willing to pay. This is called value-based pricing.

This fourth approach is in line with the 4C model from the Legacy era. Market-based pricing is a pricing method that is based on consideration of the change that occurs in the market (change). Cost-based pricing is the way firms set prices on the basis of cost calculated as a result of the internal dynamics within the company (company). Competitor-based pricing is done through price benchmarking against competitors (competitor). Value-based pricing is a pricing mechanism that considers the dynamics of customer acceptance (customer).

In the New era, the 4C model has been transformed to 5C, where the fifth C refers to the aspect of Connector. The existence of the Connector has resulted in increased transparency, owing to the availability of a lot of information to the customer. On the one hand, consumers can easily ascertain your prices and competitors' prices. They can even ascertain the elements of costs in producing a product or service. On the other hand, they want greater freedom to determine the price they would pay. This is the New era when the product results from co-creation and price has become currency.

Advances in technology have enabled companies to provide customers with greater freedom in conducting price customization. With a flexible approach to this kind of currency, the price to be paid is determined by the subscriber according to the features of the products they need. And no less important, this kind of customization would make the value received by customers increasingly relevant to their wants and needs. In general, there are two approaches to currency that can be used: adaptation and collaboration.

Currency Adaptation

Through the first approach, the company creates a customizable product that can be personalized in accordance with the wishes of the customer, resulting in the price being adjustable as well. Advances in technology have enabled customers to undertake product and price customization without any interference from the company (Gilmore and Pine II, 1997). Companies only need to set up transparent choices with a mechanism to perform customization and payments.

A practical application of the adaptation approach is seen from the "freemium" concept initiated by Anderson (2009). Technology companies such as LinkedIn, YouTube, and Facebook give consumers the freedom to choose from free or premium services. For users who require only simple services, the basic product or service comes free of charge. But if they want more advanced features, the company provides paid services. There are various packages offered to choose from, with varying levels of access to features or services, and priced accordingly.

Currency Collaboration

The second approach is facilitated through a dialogue between the company and its customers. Both sides attempt to identify the precise offering that can meet customer needs optimally. Currency collaboration is appropriate for businesses where its potential customers cannot easily articulate what they want and can begin to grow frustrated when forced to select from a lot of options (Gilmore and Pine II, 1997).

An examples of companies that have implemented currency collaboration is Tiffany & Co. An American worldwide premiere jewelry retailer and design house, the company offers a selection of engagement and wedding rings and other accessories that can be customized. Together with a jewelry designer, it helps customers create the perfect ring for their special moments. Another example of such collaboration is the innovative model adopted by Holcim Indonesia. As part of its strategy to increase the value offered to its customers, Holcim has introduced the concept of "Housing Solution", which enables customers to perform cost estimations and customizations in real time (see Box 11.3).

From Promotion to Conversation

Ahead of the curve, Ries and Ries (2002) predicted over a decade ago that the golden age of advertising will decline. This opinion was founded on several grounds: (i) the influx of advertising that would eventually diminish its effectiveness; (ii) advertising was increasingly perceived as

Box 11.3:   Holcim Indonesia's "Housing Solution"

Holcim is a pioneer and an innovator in Indonesia's fast-developing cement sector, amid an expanding market for homes, commercial buildings, and supporting infrastructure. Its products, including cement, ready-mix concretes, and aggregates, are sold in more than 8,000 retail stores across Indonesia. Holcim Indonesia's main market, the island of Java, occupies 7 percent of Indonesia's available land, and is home to 55 percent of Indonesia's population. In 2006, the Indonesian Group company identified a backlog of six million homes throughout the country, the highest housing backlog being situated on the island of Java.

Contributing to solving this difficult situation called for a special solution. Holcim Indonesia took the challenge upon itself by providing earthquake-resistant, sustainable modular houses for low- and middle-income families through an initiative called Solusi Rumah ("housing solution"). The idea was to provide all kinds of construction materials for an affordable home. This innovative system, kicked off in December 2006, aimed to empower customers by giving them consultation on project planning and supply of building materials as well as access to price information. The initiative is now in its 10th year.

Conventionally, Indonesian homes are built and renovated gradually over a period of time, and customers buy small quantities of cement according to their need. Through Solusi Rumah software, Holcim provides precast concrete, which turns out to be significantly more cost-efficient. This offers a one-stop solution to Indonesian home builders. Its unique and comprehensive services give the customers many opportunities to collaborate with the company:

- The packages include architectural services, building materials, labor, project management, and construction consultancy as well as banking services for housing mortgages.

- Using Solusi Rumah, the customers can accurately calculate material costs in real time.

- A variety of affordable house designs are available. They allow for future expansion and can be tailored to the customer's needs and budget.

Sources: "*Corporate Profile*", www.holcim.co.id; "*Solusi Rumah: Affordable Housing in Indonesia*", http://www.holcim.com/media-relations/our-major-projects/solusi-rumah-affordable-housing-in-indonesia.html.

one-sided, biased, and a company-oriented communication while people sought trusted, unbiased information that is consumer-oriented; and (iii) the advertising industry seemed to have lost its purpose, as its focus shifted from generating sales to making more creative advertisements.

As a new, more promising alternative, they hailed the rise of public relations (PRs). PR campaigns were believed to be a more effective approach in gaining customers' trust, resulting in better reception of a company's messages. The credibility factor apparently shot up because the marketing messages in PR campaigns were voiced by "third parties", or the mass media that is considered more neutral. In the book *"The Fall of Advertising & the Rise of PR"* they stated:

> The main goal of a public relations campaign is to get a company and its product mentioned and recommended by third parties. Third parties include newscasts, newspapers and magazines, which tend to be consumer-oriented. Since the media is not affiliated with the company, people are more likely to accept the opinions and ideals of the public relations campaign.

Even though it made perfect sense back then — considering the rise of several brands with minimal advertising but supported by strong PR, such as Starbucks, the Body Shop, Xiaomi, and Zalora — the trend appears to have changed. With the emergence of Web 2.0 and other supporting technologies arises another "third party", which is even more influential: the customer itself. Word-of-mouth promotion ostensibly spreads much faster and is evidently more effective in influencing customers' purchasing decisions. Online and mobile social networks and media platforms such as blogs and forums have become effective tools in facilitating exchange of information between customers and the people they trust. This ushers in a New era that marks the fall of not only advertising, but overall promotion. Welcome to the Conversation era.

This New era of marketing communications puts consumers at the core. Not only do consumers produce creative messages in various forms, such as images, articles, audios, videos, and even applications, but they also actively share them across various media platforms. And it's not just quantity, some content produced by customers is so entertaining and interesting that it could even compete with the works of a formal creative agency. And there is no dearth of media where they can publicize their messages. From social media, blogs, to instant messengers and online marketplaces and even app stores, there are plenty of platforms that provide effective means for consumers to share information among themselves. This phenomenon has been termed user-generated content (UGC), which basically includes any form of content including blogs, wikis, discussion forums, posts, chats, tweets, podcasts, digital images, and other forms created and made available by users online.

As the UGC trend catches up, companies are focusing on putting across messages that are sufficiently creative in order to be able to trigger conversations among customers, contrary to traditional unidirectional advertising, flowing from the company to the customer. These conversations help catapult marketing messages into viral content that goes on spreading fast and wide as customers share it with people connected to them via various "alternative media", as mentioned earlier. To that end, the real challenge for the company is to create content that can encourage customers to share them voluntarily.

On the basis of research conducted on a variety of viral content in the media, Kelly (2007) identified nine themes that could trigger a conversation among customers (see Table 11.1). These themes can be packaged in various forms, including text, images, and videos. Companies can choose one or several among these themes that are consistent with the character of their products and services.

From Place to Communal Activation

The final element of the marketing mix is place, often referred to as the distribution or marketing channel. It is typically the physical platform that connects companies and their customers, so that they can actually get their hands at the product or experience a service. Traditionally, distribution channels would comprise a wholesaler who would purchase products in bulk, to be resold to smaller channels or retailers who would sell to the customers directly. Distribution channels also exist in the form of dealers or branches, mostly serving as a direct channel from the company.

As with the fundamental transformation of other elements, the Internet has also led to the creation of alternative distribution channels. Online and mobile channels act as low-budget channels to deliver products and services to customers. Together with the ease to make online payments, online distribution channels are thriving across industries

Table 11.1:   Nine conversation themes.

Conversation Themes	Description	Example
Aspirations and beliefs	Something inspiring and touching emotions and big ideas that challenge and potentially create meaningful change	The story of Indian families that came out of poverty as a result of becoming Hindustan Unilever's Shaktipreneur
David vs. Goliath	The story of a small player's struggle against domination of big powers	Rivalry between Amazon.com and Barnes and Noble, or the battle between Microsoft and Linux or how Hyundai attempts to beat Mercedes/BMW
Avalanche about to roll/trends	Big, emerging trends that could damage a business or industry practice ·	The emerging trend of how latest tech products from the likes of Xiaomi are taking off; rising wave of online transportation companies (Uber, Grab, Gojek, Didi Chuxing, etc.) in Asian countries
Anxieties	Information about something evokes fear but should be kept in mind because it involves risks that must be avoided	Health message from soap manufacturers about the dangers of certain endemic diseases
Contrarian/challenging assumptions	An opposing view of the conventional wisdom that already exists in the community	A campaign from Dove that features an unlikely female endorser (fat, curly haired, dark-skinned, etc.)
Personalities and personal stories	The story about the private life of successful personalities or inspirational success stories of people (business, political, and social)	How Steve Jobs resurrected Apple after his return, or the story of how AirAsia was built by Tony Fernandes
How to/practical tips	Information relating to the tips or techniques to do something useful, but not yet widely known	Tips to perform simple financial planning for family
Glitz and Glam	The stories about the lives of glamorous celebrities featuring luxurious lifestyles	Stories of celebrities or famous personalities who prefer to use a particular brand
Seasonal/event related	Information about special events or important moments that are generally of interest to many people	The launch of new products on special dates such as December 12, 2012

and as a result, more and more companies can sell their products directly to customers. One classic example is that of "disintermediation" performed by Dell to cut middlemen and use the Internet to take direct orders from end users. By 1997, Dell's online sales had reached an average of US$4 million per day. While most of the PCs were sold preconfigured and preassembled in retail stores, Dell was able to offer its customers superior choice in system configuration at a deeply discounted price, due to the cost-savings associated with cutting out the retail middlemen. This move, away from the traditional distribution models for PC sales, played a large role in Dell's formidable early growth (Strickland, 1999).

In the New Wave era, such kind of a channeling model adopted by Dell has become quite common. The Internet has become the medium that brings together actors from various industries with their customers. But, what needs to be noted is that this New Wave is a combination of online and offline interaction. Dell too eventually learnt its lesson: that it could not simply rely on the online channel alone. That gave birth to the underlying philosophy of Dell 2.0, in which the offline channel to penetrate the enterprise and small businesses markets was reintroduced. Tesla could be a case in point on facilitating online–offline interaction, and in the process also creating a unique distribution model in the auto industry, which is traditionally served by a network of "dealers". Tesla does not deal with conventional dealerships; it has what it calls a "store and service" center model whereby it sets up showrooms at places experiencing high footfalls, such as malls and shopping streets. These showrooms help facilitate interactions with customers, which helps make reservations for vehicles. There is no inventory to choose from, but a customer can place an order for a Tesla car online, even choosing from various customizable options through its design studio.

The New Wave era calls for companies to be smarter in devising the right combination of online–offline approaches, especially for target customers who are turning increasingly communal — as discussed previously, owing to the shift from segmentation to communitization. Therefore, companies — at a tactical level also — need to implement the right initiatives, one of which is the utilization of the community that is aligned with the company's distribution channel, in terms of purpose, values, and identity. This is called communal activation.

To perform communal activation, the company should act as a facilitator that provides a real-world platform for community members to meet with each other and share ideas. Although social media and other online platforms offer convenience for community members to interact with each other, nonetheless, their existence cannot replace face-to-face meetings. Physical spaces play important roles in fostering community connections. According to Mark Rosenbaum of Northern Illinois University, communities that are developed in third places like gyms and coffee shops often provide social and emotional support equal to or stronger than family ties (Fournier and Lee, 2009).

Vice versa, if the customer is already part of a routine offline community activity, companies can support the endeavor with the creation of an online platform to further facilitate interactions among community members. One such initiative was undertaken by *Nutella*, the most famous hazelnut spread brand in the world, manufactured by Italian company Ferrero. *Nutella's* popularity in Europe was notably marked by the rise of "Nutella party" among teenagers. Such events were being organized at countrysides, at schools, or at teen activity centers. In addition to a fun gathering and other entertaining activities, the teens jazzed up the party with a ritual meal of bread spread with *Nutella* butter.

Looking at the enthusiasm of the customer community in the "Nutella party", the management of *Nutella*, while initially skeptical, eventually decided to plan some initiatives around it. One was the launch of the website www.mynutella.com, which aimed to strengthen its bond with the customers. On the website, community members could share stories about *Nutella* and how it fits into their daily lives, in the form of stories, photos, and videos. This turned out to be an example of a successful activation of the communal approach by combining online and offline platforms.

From Selling to Commercialization

In addition to the elements of the marketing mix that have undergone fundamental transformations, selling practices have also undergone a shift in the New Wave era. In this era of horizontal marketing, the use of social networks in the sales process is becoming increasingly important. It is a network of social interactions among people who are in some form of a relationship with each other — families, relatives, friends, acquaintances, clients, and so on (Christakis and Fowler, 2011). The role of social networks has become increasingly significant because in this era, recommendations play a major in driving decision-making among consumers. On the flip side, advertisements are being proven to not be as efficacious as they used to be in influencing the choice of customers. There is far greater credibility attached to the recommendations and positive feedback that customers receive from their social network, especially in comparison to advertisements in various media. These trends must be accommodated in the new form of selling tactic called commercialization. We define commercialization as a tactic that allows optimal utilization of social networks for the purpose of acquisition of new customers and retention of old customers.

The role social networks play in sales processes is much easier to identify and understand in this new connectivity era. The existence of connectors, either offline (community, social events, etc.) or online (mobile technology, social media, etc.), causes a lot of convenience for salespeople to build a sales network. The fact that customers are turning more social and hence more receptive toward other people's opinions and feedback in their decision-making process is another catalyst reinforcing the role of social networks in sales processes.

However, optimization of a social network would not mean simply making connections with a large number of people around us. Such an endeavor would be costly in terms of time, effort, and probably money too in managing so many relationships. Commercialization calls for the use of social networks in ways that are effective and efficient. To that end, the salesperson needs to understand the different types of network that exist, because each of them plays a unique role in supporting the process of commercialization. With reference to an article by Ustuner and Godes (2006) in the *Harvard Business Review*, we can map the process of commercialization into four types:

1. **Commercialization of market place network**

   In the early stages of a sale, the salesperson's main homework is to find a potential prospect. A network that can introduce the sales person to many potential customers is appropriate for this stage. This is called the market-place network.

   The sales staff of Arrow Electronics, an electronic components company listed in Fortune 500, has a unique way to get prospects through commercialization. Customers in the industry are generally known to place orders when companies begin development of new products. The problem however is that this kind of information is strictly classified in order to prevent any leak to competitors, making it rather difficult to extract it from company insiders. The salespersons at Arrow are creative enough to get this information in a "non-traditional" way. They work with real estate agents who are used to dealing with companies wanting to expand offices or locate new land for a production facility, both of which is commonly done in advance to prepare for development of new products. Networking with these real estate agents makes the Arrow salespersons obtain more updated information on prospective clients, and faster than competitors.

2. **Commercialization of prospect company network**
When the prospect has been established, the next stage is to approach to get a buy-in from the prospective customer. To make that happen, a salesperson must build a network of right people in his or her client organization. The salesperson must be able to approach the user (the party that will buy your product), technical buyer (the party controlling product specification), and of course the decision-maker (who is authorized to decide on the sale). The stronger such a network is built, the greater is the sales person's contribution to the success of the sale.

3. **Commercialization of internal network.**
This is a network among the peers within the company. The salesperson must not underestimate a network of this kind, especially if the products/solutions on offer tend to be complex. To formulate a customized solution for a customer, the salesperson certainly cannot work alone, but actively needs inputs from the technical teams that are more familiar with the complexity of the product. Similarly, when managing expectations and customer loyalty, the salesperson needs support from the customer service team and other support teams.

Companies that understand the importance of this kind of an internal network are more proactive in their intervention on related matters. Using social network analysis, a company can attempt to map the silo mentality that often emerges between different teams, especially sales and support teams. Once the silo has been identified, the company will be able to eliminate it, through either technical approaches (e.g., via intranet, which facilitates internal communication) or structural approaches (through establishment of a specific ad-hoc team tasked with promoting communication between the sales team and other teams) (Cross and Parker, 2004).

4. Commercialization of customer network.
This is a network that consists of a company's loyal customers. Examples are communities that are established by customers to engage in mutual exchanges of information or just to share feelings. Such networks of loyal customers do not only positively impact the loyalty of existing customers. They can also be leveraged to help the process of closing sales on new customers. For example, by inviting them to attend a gathering organized by the customer community, prospective customers can get direct references and recommendations from an existing base of loyal fans, thus easing the process of sales.

Once a company is able to understand the types of network and their respective roles in the commercialization process, the salesperson will be able to allocate resources more effectively.

References

Anderson, C (2009). *Free: The Future of a Radical Price*. New York: Hyperion.
Baker, C. (2002). Taiwan Semiconductor. http://www.wired.com/2002/07/semiconductor/ (last modified July 1, 2002; last accessed August 1, 2016).
Baker, WL, M Marn and CC Zawada (2010). *The Pricing Advantage*, 2nd Ed. New York: Wiley.
Christakis, NA and JH Fowler (2011). *Connected: The Surprising Power of Our Social Networks and How They Shape Our Lives*. New York: Back Bay Books.
Cross, R and A Parker (2004). *The Hidden Power of Social Networks*. Boston: Harvard Business School Press.
Fournier, S and L Lee (April 2009). Getting brand community right. *Harvard Business Review*.
Gilmore, JH and BJ Pine II (January–February 1997). The four faces of mass customization. *Harvard Business Review*.
Holcim Indonesia (2016). Corporate Profile. http://www.holcim.co.id/about-us/corporate-profile.html (last accessed August 1, 2016).
Holcim (2016). Solusi Rumah: Affordable Housing in Indonesia. http://www.holcim.com/media-relations/our-major-projects/solusi-rumah-affordable-housing-in-indonesia.html (last accessed August 1, 2016).
Info-communications Development Authority of Singapore (2016). Government. https://www.ida.gov.sg/Programmes-Partnership/Sectors/Government (last accessed August 1, 2016)
Kelly, L (2007). *Beyond Buzz: The Next Generation of Word-of-Mouth Marketing*. New York: AMACOM.

Kotler, *et al.* (2003). *Rethinking Marketing: Sustainable Market-ing Enterprise in Asia.* Singapore: Prentice Hall.

MacLarry, R. (n.d.) Singapore Moves Towards a Collaborative Government. http://dailycrowdsource.com/content/open-innovation/573-singapore-moves-towards-a-collaborative-government (last accessed August 1, 2016)

Needham, A and N Zohhadi (October 2009). Co-creation: How to innovate with consumers. *Research World*, ESOMAR.

Prahalad, CK and V Ramaswamy (2004). *The Future of Competition: Co-Creating Unique Value with Customers.* Boston: Harvard Business School Press.

Ries, A and L Ries (2002). *The Fall of Advertising and the Rise of PR.* New York: Harper Business.

Strickland, T (1999). *Strategic Management, Concepts and Cases.* New York: McGraw-Hill College Division.

Taiwan Semiconductor Manufacturing Company (2016). About TSMC. http://www.tsmc.com/english/aboutTSMC/index.htm (last accessed August 1, 2016).

The China Post (2016). Taiwan Overtakes South Korea as Top Chip-maker in Integrated Circuit Wafer Fab Capacity with 3.55 Mil Units. http://www.chinapost.com.tw/taiwan-business/2016/03/02/459646/Taiwan-overtakes.htm (last modified March 2, 2016; last accessed August 1, 2016).

Ustuner, T and D Godes (July–August 2006). Better sales networks. *Harvard Business Review*.

Wong, V (April 2, 2010). Co-Creation: Not Just Another Focus Group. http://www.bloomberg.com/news/articles/2010-04-01/co-creation-not-just-another-focus-groupbusiness-week-business-news-stock-market-and-financial-advice.

CHAPTER 12

MARKETING VALUE WITH VALUES

I'm not a tech guy. I'm looking at the technology
with the eyes of my customers, normal people's eyes.

Jack Ma — Founder and Executive Chairman of Alibaba Group

As noted previously, the third component of the marketing architecture, apart from "strategy" and "tactic", is "value", which consists of three sub elements: brand, service, and process. As discussed earlier, in the horizontal era, brand marketing — which is at the core of value — has undergone a transformation to cultivate a more human character. This chapter discusses how the other two sub-elements of value, service and process, have changed in the New Wave era: how service has been redefined into "care" and process has become "collaboration" (Fig. 12.1).

Figure 12.1: New Wave marketing value.

From Service to Care

The course of value creation is fundamentally determined by "brand" as a value indicator, "service" as a value enhancer, and "process" as a value enabler. In practice, service is not merely related to provision of after-sales support or a customer service helpline. Service is a paradigm by which a company creates continuous value for its customers (Kotler *et al.*, 2003). Advancements in technology and a continuously evolving business landscape have fundamentally shifted the concept of marketing. The question is whether the traditonal paradigm of service — as practiced in the Legacy Marketing era — still holds relevance?

In a report titled "Digital Disconnect in Customer Engagement", Accenture claimed that human interaction remains a vital component of customer satisfaction, even in the digital age. This holds true for all regions, including Asia Pacific. A research finds that up to 81 percent Australian consumers prefer to deal with human beings over digital channels to solve customer service issues (Hont *et al.*, 2016). In other words, human-to-human (H2H) interactions remain more important to consumers than machine-to-human (M2H) technology-based mecha-nisms. We call this the paradox of today's era when increasingly sophis-ticated technology is actually making customers more human. As a

Table 12.1: Service versus care.

Dimensions	Service	Care
Perspective toward customers	Customer is a king	Customer is a friend
Focus	Customer's needs and wants	Customer's anxieties and desires
Expected outcome	Repurchase	Recommendation
Management tools	Standard operating procedures (SOPs) and service scripts	Values-based principles (VBPs)

consequence, the conventional concept of service must change into a model driven by care.

There are some fundamental differences between the care-based model and the traditional concept of service (see Table 12.1). First, traditionally, a customer should always be treated as king, whose wishes must be obeyed, regardless of whether or not it is in his or her best interest. For service providers, it represented a vertical relationship where they would typically be positioned under the customer, and their satisfaction was the ultimate goal. It couldn't go any wrong — whatever is desired by the customer should be granted. The customer's dominant position in the traditional service model is illustrated from a popular anecdote about the "two rules" that were supposedly popularized by Stew Leonard, a supermarket chain in the United States. Rule number one: the customer is always right; rule number two: if the customer is ever wrong, refer to rule number one. As for the care-based concept, the customer is considered a friend, positioned in parallel with the company. This is what's being implemented at the Ritz-Carlton, as illustrated in their motto: "We are ladies and gentlemen serving ladies and gentlemen". As customers are positioned in parallel as friends, sometimes the company (as the care-giver) must give inputs when the customers want something they may not really need.

The second difference lies in the focus of attention. Service puts the customer's needs and wants as an explicit reference in service delivery. But the fact is that often there are things that customers need, but may not yet be aware or are unable to voice or express it. Therefore, in the care concept, the focus of attention is on the customer's anxieties and desires — their unspoken needs and wants. Care givers should be able to decode what their customers actually need, without having them to express it. Luxury hotels in India apply this through the provision of a "special greeting" for celebrities who check in at their hotels. While regular patrons are welcomed with their real names at the time of arrival, for celebrities, the hotel clerks would call them with a pseudonym. This is because the hotel staff is trained to respect and regard celebrities' privacy, although they need not have expressed this directly (Buell *et al.*, 2015).

The third aspect that distinguishes care from service is the expected outcome. Tradtionally, what the company is looking to achieve by service is repeat purchase. Loyalty is measured in terms of how often a customer repurchases a product or reuses a service. Care, however, is considered a measure of customer satisfaction and loyalty is measured based on customers' willingness to recommend a product or service. Net Promoter Score (NPS) is one such evaluation that measures a company's "Promoters" — loyal enthusiasts who not only keep buying from it but also urge their friends to do the same. A Bain & Company research shows that companies that achieve long-term profitable growth have NPS two times higher than the average company (Reichheld and Markey, 2011).

The last difference is in the management tools used by the company. Traditional service is generally established through standard operating procedures (SOPs) and service scripts that elaborately detail the regulations concerning behavior of service staff. The concept of care instead emphasizes the importance of empowerment; the company also uses values-based principles (VBPs) as a general guideline on behavior for all its employees. Let us look at the fourth difference in closer detail to better understand the managerial implications of the shift in the concept, from service to care.

From SOPs to VBPs

Service designers in a company are accustomed to tightly sticking to SOPs in order to standardize all the internal processes related to customer service. These SOPs typically govern the behavior of service staff: what are the typical steps to be taken to deal with a situation (do's) and what are the things to be avoided (don'ts). SOPs help provide a similar identity to various processes while ensuring a uniform level and quality of customer service for all customers.

However, excessive compliance with SOPs can create problems of its own. In order to campaign for standardization of their customer services, some companies go a step further by drafting highly detailed service scripts. In some cases, this script is so precisely created that it sets up verbatim on what customer service staff must speak to handle each situation. If the frontline staff is just made to memorize and deliver a script without understanding the essence of what it stands for, it may be worrisome for these workers would act like programmed robots. As a result, services delivered to customers would be perceived as rigid and too formal, and fail to provide a H2H touch.

In addition, standardization often cannot accommodate the plurality of customers. Each customer is after all a unique individual with unique needs, desires, and expectations. While some may appreciate a service that sticks to SOPs, there would be others who appreciate a more personal touch. This differentiation is seemingly well understood by Vikram Oberoi, chief operating officer of the Oberoi Group, an India-based luxury hotel chain that targets upmarket business and leisure travelers. As of 2014, the Oberoi Group owned and operated 31 hotels in six countries — India, Egypt, Indonesia, Mauritius, Saudi Arabia, and the UAE — as well as two luxury cruise liners. Commenting on the diversity of the customers the hotel group serves, Vikram once said:

> No two guest interactions are alike, and it is important that we always do the right thing for each guest. You can't foresee and anticipate everything that is going to happen (Buell *et al.*, 2015).

So, does it mean that the company does not need to standardize its service at all? Of course, that is not right. The Oberoi Hotel Group itself has a service SOP named "Making a Difference the Oberoi Way". Priding itself on attention to detail in delivering a great guest experience, the Oberoi specified standards for almost every task and activity, from detailed grooming standards for men and women, to the requirement that operators answer calls with a smile within three rings, to specifications for arranging packets of sugar and sweetener for coffee and candies in conference room dishes. Even the scent in Oberoi hotels was standardized by burning a customized mixture of incense on every floor (Buell *et al.*, 2015).

But the hotel certainly did not stop at SOP. The hotel implements VBP to its service called "The Oberoi Dharma". These principles dictate the general guidelines on the behavior of all its employees in various functions from all departments. As an example, one of the principles is to "put the customer first, the company second and the self last" (see Box 12.1 for the complete list). These kind of values, when understood, adopted, and inculcated by the hotel staff, would help each employee to make decisions independently, without having to rely on the instructions from a supervisor or boss. Vikram Oberoi stresses the importance

---

Box 12.1: VBPs: The Oberoi Dharma

We, as members of the Oberoi Group are committed to display through our behavior and actions the following conduct, which applies to all aspects of our business:

- Conduct which is of the highest ethical standards — intellectual, financial, and moral, and reflects the highest levels of courtesy and consideration for others.

- Conduct which builds and maintains teamwork, with mutual trust as the basis of all working relationships.

- Conduct which puts the customer first, the company second, and the self-last.

- Conduct, which exemplifies care for the customer through anticipation of need, attention to detail, excellence, aesthetics and style, and respect for privacy, along with warmth and concern.

- Conduct which demonstrates a two-way communication, accepting constructive debate and dissent while acting fearlessly with conviction.

- Conduct which demonstrates that people are our key asset, through respect for every employee, and leading from the front regarding performance achievement as well as individual development.

- Conduct which at all times safeguards the safety, security, health and environment of guests, employees, and the assets of the company.

- Conduct which eschews the short-term quick fix for the long-term establishment of a healthy precedent.

Source: www.oberoihotels.com.

of VBPs as a guide for all employees: "By applying these values, we will always come to the right decision. Focusing on our values cannot be compromised".

Care Lesson from Health Care

There are interesting lessons from the world of health care that can reinforce the importance of VBPs in service. In the book *"Delivering Knock Your Socks Off Service"*, Anderson (1998) explains that in some advanced health-care institutions, two types of rules exist: red rule and blue rule.

Red rules are those rules that must never be violated. They have been established to protect the lives and health of patients. For example, a ban on smoking in the operating room. There is absolutely no compromise or negotiation on the red rules. On the other hand, while blue rules are designed to ensure the various processes in the hospital are being run smoothly and in an organized way. For example, the rule that patients requiring treatment must fill up the registration form in advance.

In contrast to the red rule, rules belonging to the blue category *can* be violated under certain conditions. For example, when there is an emergency patient who needs urgent attention, then the rule about registration forms to be filled up in advance can be broken. Essentially, a rule can be violated if it is in the interest of a patient. The patients-first principle, keeping the interests of patient at the forefront, is a VBP that is rooted in the tradition of such hospitals. While not all hospitals may necessarily put it up in a written document, the principle has become a general guide that is understood by every health worker.

Mayo Clinic is an example of a hospital that has incorporated the principle of "prioritizing the interests of patients" in official documents of the organization. As per the written primary value, "the needs of the patients come first". Interestingly, this principle is completely internalized within the organization and used as a behavioral guide by every employee. At Mayo Clinic, when a nurse is faced with two choices, attend meetings on time or face a delay of 10 minutes so as to get a wheelchair for a patient in need, then the second choice would most certainly be opted for. And the choice can be made without having to consult with a head nurse first. This is what is described by Leonard Berry as value-based authority (Berry and Seltman, 2008).

This application of VBPs in the world of health care could arguably serve as an inspiration for the architects of services in other industries. Service standards for companies should certainly remain in place, but there are other complementary attributes that must be adopted in order for service to turn into care. These are VBPs. When values are ingrained in the DNA of service personnel, they will not just act on instructions — as a submissive robot who just follows a script or SOP. VBPs that are strongly cultivated in the general day-to-day conduct of concierge service staff will empower them to dare and take initiatives for the customer's benefits — even if they don't go by the book. The principles are infused with their daily habits, which in turn make the service staff have high empathy for customers. This is the foundation for delivering on customer care.

VBPs Internalization

Merely creating a set of VBPs will not guarantee that a company can successfully transition from providing service to care to its customers. An even bigger challenge is to internalize the principles in order to ensure the values are ingrained in the behavior of each employee of the company. On the basis of observations of some of the leading service providers in Asia, more specifically Singapore's Changi Airport, Kaufman (2012) identifies 12 building blocks that help internalize VBPs in a company:

1. Common Language
   In any company, although guided by the same vision and core values, there is often a significant difference in the terms of service between leadership team, managers, and staff. This gap certainly plays a role in complicating the absorption of VBPs across the company. By using a uniform service language, it becomes easier for companies to cultivate a culture of care among all its employees.

2. Engaging Vision
   "Many Partners, Many Missions, One Changi". That's the service vision which binds all the employees working at Changi. At the airport, all employees — from coffee shop workers to the top-level managers — are willing and proactive to serve customers, even for the simplest of things, such as providing directions to visitors

looking for souvenir shops at the airport. All the employees at the airport collectively work toward a single vision, that of creating an atmosphere of care every day.

3. Staff Recruitment

Recruitment of employees possessing the right character is a key foundation in the process of value internalization. Companies including Google and Amazon, for example, understand the importance of this first step in hiring employees with care as an integral character of their personality, making it easier to instill the company's vision of service. When CEO of Starbucks Howard Schultz was asked how he ensures everyone at the coffee shop greets customers with an ever-present smile, his simple answer was, "(Because) we just hire people who smile all the time" (Moon and Quelch, 2003).

4. Service Orientation

Implementation of the orientation of VBPs is another building block. Orientation typically represents the first formal process, critical for every new employee to get introduced to and well acquainted with the company culture. There are various approaches to service orientation, which can work to familiarize new recruits with the company values. For example, at Zappos — a US-based online shoe and clothing shop — each new employee is required to be placed in different departments in order to truly understand the company values (Frei *et al.*, 2009).

5. Internal Communication

Internal communication in the company is crucial to reminding employees of the culture of care in the firm. It serves to educate, inform, inspire, and motivate employees. It is essential because it can work to effectively promote company values and ensure that every employee gets to remember the code of conduct for their behavior.

6. Recognition and Awards

Recognition and awards are a means for the company to say "thank you" to the employees for their commitment and hard work in serving customers. But it has the most lasting effect when the direct leadership, or an immediate boss, provides this recognition. This helps to make employees more committed toward the adoption and implementation of the care culture of the company.

7. Voice of the Customer

Voice of the customer is considered a crucial building block to the culture of care in a company. Through a variety of online and offline media, a company today can obtain inputs or feedback from the customer directly, which is quite useful for the development and improvement of its services. It is highly recommended that a dedicated team takes on this task, to listen to, understand, and analyze customer feedback. Various software applications today allow companies to analyze millions of words and phrases used by customers online to comment on their products and services.

8. Measures and Metrics

In order to maintain sustainability of the culture of care, it is necessary to measure performance on a regular basis, such as through customer surveys. This helps obtain feedback to continue improvements on the quality of service. In addition, there is a need to develop performance appraisals that measure the implementation of values by every employee in their behavior.

9. Improvement Process

This includes the extent to which complaints and customer feedback are analyzed and followed up to ensure improvement in the quality of service. It is critical to identify various issues that must be addressed quickly and communicated duly to the person(s) in-charge of the related divisions. This will help in the development of a continuous process improvement for the quality and service culture in the organization.

10. Recovery and Guarantees

It is unavoidable for companies to falter at some point in providing service. But more important than the mistake is the extent to which a company is willing to compensate the customer. Internally, there should be a thorough mechanism to detect and correct errors that occur in services, and if possible, done before a customer makes a formal complaint.

11. Service Benchmarking

    Benchmarking service helps companies to refer to the "best practices" in the industry. Thus, a company will always be pushed to do better in improving the culture of care. Benchmarking service allows companies to understand and learn from the service excellence standards achieved by competitors as well as counterparts in other industries. All this acts as critical input for improved care in the delivery of services.

12. Role Models

    Finally, it is to be noted that everyone is a role model on implementing VBPs. Corporate leaders must lead by example in ensuring implementation of these principles. However, being a role model is a concern not only of the top management, but also of leaders at all levels. At Mayo Clinic, all the doctors and senior nurses are required to be examples for new employees on how to apply the principle of care in the hospital (Berry and Seltman, 2008).

In following these building blocks, VBPs that have been internalized in the real behavior of all employees in the company will help develop a new competitive advantage, amid evolving customer trends that call for a deeper human touch. As discussed previously, the implication for businesses would be to trigger an increase in customer recommendations, which is a key attribute of value engagement. In the long run, this is what drives the company's growth. Giordano, a retail company based in Hong Kong, has been able to penetrate many areas outside Asia, including Australia and Europe, through its persistence in building a culture of care internally (see Box 12.2).

From Process to Collaboration

Apart from service, the next aspect to consider in value creation is the "process". Needless to say, process is one important factor in marketing. The effectiveness and efficiency of existing processes in the

Box 12.2: Giordano International: Values Internalization

Giordano International was founded in Hong Kong in 1981 and is now one of the world's leading international retailers of apparel and accessories for men, women' and children'. The brand has grown from its single Hong Kong store in 1981 to the present network of over 3,000 stores and counters in over 40 countries in the Asia-Pacific and Middle East regions.

Giordano's success in expanding business cannot be separated from its service excellence. It has positioned itself not only as a retail clothing company, but also as a service provider, selling experience. As part of its implementation of a care-based service to customers, Giordano developed the "Giordano Experience" in which all its customers are greeted with a warm smile, have free trials on as many clothing items in the store, as well as get additional services such as fitting buttons free of cost, along with a generous policy on exchange of goods.

To support the implementation of such a customer service that is full of care, Giordano developed a set of VBPs focusing on five aspects: Quality, Knowledge, Innovation, Service, and Simplicity (Q.K.I.S.S.). To ensure that these principles are really internalized in the behavior of employees, Giordano runs some excellent programs, which are as follows:

Recruitment

Giordano strictly enforces its new the employee selection procedures. New recruits are judged not only on skills aspect but also based on compliance with reference to the values of the company.

Service Orientation

New employees are encouraged to become "intrapreneurs" possessing a high loyalty toward the company. Giordano also runs a training program for employees to understand all the details of various operations. It is intended that employees can understand the internal processes that exist in the company in order to enable them to provide optimal service and support to customers.

(Continued)

Box 12.2: (Continued)

Measures

To further ensure that every store and its employees apply the principles of care to customers, evaluations of both the store and the individuals are conducted regularly.

Rewards and Recognition

Incentives and rewards are designed for employees who appropriately demonstrate company values in their daily conduct. Internal competition is also facilitated to further motivate the employees to improve their performance; one way is to win the title of "Best Service Shop".

Sources: "Company Info", www.giordano-me.com; Kotler *et al.* (2003).

---

company — from procurement of raw materials, production processes, to delivery of products or services to the users — determine the quality of the product, the cost incurred by the company, as well as the speed of product/service delivery. Quality, cost, and delivery (QCD) are the three keywords to measure the success of existing processes in the company. Ideally, companies ought to manage as many processes in the value chain as possible so as to create high-quality products, keep costs low, and ensure timely delivery to customers.

The various elements in the marketing process are not only critical, but also complex as they relate to the efficiency and effectiveness of the supply and demand sides. What further complicates matters is that companies are supposed to manage not only the internal processes (between departments), but also processes involving external parties (e.g., suppliers, wholesalers, retailers, and logistics).

Fortunately, the development of Internet technology provides companies with many newer, more convenient ways to manage their supply chain. The Internet not only helps facilitate business transactions such as ordering, invoicing, payment, and procurement, but can also improve coordination and collaboration, both within and across companies. This has led to the development of a new trend in the form of collaboration in supply chain management as a way forward for successful and sustainable business process (Attaran and Attaran, 2007). A report published by the Global Commerce Initiative (GCI) on the future of value chain concluded the same thing: "improved collaboration between all parties in the value chain will be essential in order to achieve a more efficient and effective value chain to better serve the needs of the consumer" (GCI and Capgemini, 2008).

Collaboration could also positively affect a company's bottom line. A study by AMA Research shows that supply-chain collaboration can add as much as three percentage points to the profit margins for all types of supply chain players. Wal mart is a case in point, having experienced significant success through collaboration. Under a joint initiative with P&G, called collaborative forecasting and replenishment (CFAR), managers from both Wal mart and P&G jointly prepare forecasts on P&G products at Wal mart stores and plan replenishment strategies (Chopra and Meindl, 2001).

What exactly is meant by collaboration in the context of supply chain management? Thomson (2001) defines collaboration as a process in which autonomous actors interact through formal and informal negotiations, jointly creating rules and structures governing their relationships and ways to decide or act on issues that bring them together; it is a process involving shared norms and mutually beneficial interactions. This definition suggests a higher level of collective action than cooperation and coordination (Thomson and Perry, 2006). In the book "*Collaborating: Finding Common Ground for Multiparty Problems*", Gray (1989) points out that although both cooperation and coordination may occur as part of the early process of collaboration, collaboration represents a longer term integrated process through which parties who see different aspects of their differences constructively explore problems and solutions together.

In line with the earlier views, GCI and Capgemini (2008) describe some of the characteristics of the future supply chain, characterized by strengthened collaboration in various aspects:

- The future model will be based on multipartner information sharing among key stakeholders: consumers, suppliers, manufacturers, logistic service providers, and retailers.
- After production, the products will be shipped to collaborative warehouses in which multiple manufacturers store their products.

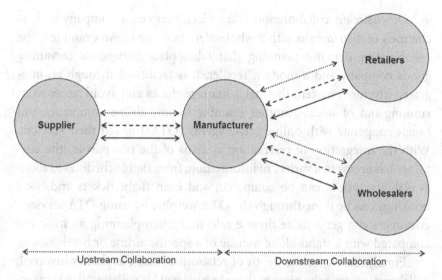

Figure 12.2: Types and levels of collaboration.

- Collaborative transport will deliver to city hubs and to regional consolidation centers.
- Non-urban areas will have regional consolidation centers in which products will be cross-docked for final distribution (collaborative non-urban distribution).

Collaboration: Two Types and Three Levels

Considering the types of parties involved, collaborations can be divided into two types: upstream and downstream. Also, based on the depth of relationships among the parties involved, collaboration can be categorized into three levels (see Fig. 12.2).

Upstream collaboration typically occurs between a manufacturer and a supplier. Collaboration could be built in the form of synchronized production scheduling, collaborative product development, and many more such mutual processes. Charoen Pokphand, Thailand's largest private company in animal feed production and livestock breeding, uses a system of partnerships with local breeders to get a finite supply of poultry. Another example is Google's Android Play Store that is used as a platform to collaborate with independent app developers from around the world.

Downstream collaboration takes place between a company and its channels of distribution, either wholesalers or retailers. An example is the collaborative demand planning that takes place between a consumer goods company and a modern retailer. It is facilitated through an integrated inventory system that helps manage stocks and avoid stores from running out of stock. Another example is how airline companies and hotels cooperate with online travel agents (OTAs) to sell their services. With the integration of reservation systems of the two parties, the customer has access to a variety of information, from flight schedules to room availability; prices can be compared; and even flight tickets and hotel bookings can be done through the OTA website. By using OTA services, customers can get a more diverse selection when planning an itinerary, compared with a stand-alone website of a specific airline or hotel.

Finally, based on the depth of relationships of the parties involved, collaboration can take place at three levels: level I is collaborative transaction management, level II is collaborative event, and level III is collaborative process management. Ahmed and Ullah (2012) describe the three levels as follows:

- **Level I:** Collaborative transaction management is characterized by high-volume data exchange and task alignment centered on operational issues/tasks. The relationships categorized as Type I include scorecard collaboration initiatives.

- **Level II:** Type II is characterized by joint planning activities regarding events (e.g., new product introductions) and items of collaborative focus, such as promotions.

- **Level III:** Collaborative process management is differentiated by a more strategic collaboration that relies on knowledge sharing as well as joint decision-making. It is characterized by joint problem-solving, long-term joint business planning, and more fully integrated supply chain processes.

References

Ahmed, S and A Ullah (2012). Building supply chain collaboration: Different collaborative approaches. *Integral Review*, 5(1), 8–21.

Anderson, K (1998). *Delivering Knock Your Socks Off Service*. New York: AMACOM.

Attaran, M and S Attaran (2007). Collaborative supply chain management: The most promising practice for building efficient and sustainable supply chains. *Business Process Management Journal*, 13(3), 390–404.

Berry, LL and KD Seltman (2008). *Management Lessons from Mayo Clinic: Inside One of the World's Most Admired Service Organization*. New York: McGraw-Hill.

Buell, RW, A Raman and V Muthuram (March 24, 2015). Oberoi Hotels: Train Whistle in the Tiger Reserve. *Harvard Business School Case*. Boston: Harvard Business School Publishing.

Chopra, S and P Meindl (2001). *Supply Chain Management: Strategy, Planning, and Operation*. Upper Saddle River: Prentice Hall.

Frei, FX, RJ Ely and L Winig (October 20, 2009). Zappos.com 2009: Clothing, Customer Service & Culture. *Harvard Business School Case*.

Gray, B (1989). *Collaborating: Finding Common Ground for Multiparty Problems*. San Francisco: Jossey-Bass.

Giordano (2016). Company Info. http://giordano-me.com/about-us/company-info/ (last accessed August 1, 2016).

Global Commerce Initiative (GCI) & Capgemini (2008). *2016: The Future Value Chain*. Paris: Global Commerce Initiative.

Hont, R, D Klimek and S Meyer (2016). Digital Disconnect in Customer Engagement. *Global Consumer Pulse Research*, Accenture.

Kaufman, R (2012). *Uplifting Service: The Proven Path to Delighting Your Customers, Colleagues, and Everyone Else You Meet*. Ashland: Evolve Publishing.

Kotler, *et al.* (2003). *Rethinking Marketing: Sustainable Market-ing Enterprise in Asia*. Singapore: Prentice Hall.

Moon, Y and JA Quelch (July 31, 2003). Starbucks: Delivering Customer Service. *Harvard Business Case*.

Reichheld, F and B Markey (2011). *The Ultimate Question 2.0 (Revised and Expanded Edition): How Net Promoter Companies Thrive in a Customer*. Boston: Harvard Business Review Press.

Thomson, AM (2001). *Collaboration: Meaning and Measurement*, PhD diss., Indiana University, Bloomington.

Thomson, AM and JL Perry (December 2006). Collaboration Process: Inside the Black Box. *Public Administration Review*.

Chapter 10. Marketing Strategy for Value Exploration

- According to the Legacy concept, marketing strategy consists of three main elements: segmentation, targeting, and positioning. Segmentation is the way companies look to creatively segment a market (mapping strategy) while targeting refers to the company's strategy of adapting its resources to the needs of the target market (fitting strategy).

- In the New Wave era, instead of traditional segmentation, companies need to do "communitization", which helps them view consumers as a group of people who care for each other, people with common purposes, values, and identity.

- The strategy of communitization should be supported by "confirmation" wherein three criteria must be considered: community relevance, activity level, and the number of community networks.

Chapter 11. Marketing Tactic for Value Engagement

- In the Legacy era, marketing tactics consisted of three main elements, namely differentiation (uniqueness offered by the company to its target market), marketing mix (product, price, place, and promotion), and selling (effort to build and maintain long-term and mutually beneficial relationships with the customer).

- With the development of digital technology, the practices of traditional marketing mix have transformed: product is co-creation, price is currency, place is communal activation, and promotion is conversation.

- In addition to the marketing mix that has changed as discussed above, selling practices have also undergone a shift. In the era of horizontal marketing, the use of social networks in the sales process is becoming increasingly important. This is called commercialization.

Chapter 12. Marketing Value with Values

- In Legacy Marketing, after "strategy" and "tactic", the third component in the marketing architecture is "value", which consists of brand, service, and process.

- In the New Wave era, services that rely on standard operating procedures (SOPs) should instead employ "care" in the service delivery process, which means seeing customers as friends, focusing on their anxieties and desires, ultimately aiming to create word-of-mouth recommendations, and using values-based principles as management tools.

- Furthermore, process that tends to be vertical is beginning to change into "collaboration" which is more horizontal, both upstream and downstream.

Postface

Globalization has helped nurture business entities that are able to develop their markets out of the political boundaries of a state. In the early days of globalization, there was a distinct difference between a local brand and a foreign brand. The local products were usually cheaper and of lower quality but suited the local conditions better. The imported products, particularly from the West, were not just more expensive but were also more problematic due to non-Asian product specifications. Though the reverse could be true as well. An Asian global company attempting to go international could often stutter when required to adapt to new, higher standards.

It calls for Asian players looking to go global to remain cautious about maintaining a balance between standardized processes and their effectiveness for the local markets. Even though standardization improves efficiencies and consistency in managing international operations, there are observers who find merit in adapting to local markets. One of the strongest arguments in support of standardization was made by Levitt (1983), a Harvard marketing professor, when he stated, "Only global companies will achieve long-term success by concentrating on what everyone wants rather than worrying about the details of what everyone thinks they like". His argument rested on the observation of the world as a collective market where the needs of the customers are basically alike, largely owing to more or less similar desires and lifestyles. He, therefore, cautioned multinational companies against deliberating too much on cultural nuances and idiosyncrasies of customers in different regions. Instead, they should simply focus on satisfying universal desires.

Levitt believes that development of IT and transportation had led to the creation of a more homogenous world where people basically had similar inherent desires — of things that made their lives easier, saved their time, and improved their purchasing power. He, therefore, opined that multinational marketers must consider how standardization of production, distribution, marketing, and management helps achieve economies of scale and lower costs, thus offering greater value to customers.

However, as we have seen, with the emergence of regionalization, the global value that the customer receives must not be entirely standardized. There should be a coordinated regional strategy, as each region has different characteristics relative to another. Finally yet importantly, the tactics in each country within each region should also be localized. Therefore, for Asian companies — especially which are going to expand their businesses beyond the local market — we propose that they adopt the 3C formula that we called the glorecalization mindset. And in order to make a place in the minds and hearts of the increasingly digital customers, the formula must be implemented through a new, more horizontal wave of marketing.

In the 3C glorecalization formula, the first C stands for consistent global value. The value offered by a company to its customers consists of three New Wave elements: character (the new brand), care (the new service), and collaboration (the new process). It is important for marketers to standardize these three elements considering the high costs incurred in developing them. A brand that is well known for a character recognizable across the world acts as a great strength for it, which is why the element of character must be standardized so as to build the same association, perception, and image in the minds of customers, no matter where they are.

In order to build such a consistent global value, MNCs should not rely only on branding-with-character activities. They must also pay attention to the two other value elements that need to be standardized: care and collaboration. Especially in the case of care, standardization does not mean having all the employees in the company to practice the same method of service. Standardization of care is done through the implementation of values-based principles that are consistent across the various locations of the company. Each employee should feel empowered to take bold decisions more independently — in line with the company's values-based principles — in order to provide the best value to customers. This helps reinforce the unique character of the company in the eyes of customers.

At the same time, the process of collaboration also needs to be standardized so that the company creates a consistent pattern of partnership wherever it operates. Best practices that have been proven in a country or region can be duplicated as global standard. Standardization can be done both in terms of its type (upstream or downstream collaboration) and level (Level I: collaborative management transaction, Level II: joint planning activities, or Level III: collaborative process management).

The second "C" of the glorecalization mindset is coordinated regional strategy. The New Wave Marketing strategy consists of communitization (the new segmentation), confirmation (the new targeting), and clarification (the new positioning). As discussed earlier in a previous section of the book, Asia has diverse cultural communities. Therefore, the businesses in Asia that implement a coordinated regional strategy will best serve its customers. In fact, despite the sociocultural diversity, there are three communities (subcultures) that cast a major influence on the dynamics in Asian market: youth, women, and netizens. Resurrection of the three subcultures is a commonly occurring phenomenon in Asia, and hence companies need to have a common strategy at the regional level as well.

The third "C" of the glorecalization approach is customized local tactic. The New Wave tactic consists of codification (the new differentiation), New Wave Marketing mix, and commercialization (the new selling). Codification is about how you differ yourself authentically from your competitors. It has to be customized at the local level. Then, it should be translated into the New Wave Marketing mix and commercialization techniques, which must also be customized locally.

To summarize, there are three Cs that must be balanced by Asian companies eyeing the market beyond their home — Consistent global value, Coordinated regional strategy, and Customized local tactic. In the following chapters, you will read about successful Asian companies that have implemented the formula effectively and have made remarkable gains from these approaches: whether as a local champion, regional player, or even as a multinational company.

Reference

Levitt, T (May–June 1983). The globalization of markets. *Harvard Business Review*, 61(3), 92–102.

CHAPTER 13
ASIA'S LOCAL CHAMPIONS

*Giants — "new tech," CRM, etc. notwithstanding — will
always be clumsy and impersonal relative to an "intimate local"
who is really out to make a dramatic difference.*

Tom Peters

In any market, indigenous businesses can essentially be regarded as the toughest niche players. The phenomenon of glocalization also underlines how global companies tweak their offerings according to local tastes, in order to compete better with home grown players. Multinationals today would be much less anxious about their peers as they would have — more or less — similar business models and hence adopt similar strategies. Big global businesses, with sophisticated systems in place and standardized products, also tend to struggle with cultural shocks and blocks when entering new, niche local markets. On the other hand, smaller domestic players that are extremely agile in meeting the needs of local customers are difficult to predict, and therefore almost unbeatable in the markets that they are entrenched (Kotler *et al.*, 2007).

What, then, are the winning strategies of these local champions that command the respect and loyalty of customers in a market where consumers are spoilt for choice by a wide range of products and services? How do successful local brands continue to do well in a globalized and highly competitive environment? In order to be a local champions, relying on nationalist sentiment is certainly not a sustainable strategy. The better understanding of the local market should be able to translate into products and services that can address the anxieties and desires of local consumers. This approach should be aptly supported by a strong marketing organization that houses local culture professionals. In addition, the digital technology revolution that has swept across Asian countries also presents an opportunity for local players to develop marketing strategies and tactics that are low budget but high impact.

Although most of the local champions in Asia — especially from developing countries — emerged as strong players largely because of the monopoly they enjoyed owing to government regulations, the Asian market has since started to become increasingly open, resulting in tougher competition. In this scenario, the strategy, tactics, and values offered to the consumer are the keys for a local champion to maintain its dominance. The cases compiled in this chapter demonstrate the efforts of local champions in the face of increased competition in the country — invasion from both regional and global companies as a result of the domestic market opening up. The cases also highlight how their efforts help realize a value offering that is able to appeal to a growing pool of digital consumers in their country.

Lao Airlines — Lao People's Democratic Republic

Lao Economic Condition and ASEAN Aviation Market

Laos — or officially the Lao People's Democratic Republic (LPDR) — is a one-party socialist republic. Despite being known as a lower middle income economy with a gross national income (GNI) per capita of $1,600 in 2014, LPDR is still one of the fastest growing economies in the East Asia and Pacific region. GDP growth averaged 7 percent over the last decade, with increasing use of the country's natural resources — mostly water, minerals, and forests — contributing one-third to growth. Construction and services also expanded, with growing regional integration boosting tourism and attracting foreign investments (The World Bank, 2016).

The economic outlook remains broadly favorable, supported by the power sector and the growing Association of Southeast Asian Nations (ASEAN) integration. As a member of ASEAN, LPDR is increasing its integration into the regional and global economies. LPDR is also the chair of ASEAN in 2016, an honorary position previously held by Malaysia. The launch of the ASEAN Economic Community (AEC) at the end of 2015 is projected to further facilitate movement of goods, services, capital, and high-skilled labor in the regional block. The integration of ASEAN as a single market is also expected to further bolster LPDR's economic condition.

One industry that has been at the center of attention during the implementation of AEC is air transportation. The aviation industry in ASEAN has recorded significant growth over the past few years. The total seat capacity of ASEAN airlines experienced double-digit growth in the four-year period of 2009–2013, and the share of low-cost carriers (LCCs) in the region increased significantly from 13.2 percent in 2003 to 57 percent in 2014. ASEAN has established itself as one of the world's fastest growing aviation markets and has huge potential for more rapid growth. This industry growth is well supported by the increasing demand from local and regional consumers. Southeast Asian passenger traffic has grown by more than 9 percent since 2010, with intra-Southeast Asian traffic projected to increase by 7.7 percent over the next 20 years. This is happening for a clear reason. Nearly all of the 10 countries that comprise ASEAN have robust economies and expanding middle classes, resulting in a favorable environment for airlines (Civil Aviation South East Asia Summit [CASEA], 2016).

Considering how crucial aviation industry in ASEAN is, the ASEAN Open Sky Policy that calls for the development of a Roadmap for Integration of the Air Travel Sector (RIATS) has been formulated. This roadmap aims to set out the goals and timelines for ASEAN to complete all the necessary frameworks for the realization of the Open Sky Policy, which commenced in 2015. The frameworks required to make the ASEAN Open Sky Policy operational have since been developed, including the ASEAN Multilateral Agreement on the Full Liberalization of Air Freight Services (MAFLAFS), the ASEAN Multilateral Agreement on

Air Services (MAAS), and the ASEAN Multilateral Agreement on the Full Liberalization of Passenger Air Services (MAFLPAS) (ASEAN, 2015). As a result of these agreements, an airline assigned by any ASEAN member state can now operate both passenger and cargo scheduled services between the home country and any international airport in a member state, and then to the international airport of another member state, without any limitation on capacity and schedule. Achieving open skies in the region is an important part of the bigger plan to establish an ASEAN Single Aviation Market (ASAM) aimed to expand and deepen integration in all aspects of the aviation sector, including air services liberalization, aviation safety and security, and air traffic management. Such integration paves the way for the creation of numerous opportunities for industry players to spread their wings in ASEAN. This is not without challenges in light of the greater competition. The increased competition climate is a result of more independent foreign players entering the domestic market. This strengthening competition is a consequence of an increasingly free business climate for foreign players to enter a given market.

Lao Airlines: History and Competition

Lao Airlines State Enterprise is the national airline of Laos, headquartered in Vientiane. It operates domestic as well as international services to countries such as Cambodia, China, Thailand, Vietnam, Singapore, and Korea. New routes are planned for the future, including within ASEAN as well as to Hong Kong, Taiwan, and Japan. Its main operating base is Wattay International Airport in Vientiane (Lao Airlines official websites, 2016).

The company's history began in September 1976 as the Civil Aviation Company was formed from the merger of existing airlines, Royal Air Lao and Lao Air Lines. The company became Lao Aviation in 1979. The national carrier initially started with a mixed fleet of Western aircraft, including the Douglas DC-3 and DC-4, operating on international and domestic routes, as well as a fleet of helicopters for more remote regions. In 2000, a joint venture with China Yunnan Airlines and the Lao government was formed, which renationalized Lao Aviation. In 2003, the airline was rebranded to become Lao Airlines.

Lao Airlines is a dominant player among other domestic airlines in Laos. Its local competitors include Lao Skyway and Lao Central Airlines. Lao Skyway, formerly known as Lao Air, is a private airline established on 24 January, 2002 as a helicopter charter service company. Today Lao Skyway operates a wide range of domestic flights. It has plans to expand its operations with more domestic destinations while also looking into expansion of international routes.

Lao Central Airlines was a privately owned airline based in Vientiane and was the second biggest among Lao airline operators in terms of fleet size. The airline was established in May 2010 to serve the domestic and regional markets. It was positioned as a premium airline offering full on-board services to passengers with unique Lao experience. Its mission was to be a leading airline in Asia, emphasizing safety, customer service, and value for money while utilizing leading technology and systems. Lao Central Airlines operates both domestic routes and scheduled flights to Bangkok, Thailand. In 2013, new destinations were added to include Hanoi, Kunming, Siem Reap, and Phnom Penh. Unfortunately, Lao Central Airline ceased operations in 2014.

Local Tactics

As it is strongly positioned in the domestic market, Lao Airlines' main focus should be on the retention of existing customers. The entry of foreign players as a result of ASEAN Open Sky Policy should be closely anticipated and prepared for, with concrete steps. This is already being realized by Lao Airlines. The airline officially launched a frequent-flyer program (FFP) in February 2014. The loyalty program is called Champa Muang Lao, offering plenty of benefits to regular flyers, such as free tickets, privileged services, and added convenience.

In addition, although Internet penetration in Laos is still low — reaching around 14.3 percent as of 2015 — Lao Airlines has already undertaken initiatives to optimize its website functions to better utilize it as a platform aimed at building deeper customer relationships. Airline companies are already at the forefront in adopting digital technology advancements to support their business processes. Lao Airlines does not want to be left behind; it is also actively looking to provide convenience to its customers when making online bookings through its website.

In addition, the growth of online travel agencies (OTAs) in Laos spells opportunities in the aviation industry. An increasing number of digital consumers also contribute to an expanding pool of flyers. A few prominent travel agencies offering online services in Laos include tourismlaos.org and laostravel.com. In the horizontal era of New Wave marketing, these OTAs could serve as potential partners to collaborate with and take advantage of the evolving dynamics in the travel distribution business. In the case of Lao Airlines, a downstream collaboration could be of particular interest, where OTAs act as an extension of the airline to reach more customers. Needless to say, such a collaboration would be optimal if aptly supported by an integrated online booking system.

With the help of such initiatives, Lao Airlines is expected to become more prepared to face the impending foreign competition in the domestic market, especially from the airlines based in neighboring countries. In addition, an approach to engage with local communities will be beneficial for Lao Airlines to understand the anxieties and desires of domestic customers. As it gains from the knowledge of the local market, Lao Airlines will be able to design a loyalty program that is most appropriate for the local traveler.

UFC Group — Mongolia

UFC Group was founded in 1942 under the name "Idesh Tejeeliin Kombinat" (literally meaning "foodstuffs combine") as a state-owned enterprise of the Mongolian People's Republic, located in Uvs Province. It remained in government hands until 1997, when it was bought out by private owners and renamed "Uvs Hüns" ("Uvs foods"). As it expanded its businesses, it began using its present name UFC Group in 2006. In 2011, the Mongolian Chamber of Commerce and Industry named UFC Group as one of Mongolia's top 10 companies.

UFC produces and distributes a variety of 100 percent natural and ecologically pure products, including vodka, soft drinks, pure natural sergeesh juice, sea buckthorn juice, pure mineral water, and iodized salt. Other than beverages, UFC Group also produces breads and biscuits from natural ingredients. In 2009, the company received the ISO 9001 certification for its laboratory; all the products go through its laboratory before arriving at stores for customers.

UFC's premium vodka brand is known as *Chinggis Silver*. The *Chinggis* brand is today considered a quality product not only in the domestic market, but also internationally. It is exported to various markets including Korea, Germany, Belgium, England, and Sweden. Another vodka brand of theirs, *Moritoi Chinggis* (literally meaning "Chingis Khan on a horse"), received a "Grand Gold" designation from Brussels-based Monde Selection in both 2010 and 2011 (UFC Group official website, ba.k1 2016).

One more superior product from UFC is a natural juice processed from sea buckthorn oil. Sea buckthorn are wild deciduous shrubs growing on the plains, 15,000 meters above sea level. Sea buckthorn (*Hippophae L.*) fruits and leaves are highly nutritious and have great pharmaceutical value, being rich in nutrients including vitamins A, B1, B2, C, E, P, carotenoids, flavonoids, and phytosterols. The Mongolian sea buckthorn has long been used as a traditional medicine. Today sea buckthorn is used in about 200 industrial products, including cosmetics, life-saving drugs and herbs to treat cancer, heart ailments, hepatic disorders, bums, and brain disorders. Due to high contents of antioxidants, sea buckthorn oil is also extensively used for anti-inflammatory, antibacterial, antiradioactive, antiaging, and analgesic conditions, and for the promotion of tissue regeneration.

UFC's Local Actions

In the natural beverages industry — one that UFC operates in — the availability of abundant raw materials is an important factor to maintain business sustainability. In view of increasing demand, even though UFC Group cannot rely solely on its own plantations to meet its raw materials needs, it does serve as an important factor in building competitive advantage. In this connectivity era, competitive advantage can also be built through collaborations with other stakeholders — governments, other companies, and suppliers.

Manufacturing UFC's flagship products — natural sea buckthorn juice and oil — requires raw materials that cannot be found anywhere else. This is why UFC needs to collaborate with various parties to ensure supply. Fortunately, the government of Mongolia puts special attention on plantations of such horticultural products of great value. The cultivation of sea buckthorn in Mongolia has been on the rise, in view of the framework created within national "sea buckthorn" and "Green Wall" programs. Before the national sea buckthorn program was put in place, until 2009 or so, 80 percent of 1,200 hectares for horticulture cultivation was used in growing sea buckthorn. Following a ratification in March 2010, the cultivation area doubled in that year to 2,210 hectares. Even as the government sponsors a certain share of sea buckthorn plantations, the investment from the private sector at both personal and enterprise levels is growing. In 2011, the total area used for sea buckthorn cultivation reached 4,000 hectares and further expanded to 6,000 hectares in early 2012. The national "Seabuckthorn" program aims to increase the cultivation area to 10,000 hectares in 2012 and 20,000 hectares by 2016 (Batmunkh, 2014).

In addition to the government of Mongolia and UFC as dominant industry players, there are several other major sea buckthorn cultivation and processing entities including Uvs seabuckthorn LLC, Entum LLC, Gangar Invest LLC, Khaan Jims LLC, and Tovkhon Jims LLC. Furthermore, there are numerous small and micro-enterprises and households that grow sea buckthorn and produce sea buckthorn juice (Batmunkh, 2014).

There are existing collaborations between numerous parties engaged in sea buckthorn cultivation in Mongolia; however, most of these partnerships are not quite fruitful. There is little feedback mechanism in the supply chain and the end results from the collaborative activities are not actively shared among all the participants — the benefits hardly trickle down all the way. Limitations of modern cultivation and harvesting machinery technology also result in only 50–70 percent of the crop being harvested. This indicates that existing internal resources are not being used optimally.

In this era of connectivity, UFC can take advantage of information technology to support the process of collaboration with companies and sea buckthorn local growers. Provision of accurate information about the weather and technological developments on cropping and cultivation will also be able to support the improvement process. Exchange of information on market prices, availability of raw materials, and international demand will help sea buckthorn juice and oil producers in maintaining production capacity to match market demand. If the supply and demand sides can be optimized, all parties in the country will benefit from this.

On its part, the UFC Group is already aiming to capitalize on digital channels to increase market awareness, especially internationally, of its pure and natural products that are made of sea buckthorn. The company tries to communicate the various benefits and advantages of its product range. However, one limitation of the website is that the content is still presented in the local language — English language translation should be offered to make the content more universally appealing.

Hua Ho Department Store — Brunei Darussalam

Hua Ho Department Store, founded by Pehin Dato Lau, is one of Brunei Darussalam's largest supermarket chains and a leading provider of retail products, groceries, and fresh produce. Pehin Dato Lau first set up shop in a straw hut in a rubber plantation and sold his agricultural products on a bicycle, selling them to residents in the area. Hua Ho was first established by Pehin Dato Lau in 1947, and he opened his first supermarket in 1982. At present, it has sprung up nine more outlets, all strategically located, from Sengkurong, Gadong 2, Mini-Mart, Kiulap, Yayasan, Delima (Serusop), Manggis, Bunut to Hua Ho Petani Mall in Tutong. Its success was accredited largely to a commitment to providing the Bruneian population with the best products at affordable prices, along with quality service.

As a Chinese community leader who is now 90, Pehin Dato Lau still remains active in liaising between the Brunei government and the Chinese community to enhance good relationship between the two parties. In recognition of Lau's efforts and commitments to Chinese society and government activities, on 21st April 2004, he was bestowed with the title of Pehin Kapitan China Kornia Diraja by His Majesty, the Sultan of Brunei Darussalam. Again on 15th July 2006, during the occasion of the Sultan's 60th birthday celebration, Lau was bestowed the title of Dato Paduka, which is a meritorious recognition. On 29th August 2008, in recognition of his business achievement in Brunei Darussalam, Enterprise Asia, a Kuala Lumpur-based non-governmental organization, conferred him the Asia Pacific Entrepreneurship Lifetime Achievement Award (Suryadinata, 2012).

In addition to retail business, Pehin Dato Lau has set up several Hua Ho Agricultural Farms to supply vegetables, fruits, chickens, and eggs.

The department store has also started manufacturing under its own in-house brand, *BONUS*. It had started with Bonus Facial Tissue and Hua Ho RO water. Today the range has expanded to include other supermarket items such as baby wipes, detergents, hand wash as well as a variety of electronic products such as electric oven, kettle, and fan (Too, 2012). In 2000, he also set up a Hua Ho Cultural Foundation to help preserve and promote Chinese culture. The activities of the foundation include Chinese calligraphy classes and financial support for students from poor families.

Local Loyalty Program

In a bid to show gratitude and reward its loyal customers, the supermarket came up with its own rewards points program called "H2" where customers who shop at the department store are able to collect points and redeem them for a variety of products sold in the store. The use of the H2 card is applicable in six Hua Ho outlets, namely. Kiulap, Delima, Tutong, Gadong 2, Mini-Mart, and Mulaut. In 2008, Hua Ho Department Store launched the SYMB Bonus Card for its four other outlets (Sengkurong, Yayasan, Manggis, and Tanjong Bunut). These two loyalty cards operate through different rewarding systems that ultimately serve the same aim: to provide its valuable customers with the most lucrative rewards and the best shopping experience.

In executing its loyalty programs, Hua Ho also collaborates with other companies. One example of such a successful collaboration is with Baiduri Bank, a Brunei-based commercial bank, through a program called "The BIG Shopping Win". The program offers Baiduri cardholders a chance in the lucky draw when they use their Baiduri credit or debit cards together with their Hua Ho H2 privilege card at Hua Ho Department Stores in Delima, Gadong 2, Kiulap, Mulaut, and Tutong. Every receipt of a minimum of BND 50 from participating Hua Ho Department Stores entitles the cardholder one entry form for a chance in a grand lucky draw (Borneo Bulletin, 2016).

In addition to using a conventional approach, advances in digital technology have paved the way for retailers including Hua Ho to devise more creative loyalty programs. Brunei Darussalam is one of the countries in Asia where the Internet and mobile phone penetrations are high, at 74.2 and 115.2 percent, respectively (GSM Association, 2015). By using digital technology to support loyalty programs (e.g., by SMS alerts, check points through the phone or website), Hua Ho can strengthen its position among the growing section of digital consumers in Brunei.

In view of the large number of Internet and mobile phone users in Brunei Darussalam, Hua Ho should also closely monitor the emerging opportunity in e-commerce. There is a growing trend in the world and even Asia wherein retail markets are increasingly shifting from physical retail toward fast-growing e-commerce channels. E-commerce is fast gaining prominence among retailers and brand owners. For example, China is on its way to emerge as the world's largest e-commerce market. A report from PricewaterhouseCoopers (PWC) finds that electronic goods retailers are the main beneficiaries of e-commerce (PWC, 2015). Hua Ho Department Store, which owns its own range of electronic products, should certainly not ignore this trend.

Macau.com — Macau

Macau: History and Economy

Macau, or Macao, is a small peninsula in mainland China, across the Pearl River Delta from Hong Kong. Also called the Macao Special Administrative Region (Macao SAR) of People's Republic of China, it lies 65 kilometers to the west of Hong Kong and is also bordered by the Chinese Guangdong province in the north and the South China Sea in the east. A Portuguese overseas territory until 1999, it is also known as Asia's Las Vegas and is one of the most densely populated regions in the world.

Macau was administrated by the Portuguese Empire and later its inheritor states, starting in the mid-16th century until 1999 — being the last standing European colony in Asia (BBC News, 1999). The first traders from Portugal arrived in Macau in the 1550s, following which the Ming dynasty in China rented it to Portugal as a trading port in 1557. Macau was governed by the Portuguese Empire under Chinese authority and sovereignty until 1887, when Macau became a colony. Eventually, on 20 December 1999, sovereignty over Macau was transferred back to China.

Under the policy of "one country, two systems", the State Council of the People's Republic of China is responsible for military defence and foreign affairs while Macau maintains its own legal system, the public security force, monetary system, customs policy, and immigration policy.

As one of the richest cities in the world, Macau's gross domestic product (GDP) per capita based on purchasing power parity (current international $), as of 2015, was $139,767 — the second highest in the world after Qatar, based on the World Bank data. Tourism is a major economic industry. Up to 60 percent of Macau's economy depends on the casino industry and other related sectors such as hotels, shops, and restaurants (CNN Money, 2016). The other major economic activity, at one time, was related to textile manufacturing, especially export oriented, though textiles and apparel exports have been on the decline since the elimination of the textile quota system at the end of 2004. Textiles and apparel today account for approximately 7 percent of exported goods.

In accordance with Macao SAR Government's strategy of positioning and developing Macao as a World Centre of Tourism and Leisure, the Macao Government Tourism Office (MGTO) serves as the public entity responsible for implementing, analyzing, and assisting in formulating the tourism policies of the country to enhance its reputation as a quality destination. Together with local trade, MGTO promotes Macao's tourism products and services not only in the leading and emerging tourism markets but also evaluates and seeks to develop potential markets to attract diverse visitor sources for Macao. To achieve this effectively, there are 13 MGTO representatives and 3 Macao SAR delegations around the world that tailor-make promotion schemes and activities for each market's needs.

The office works hard to strengthen its connections with regional and international tourism organizations to achieve Macao's tourism development targets. Locally, MGTO plays an important role in fostering the improvement and diversification of tourism products as well as promoting, coordinating, or facilitating a variety of tourism projects and mega events.

Macau.com: Promoting Local Destinations

Private players also play a key role through their efforts to promote the destinations and tourism potential of Macau. Various companies engaged in the field of travel, tourism, and hospitality have been instrumental in backing the government's efforts to introduce Macau to foreign countries. Macau.com is one such leading company actively campaigning for Macau online in the overseas market. It is a destination marketing and travel company that focuses on information and trip planning tools for visitors coming to Macau. The company markets accommodation, shows, restaurants, entertainment, and attractions in Macau and the Pearl River Delta region. It concentrates its business on the inbound market, primarily coming from Hong Kong, Taiwan, Japan, South Korea, Australia, and Southeast Asia.

Established in 2006 with GoMacau.com as the brand name, it later acquired Macau's Number 1 Website in June 2007 and relaunched it as Macau.com. The two brands complemented each other's businesses well, which ultimately helped expand GoMacau's consumer reach significantly. The company is also a member of Ignite Media Group, a Macau-based media conglomerate with a portfolio of comprehensive media resources across the region.

Macau.com already serves as a natural starting point for visitors seeking information about Macau. The website serves as a go-to online portal for tourists seeking information on Macau, helping them plan and schedule their visit. The website compiles a whole lot of information on things to do based on interests such as entertainment, spa, and nightlife; there is a calendar that can help schedule visits as per the hot and happening events in the city, and much more. The online portal is a hugely convenient resource for those who want to get quick information about Macau and is accessible from anywhere. All of this, however, must be supported by a memorable offline experience as well. Therefore, Macau.com frequently offers many pioneering promotional activities and events, some of the exciting packages included the Macau Grand Prix and the Pete Sampras and Roger Federer Tennis Showdown.

The practice of collaboration has become inevitable in this era of horizontal marketing. Aiming to establish its superiority as a local champion, Macau.com actively collaborates with various parties in the tourism business. In December 2006, Macau.com signed a strategic partnership with Viva Macau Airlines whereby the two companies committed to jointly promote Macau as a travel destination. Further, in November 2007, Macau.com set up a partnership with Macau Fisherman's Wharf — an integrated waterfront hotel, convention, dining, and retail and entertainment complex for cooperation in promoting Macau's event market. In March 2012, Macau. com announced another partnership with Expedia Affiliate Network to give its users access to over 149,000 hotels worldwide.

References

Association of Southeast Asian Nations (ASEAN) (2015). ASEAN Single Aviation Market: One Sky, One Region. www.asean.org (last accessed May 13, 2016).

BBC News (December 18, 1999). Macau and the End of Empire. *BBC News*. http://news.bbc.co.uk/2/hi/asia-pacific/566301.stm (last accessed May 16, 2016).

Batmunkh, D (2014). Some Ways to Develop Sea Buckthorn Cluster Aimed at Improving the National Competitiveness of Mongolia, *ERINA Report*, No. 114, November 2013.

Borneo Bulletin (January 7, 2016). 'BIG Shopping Win' at Hua Ho Dept Stores. *Borneo Bulletin*. http://borneobulletin.com.bn/big-shopping-win-at-hua-ho-dept-stores/ (last accessed May 15, 2016).

Civil Aviation South East Asia Summit (CASEA) (2016). Concept. http://civilaviationsea.com/index.php?r=page/Category/index&class_id=13 (last accessed May 13, 2016).

GSM Association (2015). *The Mobile Economy: Asia Pacific 2015*. London: GSM Association.

Kotler, P, H Kartajaya and Hooi, DH (2007). *Think ASEAN*. Singapore: McGraw-Hills.

Lao Airlines official websites. http://www.laoairlines.com/ (last accessed May 12, 2016).

Macao Government Tourism Office (MGTO) official website. http://en.macaotourism.gov.mo/main/aboutus.php (last accessed May 16, 2016).

PricewaterhouseCoopers (2015). *2015–16 Outlook for the Retail and Consumer Products Sector in Asia*. Hong Kong: PricewaterhouseCoopers.

Suryadinata, L (2012). *Southeast Asian Personalities of Chinese Descent: A Bibliographical Dictionary*, Vol. 1. Singapore: Institute of Southeast Asian Studies.

Too, D (July 18, 2012). Hua Ho's New Branch to Target Malaysian Shoppers. *The Brunei Times*. http://www.bruneitimes.com.bn/business-national/2012/07/18/hua-hos-new-branch-target-malaysian-shoppers (last accessed May 15, 2016).

UFC Group official website. www.ufc.mn/ (last accessed May 14, 2016).

The World Bank (April 2016). Lao PDR Overview. http://www.worldbank.org/en/country/lao/overview (last accessed May 13, 2016).

CHAPTER 14

ASIA'S REGIONAL PLAYERS: ASIA VISION, LOCAL ACTIONS

Asia's leading online fashion destination.

Zalora's tagline

Statistically, more than half the world's population lives in Asia (GSM Association, 2015). This makes Asia one of the most potential markets for companies from various industries. Moreover, the region has been dubbed the global economic engine, recording a robust 5.4 percent growth in 2015–2016 (International Monetary Fund, 2015), against an estimated global growth rate of 3.6 percent in 2016. Growth will be driven by rising middle-class wealth and supported by governments around the region that are implementing structural reforms and strengthening macro policy frameworks.

Asia is not an easy market to be conquered, especially for global players, who mostly hail from the West. No wonder then that some multinational companies have had to leave. The economic crisis that hit the United States and Europe in 2008–2009 dealt a hard blow to some global players in Asia, especially those in the banking industry. Capital and profitability pressures in their home market forced several major banks from Europe and the United States to withdraw entirely from certain markets and shut down their Asian operations. The phenomenon actually presented an opportunity for banks in Asia looking to strengthen their position in the regional market. A report from EY on Banking in Asia Pacific (2015) states, "As international players downsize and withdraw from the region, regional banks from Japan and ASEAN are building their presence. These strong, well-capitalized local institutions have spent the last five years expanding their regional footprints, following intra-region trade flows and the geographic expansion of their customers".

The opportunities for local companies in Asia to branch out into the region are certainly not confined to the banking industry. Local champions from Asia that have built solid business foundations in their country of origin are well positioned to leverage the opportunity to enter the broader regional markets. These are the companies with a great vision in Asia — perhaps eventually for the world — but they can adapt their tactics effectively in accordance with local tastes.

This chapter, presents the case of some such Asian companies that are beginning to or have successfully expanded business outside their domestic market. These businesses have managed to successfully integrate strategies at the regional level with the marketing tactics at the local level. In the context of the digital era, this chapter also covers initiatives of the businesses in crafting marketing programs that are more horizontal in nature, in view of the Internet and mobile technology.

Zalora — Singapore

E-commerce has long taken off in markets such as the United States, the United Kingdom, and Europe. Online fashion websites including ASOS and Zappos have established a strong presence in the retail sector, though there are not many counterparts as strong in Asia yet. Even as e-commerce was gaining steam over the past decade in the West, in Asia, the space was filled by a few blogshops run by small players in countries including Singapore and Malaysia, selling clothes and accessories online. That began to change with the launch of Zalora in March 2012.

Based in Singapore, Zalora is an online fashion retailer that has expanded across the region to Brunei, the Philippines, Thailand, Vietnam, Indonesia, Hong Kong, Australia, and New Zealand.

The online portal sells clothing and footwear from over 400 popular fashion labels including *Mango, Nike, Puma, Casio, Calvin Klein,* and *Levi's.* The variety on offer and convenience of product purchase with just a few clicks soon made the website catch up, especially among millennials. The company is backed by Rocket Internet, a German Internet company based in Berlin owning shareholding in several successful ventures in the United States and Europe, and now proactively targeting other regions including Asia. With approximately $100 million in funding from Rocket Internet's financial partners — including big names such as JP Morgan — Zalora built up a customer base of 500,000 across all the countries it was present in within just a year of its launch, with a geographic reach spanning 16,000 cities and towns in Asia (Kotler *et al.*, 2014).

Global Brand, Regional Vision

Zalora swiftly went on to become one of the fastest growing online fashion retailers in Asia, supported by a host of branded offerings — even from brands such as *Kate Spade* or *Steve Madden* — which were earlier not available to customers in their regions. Zalora soon diversified into selling beauty, hair, and skincare products. Free shipping is offered on orders exceeding a certain amount to incentivize customers to make purchases in large quantities. The website also offers a generous 30-day free-return window to deal with concerns that customers are not able to try on the items before purchasing them.

The company uses a range of digital marketing tactics to win new customers and engage the existing ones. New visitors on its website are encouraged to sign up for newsletters informing them about attractive deals on offer. The website offers comprehensive sizing and conversion charts to aid customers in selecting the right sizes of clothing and footwear. That may not have been anything novel to customers in the United States or Europe but in Asia, customers were being newly exposed to all such ways in which e-commerce made their purchases simpler and more convenient. As the Regional Marketing Director of Zalora puts it, "the record-breaking sales is evidence that people are seeing the benefit of having thousands of products to choose from right at their fingertips, and want to be up-to-date with the best in fashion and trends, no matter where they live or what they do" (Anjum, 2013). Zalora offers both domestic and international brands, making each of its country website unique and tailored specifically to consumers in the country.

Zalora eventually launched its private label Ezra in October 2013 in addition to other brands on offer. Ezra started out on the Singapore site, featuring only womenswear collection, and was later extended to include men apparels and footwear. The brand is also available in other regional markets, including Indonesia, the Philippines, and Malaysia. Priced reasonably, the label has gained popularity among men and women and Zalora has expanded the brand's catalogue to include accessories as well. The brand serves as an extra revenue stream for Zalora and its popularity among buyers also helps create loyalty toward Zalora as a fashion retailer amid stiff competition from a range of other online fashion websites.

Zalora has developed strength not only based on its diverse product range offering a mix of local and international brands, it is also particular about its quality of service, all in all, providing an exceptional experience to customers. Following an approach similar to Inditex — a Spanish multinational clothing company with 7,000 stores in 88 markets globally — Zalora has benchmarked its distribution model on the "fast fashion" concept, producing new clothings in small batches regularly. The company has set up warehouses closer to where it sources products from, thus allowing it to bring new collections of styles and fashion more quickly on its websites. The experience is further uplifted by a quick, hassle-free delivery service propped up by proactive customer support. Zalora operates 24-hour customer service helplines and deliveries are mostly targeted within the stipulated one to three days' time frame by leveraging its vast network of warehouses at each location. Customers who wish to cancel their orders are also given the option to do so provided they make their cancellations in time. Zalora's wide range of products and emphasis on quality service ensure that customers have a pleasant shopping experience, right from visiting Zalora's homepage to receiving their orders at their doorstep.

Local Action: Customized Offline and Online Initiatives

Zalora's popularity in Asia is closely associated with its ability to address the needs and concerns of its customers. While the company offers contemporary methods of online payment including credit cards or PayPal, it does not shy away from adapting to more traditional ways of payments in regions where online payments have not caught on. In addition, it offers a cash on collection option, which has gained prominence in markets such as Taiwan and Japan. In offering this service, Zalora teams up with convenience store chains, such as 7-Eleven for the Singapore market, and lets its customers pick up their items and make payments for them at an outlet of their choice. While there are currently limited pickup points in Singapore, the service may expand across all 570 7-Eleven outlets in the country if it proves to be a popular option among consumers. Recognizing that some consumers in Asia jump directly into owning mobile devices such as tablets instead of desktops or personal computers, Zalora launched mobile versions of its websites as well as an iOS app, both of which are said to have performed above expectations.

Zalora actively targets young middle-class and young professional buyers in most of its markets, which is why it spends big on digital marketing, especially social media and search engine marketing. The company hires social media marketing specialists for the specific job of coming up with engaging, interactive content on social media and other forums to engage customers. The company's official Facebook page has amassed over 6.5 million likes and its Twitter pages from various countries (Singapore, Malaysia, the Philippines, and Indonesia) collectively boast of hundreds of thousands of followers. The pages are updated daily with new posts and dozens of tweets, showcasing their promotions, new product ranges, and even fashion tips. Each of Zalora's individual country's Instagram accounts has garnered a steady stream of followers, and new styles with Zalora's products are being featured on its Pinterest pages. Zalora has also its own YouTube video channel with fashion videos, styling tips, and tutorials. This demonstrates the company's understanding of where and how its potential buyers are spending their time online. Hence its approach in implementing social media marketing has been largely successful in enabling it to gain new followers and fans, and in building its brand image cost-effectively too.

Zalora's ability to localize its offerings and marketing tactics is another value proposition that has helped in its success. Starting in 2014, the company collaborated with local singer-songwriters in Singapore on a 24-hour brand campaign titled "Zalora loves local", wherein the artists performed on their songs while clad in Zalora's fashion apparels. These performances were broadcasted on Zalora websites. As Zalora explained, "We are aiming to reach out to the local masses for this campaign, and in particular music lovers. By taking a very localized approach with this campaign, we want to speak to our young Singaporean community, who will hopefully understand and relate with the campaign" (Singapore Business Review, 2014). The music lovers who participated in the Zalora campaign make an example of a hub-type community, where the artists and the singers are at the center of gravity. This is an example of communitization strategy that demonstrates how Zalora applied New Wave marketing.

In a similar campaign, Zalora Philippines struck a deal with Out There Media, a mobile advertising provider, to develop a mobile marketing strategy aimed at promoting Zalora among youth and netizen communities. These communities constitute an example of "pool" type of communities in which the members likely have shared values. Zalora subscribers received discount vouchers that could be shared with their friends. In this way, Zalora implements specific local tactics for each of its markets in order to create differentiation from other global players.

Zalora has indeed benefited from early mover advantage in South east Asia where there is a vast untapped potential considering the rising Internet penetration and smartphone usage. The company has become one of the most prominent online fashion retailers within a relatively short span of time but that success has not mirrored throughout the region. Zalora has had to shut down operations in Taiwan within a year of its launch, as it lamented high costs in penetrating the already matured Taiwanese online retail market, which is dominated by players such as Yahoo! Taiwan and PChrome. Furthermore, Asia as a market cannot be looked at simply as one large market due to the heterogeneity among the countries in the region. There are stark cultural, economic, and political differences between each country in the region, making it imperative for physical operations to be present in each of the countries that Zalora intends to enter.

The company though has, to a large extent, managed to turn over those very challenges into opportunities. The ability to truly understand the nuances of the local market has been effectively harnessed with the help of a dedicated team of domestic and foreign professionals, which helps ensure that everything from management expertise to local tactics is implemented effectively. Zalora offers dual-language websites in countries where English is not the main language. Each country website has a team of localized social media specialists managing various online platforms. Zalora's Singapore blog, for example, features totally different content from its Indonesia blog. The company has established independent operations in each of these countries in Asia where it operates, and all these individual websites can leverage Zalora's growing prominence regionally.

ACLEDA Bank — Cambodia

In the aftermath of the global financial crisis, leading Asian banks have registered strong performance, even surpassing the growth in the global banking sector. Across Asia, the rise of "local champions" that are reporting strong gains from their product portfolios that include retail and investment banking, credit, and insurance has been witnessed. In view of emerging players and already stiff competition, consolidation in the banking sector is more pronounced, especially in ASEAN, on the back of the ASEAN Economic Community (AEC), which promotes free flow of goods and services in the region.

The ASEAN Banking Integration Framework will introduce greater competition by enabling easier access to markets within the region. Being able to operate across borders should enable banks to take advantage of economies of scale to increase efficiency and reduce costs (EY, 2015).

One such local champion that is fast spreading its wings in the regional market is ACLEDA Bank Plc., which is a public limited company, formed under the Banking and Financial Institutions Law of the Kingdom of Cambodia. Originally founded in January 1993, it began as a national non-governmental organization (NGO) for micro and small enterprises' development and credit (ACLEDA Bank official website, 2016). Two factors, namely expansion of its network to cover all of Cambodia's provinces and towns and its ability to operate at a profit to ensure its sustainability, led both its board and international partners to conclude that it should be transformed into a commercial bank. According to the National Bank of Cambodia, ACLEDA Bank is now the largest domestic commercial bank in terms of total assets.

Regional Expansion and Communitization Strategy

Having cemented its position in the domestic market, ACLEDA Bank began expansion in some of the neighboring countries in Southeast Asia. In 2008, ACLEDA Bank expanded its business to Laos, becoming the first Cambodian bank to begin operations within the country. It chose Laos as the first location of its regional branch due to the country's economic situation and cultural similarity to that in Cambodia. Fast forward to 2016, it operates several branches in six major provinces in Laos. The expansion undertaken by ACLEDA in Laos is a consequence of encouraging financial performance in the country. On the basis of the annual report issued by ACLEDA Bank Laos in 2015, the bank has its fourth consecutive year of growth in terms of income by 22 percent. Over the year, its lending grew by 20.57 percent and deposits by 10.45 percent. The loan portfolio increase stemmed mainly from an increase in loans to small enterprises.

In 2013, ACLEDA opened its first branch in Myanmar, following the lifting of international sanctions on the country in early 2012 (Becker, 2013). A country that was marked by extensive socialist control — with international sanctions placed against it throughout the past two decades — Myanmar has started implementing significant reforms that have led the country onto its current growth. As an indication of growth potential, ACLEDA MFI Myanmar has already opened six new offices, with one branch and four sub-branches located in Yangon Region and one branch located in Bago Region.

By the end-March 2015, authorization was received from the Microfinance Business Supervisory Committee of Myanmar to operate in 45 townships in Yangon Region and 28 townships in Bago Region. In these areas, the community of micro-entrepreneurs became the bank's main target market, offering its micro-business loans and deposits to these customers. As of 2016, ACLEDA MFI, the subsidiary operating as a micro-finance institution and which has been opened for just over two years, has achieved a strong performance in credit. It has more than 32,863 active borrowers for a combined loans of US$8.8 million. To support further development, its Head Office in Yangon Region and all its branches are using in-house systems developed by ACLEDA Bank Cambodia.

One differentiation between ACLEDA and its local and regional rivals is the selection of low-income people as customers. ACLEDA Bank's CEO, In Channy, once said: "We are targeting the low-income community, generating business activity in the local community rather than existing large corporations. We are believers in the model of starting at the grass roots level, bringing them up and [then] they become customers of a larger institution" (Becker, 2013).

In order to win hearts in a community inhabiting the bottom of the pyramid, ACLEDA Bank utilized more horizontal, New Wave approaches. The company is not positioned above the customers, but in a position parallel to them. Corporate sales staff is trained to act as consultants who can advise customers on how to take advantage of the funds obtained. This is an example of the co-creation process where transparency of information is a key to building relationships with consumers as active partners (see Chap. 11). In this context, ACLEDA's CEO once stated: "We ask customers to share with us and we share with them too and when they tell us the truth we give them access to financial services. We tell them right from the beginning how transparent we are and we lend based on information — other banks lend based on collateral. That's how we are different".

Digital Consumers and Digital Competition

The development of digital technology has radically changed the global business landscape. Some major banks in Asia's developed countries are having to struggle in the face of new and upcoming challenges in the form of mobile money, peer-to-peer lending, as well as online-only banks (see Chap. 3). The trend would, sooner or later, catch up in Cambodia as well, given the high Internet and mobile penetrations in the country. In 2014, almost 94 percent of Cambodians claimed to own their own phone, and more than 99 percent were reachable through some sort of phone. The proportion of citizens using more than one phone was only 12.5 percent, while one Cambodian in four uses more than one operator (Phong and Sola, 2014). The data are evidence of rising mobile adoption in the region — in just one year, mobile penetration has grown to 154 percent (GSM Association, 2015).

Despite the high mobile phone penetration, in Cambodia — as with other developing Asian counterparts including Laos and Myanmar — Internet usage in the country remains low. In 2015, only 31.8 percent of the population in Cambodia were Internet users, while the percentage was 12.6 for Mynamar and 14.3 for Laos (GSM Association, 2015). The data are consistent with those relating to the usage of smartphones, which is still low. Nevertheless, in line with the commitment of governments in Asia to continue to improve the infrastructure in the field of information technology, it is expected that Internet penetration will continue to increase in the future. This could pose both an opportunity and a challenge for the banking players such as ACLEDA Bank in Asia.

To seize the opportunities in Asia, EY — a global leader in assurance, tax, transaction, and advisory services — suggests that players in the banking industry need to:

(1) Invest in digital channels to meet customer needs — but not at the expense of personal interactions with customers. Banks must find the right balance between self-service and providing the "human touch" to sell higher value products and services. In the case of ACLEDA, short message service (SMS), which does not require advanced mobile technology, can be used to improve mobile service for its microclients.

(2) Invest in technology-driven models — not only to reduce costs and drive efficiencies but also to respond to new entrants from the fintech sector using technology to provide faster and cheaper solutions for customers. Some banks in Asia collaborate with telco companies to offer new services to customers. A similar initiative can be undertaken by ACLEDA Bank.

Vinamilk — Vietnam

Founded in 1976 under the name of Southern Coffee-Dairy Company, a subsidiary of the Food General Directorate, Vinamilk today is a long- established Vietnamese company that has grown rapidly since its establishment. Its vision is to become a world-class brand in the food and beverage industry, where people put all their trust in nutrient and health products. The company currently makes up about 37 percent of the milk processing market share. On the basis of the Annual Report released in 2015, over a period of 10 years (2005–2015), Vinamilk's revenue has grown by 7.1 percent.

The company's principal business activities include processing, producing, and trading of fresh milk, packed milk, powdered milk, nutrition powder, yogurt, condensed milk, soy milk, beverages, and other dairy products. Growing dairy cows is also important part of its business, as it supplies fresh milk as raw materials to produce the company's dairy products. Its products are known not just in Vietnam, but are also being exported to other countries such as Cambodia, the Philippines, Australia, and some countries in the Middle East. Export sales contribute about 13 percent of the total consolidated revenue.

Although still 48 percent government-owned, Vinamilk achieved great success by virtue of the initiatives of its chairperson Mai Kieu Lien. Following the move to privatize state firms starting in the 2000s, Lien became actively involved in the company's affairs eventually playing a key role in its success. During the privatization, Vinamilk was hardly perceived as lucrative, but Lien sensed a strong potential in the business and engaged a professional branding and marketing firm to stoke investors' interest in buying the company's shares. She also flagged off diversification of the product range into new categories including formula milk for babies, powdered milk, and yogurt. Lien, supported by an exemplary management team's efforts, eventually managed to beat her main rival Dutch Lady. The company is not only successful in beating domestic rivals but also stands tall in the face of competition from foreign brands. Vinamilk has today become a strong Vietnamese brand, building a strong foothold in the domestic market on the back of rising consumer preference for nutritive dairy products.

Competitive Advantages

Vinamilk's journey to success wasn't without roadblocks; the management team, which had steadily supported Lien's vision for Vinamilk, decided to make an exit in 2009 in view of compensation woes and joined a new rival TH Milk. The new competitor had big ambitions for the market and acted swiftly, for example, competing in the area of fresh milk production by importing 28,000 cows in the country. Vinamilk responded by setting up a large dairy plant with an investment of US$120 million as well as by boosting sourcing from overseas. The main challenge stemmed from competition, not least from brands, such as Friesland, that became more aggressive in terms of investments in cow farms, factories, and advertisement campaigns in a bid to expand market share. Over the past several years, newer players have emerged including Moc Chau and Ba Vi milk in the liquid and yogurt market segments, resulting in greater competition.

Vinamilk, however, has managed to stay strong owing to one of its competitive advantages in the form of a wide range of products. The company has four major brands: Vinamilk in liquid milk, yogurt, and ice cream; Vfresh for fruit juices and soy milk; Dielac for powdered milk; and Ridielac for nutrition powders and condensed milk. This diverse product range helps the company meet demands of a wide array of customers, and the company is also adept at gauging evolving customer needs. In view of the changing lifestyles in favor of healthy products, Vinamilk has come up with newer value-added, healthier products. For example, it came out with a new product that contained collagen, as well as powdered milk with extra nutritional content.

Aside from its product leadership, wide availability is another competitive strength of Vinamilk. As of December 2015, it had 243 exclusive distributors nationwide, far more than its closest competitors Friesland and Nestle. These intermediaries serve directly to more than 212,000 retailers (Vinamilk Annual Report 2015). A strong network of distribution channels helps Vinamilk penetrate the market swifter and easier, with its new products.

Product Development and Market Expansion

In recognition of the emerging opportunities, Vinamilk made a surprise entry into a whole new segment in 2011 — producing fruits and vegetable juices. This helped the company to diversify into an entirely new market with high growth potential as consumers adopt healthier lifestyles and are willing to spend more for healthy food products. The new product line, shortly after its launch, became a success in the market, clinching 25 percent share in 2011 in off-trade value terms. A critical factor that contributed to this success was Vinamilk's existing brand presence and an extensive distribution network.

Following the success of its juice range, the company expanded into fruit juices for children in February 2012, a first-of-its-kind product in Vietnam. The underdeveloped market turned out to have huge potential and was effectively leveraged upon, under the leadership of brand manager Nguyen Trong Tan. The new fruit and vegetable juice business faces keen competition from international companies such as Coca-Cola with its *Minute Maid limeade*, and PepsiCo with its *Tropicana Twister*. It may be too early to evaluate the success of Vinamilk's new product range but the company manages to hold a sizeable market share in Vietnam, due to its familiarity with the market and strong brand recognition.

In addition to continuous product development, Vinamilk also makes quite aggressive market expansion. In April 2013, the company put two additional modern dairy plants in the southern province of Binh Duong into operation. The first factory was estimated to be able to come out with 400 million liters of milk annually in the first phase, and is expected to double production from the second phase. The second factory is expected to produce around 54,000 tons of powdered milk, which is four times the current output. On January 2014, Vinamilk was granted an investment certificate to build a joint-venture business in the name of Angkor Dairy Products Co., Ltd. in Cambodia. The business objective was to build the dairy manufacturing factory to serve the Cambodian market. And after setting up a subsidiary in Poland in 2014 to tap the European market, the company opened a branch in Russia at the beginning of 2016, after Vietnam signed a free trade pact with the Eurasian Economic Union in 2015 (Nikkei Asian Review, 2016).

Into Vietnam's Digital Consumers

Vietnam, akin to its other emerging Asian counterparts, is a mobile- and Internet-friendly nation. The country's young population with high mobile usage and Internet penetration (30 percent of the population) means the social media are quite popular, including Facebook, with 20 million users. The rising phenomenon of digitalization is therefore turning the tables by placing greater power in the hands of consumers than brands. Internet and the social media allow customers to share their product or service experience with a click, sharing it with tens of thousands in their online networks. Even though smartphone use in the country continues to be low as of now — with only 20 percent of the population owning one — the number is growing nevertheless and fast. Young millennials in the country actively use smartphones to check e-mails, browse Internet, watch YouTube, and connect with others on social media, especially working professionals and businesspersons.

Companies will therefore likely design marketing content and activities such as Internet videos, social media marketing, online advertising, and e-mail marketing that are compatible with different mobile devices to reach these consumers (Masso Consulting, 2014).

In terms of technology adoption, Vinamilk is in the leading position for dairy farming and food processing technologies. By utilizing some of the latest techniques and tools, Vinamilk continues to develop new product formulations. The continuous development of Internet and mobile technologies also needs to be followed closely by Vinamilk and other industry players in Vietnam. The emergence of digital consumers is a phenomenon that is changing the dynamics in almost all industries. Establishing and maintaining customer relationship through the use of online platforms is one initiative that needs to be taken to strengthen the company's presence in emerging communities.

On its part, Vinamilk has already begun marketing communications using the social media. Vinamilk's Facebook page has been liked by more than 264,000 people. The YouTube channel has nearly 14,000 subscribers. Considering the fact that the brand is predominantly targeting the domestic market, the content on social media is still put up in the local language. However, if Vinamilk is looking to build brand strength and character across the region, it would perhaps need to make more efforts in providing content that is more universal and that can be understood by all people (including providing the content in English). Beyond that, the high penetration of mobile technology in Vietnam (103.6 percent) also presents separate opportunities that are worthy of consideration, going forward.

Advances in digital technology can also be used by Vinamilk to begin applying the more horizontal principles of New Wave marketing. Product innovation, which has conventionally been Vinamilk's strength, can be further capitalized upon by the application of co-creation which encourages consumers involvement of in the product development process. Digital platforms can greatly assist in the execution of co-creation because of the flexibility it provides to consumers in sharing inputs on ideas and improvements, any time and from anywhere. Vinamilk's large customer base can also be optimized as an alternative channel of distribution. Through communal activation, such companies will be able to build greater loyalty among existing consumers while stepping up acquisition of new consumers. These are some of the possibilities that can be explored by Vinamilk to strengthen its position in the local market and to increase its penetration in the region.

The development of digital technology that is sweeping the world and Asia is going to fundamentally change the face of competition in the future. As Vinamilk continues to pave its way to expand and capture a larger share of both domestic and regional demands, it will face numerous challenges from increasing competition. But if it continues to play its cards right, Vinamilk's technological adaptability and product diversity will help to keep its business booming despite the numerous challenges it has to overcome.

Kurumba Maldives

Tourism Industry in Maldives

The tropical country of Maldives inarguably derives the largest economic benefit from its tourism industry. The country welcomes over a hundred thousand visitors every month, earning significant money in foreign exchange and generating employment in the services sector. The country attracts the highest number of visitors from China, followed by Europe including Italy, Germany, and France.

Tourism began in the Maldives in 1972. A United Nations mission on development that visited the Maldives Islands in the 1960s did not recommend tourism claiming that the islands were not suitable. Ever since the launch of the first resort in Maldives in 1972, however, tourism in

Maldives has flourished. The arrival of the first tourist group is estimated to have occurred in February 1972.

The tourism industry in Maldives began with the opening of only two resorts with a capacity of about 280 beds in an island resort. It was the Kurumba Island Resort, which was the first such resort in Maldives, followed by Bandos Island Resort. Today, there are over 105 resorts dotting the different atolls in the country. The number of tourists in Maldives has consistently risen as visitors throng the island, attracted by its white sandy beaches and crystal clear waters. In 2009, local island guesthouses started popping up in the Maldives. This was due to a change in regulations that began to officially allow tourists to stay among the local population, rather than just on privately owned resort islands.

Under the Tourism Act, Law 2/99 of the Maldives, all establishments providing accommodation to tourists are required to register with the Ministry of Tourism (MoT). Accommodation facilities are classified into resorts, hotels, guest houses, and safari vessels. The Maldives resorts with its unique "one-island-one-resort" concept make the resorts sector as the most attractive form of accommodation in the Maldives. At the end of 2013, there were 110 islands with 23,677 beds registered as tourist resorts in the Maldives, accounting for 79 percent of the total bed capacity that year. Hotels are located in inhabited islands. At the end of 2013, there were 19 hotels with 1626 beds, contributing 5 percent to the total bed capacity during the year. Guesthouses offer low-cost accommodation for travelers visiting the local islands. In 2012, there were 75 guesthouses with 1,101 beds registered in the Maldives. This number increased to 135 with 1,930 beds by the end of 2013. The live-aboard floating beds, commonly known as safari vessels, are one of the most popular forms of accommodation among tourists who visit the Maldives for diving. Although in terms of numbers safari vessels are the leading form of accommodation, their bed capacity represented only 9 percent of the total capacity of the country in 2013 (Ministry of Tourism Republic of Maldives, 2014).

Tourists also come to the Maldives from various countries and not just from Europe. Some Asian countries from where travelers visit Maldives include China, Japan, India, and South Korea. The number of visitors from each country keeps going up or down in accordance with the conditions of the economy. Economic recession that hit the European region, for instance, negatively affected the number of tourists coming from that region.

Kurumba Maldives: Company at a Glance

Kurumba Maldives was established in 1972 as the first resort that was set up in the island nation. "Kurumba" came from the local word for coconut. From its humble origins accommodating only 60 guests a month, Kurumba is now able to provide accommodation to 14,000 guests. Kurumba expanded to accommodate more people after the airport was extended to take in long-haul flights. It has also transformed from a venture managed by a handful of founding friends into a company with 450 employees.

In 2003, Kurumba underwent a complete transformation yet again, to meet the demands of the 21st century. The result was a world-class resort with 180 rooms, including the royal residence, presidential suites, pool villas, family villas, and beach and garden superior rooms. Kurumba has matured into one of the most popular accommodations in Maldives, setting the benchmark for hospitality in the country and in the region at large. In 2016, Kurumba was awarded "Maldives' Leading Resort" title and "Indian Ocean's Leading MICE Hotel" from World Travel Awards (Kurumba Maldives official website, 2016).

As a cosmopolitan Maldives resort, Kurumba offers its guests with a wide variety of accommodation, diverse choice of restaurants and bars, vibrant live entertainment, various social events, and lots of activities to choose from. The island resort has also developed both natural and artificial environments in and around its premises, which support a host of guest activities. It is protected by seawalls around the island. This is a common practice in a world-class resort to preserve the beach from erosion all year round. At the same time, they allow a safe swimming experience for everyone, especially during windy and rough conditions, and ensure that no strong currents are felt near the beach. Meanwhile, to accommodate the communication needs of its guests, Kurumba cooperates with the Dhiraagu telephone network. This operator uses a GSM 900 network, which is well suited to many international cell phone operators.

Kurumba: Care That Creates Conversation

Since its inception, Kurumba has applied the principles of New Wave marketing. When M.U. Maniku and her friends were working on the idea of a new resort in 1972, the business concepts and services were actually developed in conjunction with customers. This practice embodied the concept of co-creation involving both the company and customers in the process of value creation. Maniku once said "We knew nothing about tourism. It was tourists who helped us build the industry here. We listened to them and gave them what they wanted. Luckily for us, they wanted simplicity in natural surroundings and that was what we had to offer and all we could afford".

In terms of service, Kurumba does not merely provide what is needed by the guests but also attempts to understand their anxiety and desire. Therefore, the resort ensures that it provides complete information on whatever could be of interest to guests through the website as well as brochures: from the technical issues at the time of arrival from the airport to the issue of dress code while in the resort and when out for sightseeing. Most of the potential queries of guests have been addressed in advance through the online platform, so that the visitors feel prepared on their arrival.

The staff at Kurumba is also empowered in order to deliver care to their guests. They are not obliged to always stick to rules at the resort as long as it's for the benefit of guests, taking into account the diverse backgrounds visitors come from. A staff member — whatever his or her position — is well trained to be able to make a decision that is in the best interest of the guest. The management at Kurumba seems well aware that their staff is one of their main assets and hence the company is also concerned about their care, welfare, and needs. Training and competence development are taken seriously as standard procedures for all employees. Not surprisingly, Kurumba Maldives was ranked third in the Maldives Top Employer Award 2014 by Job-Maldives.com.

Through the care delivered to guests, Kurumba believes that its impact will be more powerful than paid advertisements in the media. With the advent of digital technology, consumers are more trusting of other people's opinions of products and services than advertisements. Kurumba strives to provide the best experience to every guest at its resort and hotel. This extraordinary experience gained by guests encourages them to give positive recommendations through various online platforms, including TripAdvisor, a travel website that lets users review travel-related providers.

And it really works. In 2015, Kurumba Maldives was recognized by TripAdvisor based on the positive reviews given from its guests. Among other awards, Kurumba was ranked number one in the category of All Inclusive Resort worldwide, number one in All Inclusive Resort in Asia, Top Luxury Hotel in the Maldives, and Top Hotel for Service in Maldives. The care provided to guests also encourages positive conversation with other potential consumers. This is exemplified by the review from one of the guests who stayed in Kurumba, on TripAdvisor on May 11, 2016: "I will come back again and will only recommend this hotel to my family and friends, we paid a fortune here, but it was totally worth it! Kurumbians keep it up, you are the best!"

References

ACLEDA Bank official website. http://www.acledabank.com.kh/kh/eng/ (last accessed May 12, 2016).

ACLEDA Bank Laos. *Annual Report 2015*. http://www.acledabank.com.la/la/eng/bp_annualreport (last accessed May 12, 2016).

Anjum, J (December 16, 2013). Zalora Achieves Record Breaking Sales Across the Region. *CIO Asia*. http://www.cio-asia.com/print-article/48560/ (last accessed May 11, 2016).

Becker, SA (March 1, 2013). ACLEDA Opens in Myanmar, Expands in Laos. *The Phnom Penh Post*. http://www.phnompenhpost.com/post-plus/acleda-opens-myanmar-expands-laos (last accessed May 12, 2016).

EY (2015). *Banking in Asia Pacific: Size Matters and Digital Drives Competition*. Asia Pacific: EYGM Limited.

GSM Association (2015). *The Mobile Economy: Asia Pacific 2015*. London: GSM Association.

International Monetary Fund (2015). *Regional Economic Outlook 2015*. Washington: International Monetary Fund.

Kotler, P, H Kartajaya and Hooi, DH (2014). *Think New ASEAN*. Singapore: McGraw-Hill.

Kurumba Maldives official website. http://www.kurumba.com/maldives-resort-information (last accessed May 12, 2016).

Masso Consulting (February 2014). Vietnam 2014 Trends in Marketing and Branding. *Vietnam Economic Times*. http://massogroup.com/knowledge/insights/8439-vietnam-2014-trends-in-marketing-and-branding.html (last accessed May 11, 2016).

Ministry of Tourism Republic of Maldives (2014). *Tourism Year Book 2014*. Malé: Statistics & Research Section Ministry of Tourism.

Nikkei Asian Review (February 9, 2016). Vinamilk Revenue up 14% in 2015 on Strong Overseas Business. *Nikkei Asian Review*. http://asia.nikkei.com/Business/AC/ Vinamilk-revenue-up-14-in-2015-on-strong-overseas-business (last accessed May 11, 2016).

Singapore Business Review (January 22, 2014). See How Zalora's 24-hour Online Ad Campaign Boosts Singapore's Music Scene. *Singapore Business Review*. http://sbr. com.sg/media-marketing/exclusive/see-how-zaloras-24-hour-online-ad-campaign-boosts-singapores-music-scene (last accessed May 11, 2016).

Phong, K, and J Sola (2014). *Research Study: Mobile Phone in Cambodia 2014*. USAID & The Asia Foundation.

Vinamilk Annual Report 2015. https://www.vinamilk.com.vn/static/uploads/bc_thuong_ nien/1462532728-0504c9670b04eb86f6e9c18594aebb97390c093fbbe21a262264a 324c22d978d.pdf (last accessed May 10, 2016).

CHAPTER 15

ASIA'S MULTINATIONAL COMPANIES: GLOBAL VALUE, REGIONAL STRATEGY, LOCAL TACTICS

*In one of our early planning sessions, my vision was
to create the largest food company in the world. That was when
we had 5 stores. Some people thought I was overly optimistic.*

Tony Tan — Founder and CEO of Jollibee

Not many companies are truly global. Instead, most companies are usually strong only in some regions in the world. The regional scale that provides profitable opportunities make regional markets attractive. However, even large companies with popular brands, abundant resources, decades of experience, and world-class management teams may still find it challenging to grow in markets and geographies away from their homes.

But some Asian companies decided to venture out of their comfort zones and even spread their wings in the international market. As they succeed in building a strong business foundation locally and regionally, some businesses take big risks in launching their products and services to customers outside Asia. It has not been smooth sailing for all. The dynamics of the global market with all the ups and downs have forced some of those Asian companies to give up and return to their home turf. A few though have managed to survive and even grow into global players that are recognized worldwide.

This chapter discusses some Asian companies that have managed to maintain and develop their presence in the global market. Three companies have been selected from different Asian countries — Philippine's Jollibee, South Korea's Samsung, and Japan's Honda — to demonstrate an overview of the implementation of concepts discussed in this book. By analyzing the values on offer, the strategies, and tactics used, the book aims to learn how the "glorecalization mindset" has been realized, especially in winning the hearts and minds of the global consumer who embraces a digital lifestyle.

Jollibee

Jollibee was founded by Tony Tan and his family. It has a humble beginning as an ice-cream parlor that later grew into an emerging global brand. Jollibee's success story in conquering the Philippines market is supported by its ability to infix the Philippines taste to its fast-food range of products from burger, fried chicken, noodle, sandwich bread, breakfast menu, to a variety of drinks and desserts. Good products will go down the drain if they are not supported with good service. To accommodate urban citizens, aside from the good 30-min delivery service, some of Jollibee shops also open 24 hours and with the *drive thru* service. Even for kids, Jollibee offers birthday packages with many thematic choices.

The threat of new entrants to the industry is considered low to medium. New entrants to the fast-food industry would need to face high entry barriers. Besides the need to have economies of scales, high capital requirements when opening a fast-food chain, as well as products that differ from the rest of the competition, the new entrants would also have to compete against the high standards and the strong loyal customer base Jollibee has established in the industry.

The threat of substitute products is considered to be medium to high. Products from local street food as well as food from its direct competitors in the industry can be considered major substitutes. The intensity of rivalry among competitors is considered to be medium to high. The fast-food industry can be described as a lucrative segment with high profitability. Within the Philippines, there are already other fast-food players competing with Jollibee.

In terms of global market, Jollibee is a mouse among the elephants but in the Philippines, Jollibee controls over 80 percent share of the hamburger market and 55 percent share of fast-food market as a whole. It was able to attain a competitive advantage in the Philippines over McDonald's by entering the market first; retaining tight control over operations management, which allowed it to price below its competitors; and having the flexibility to cater to the taste of its local customers.

International expansion

Jollibee has embarked on an aggressive international expansion plan. The company started with five branches in 1978 and has grown to a strong network of 890 stores in the Philippines and 133 stores internationally (Yoo-chul, 2016). It is the largest fast-food chain in the country with international locations in Brunei, Hong Kong, Kuwait, Qatar, Saudi Arabia, Singapore, Vietnam, the United Arab Emirates, and the United States.

In 1993, the company acquired 80 percent of Greenwich Pizza, enabling it to penetrate the pizza–pasta segment. From a 50-branch operation, Greenwich has established a strong presence in the food service industry. In 2000, the company acquired Chowking, allowing Jollibee to be part of the Asian quick service restaurant segment. In 2004, Jollibee acquired the Chinese fast-food chain Yonghe Dawang for $22.5 million.

Jollibee entered into a joint-venture contract with US-based Chow Fun Holdings LLC, the developer and owner of Jinja Bar & Bistro in New Mexico. In 2010, Jollibee acquired 70 percent share of Mang Inasal, a Filipino food chain specializing in barbecued chicken. In 2013, Jollibee opened its stores in Virginia Beach, Virginia, and Houston, Texas. It returned to the United Arab Emirates market by opening a store in Dubai in 2015, and a second one in February 2016. It was Jollibee's second expansion to the Emirati market after its first trial failed in 1995.

Consistent global value: Jollibee character and family-oriented values

The large bee mascot dressed in a blazer, shirt, and chef's hat was introduced by the brand in 1980. It is probably the most widely recognized character in the Philippines and also acts as a universal identity for Jollibee, which is currently expanding into the global market. Beyond the attractive visualization, Jollibee's character also reflects the company values offered to customers and employees. Officially, there are eight values-based principles that Jollibee Foods Corp (JFC) calls foundation to its business practices: customer focus, excellence, respect for the individual, teamwork, spirit of family and fun, humility to listen and learn, honesty and integrity, and frugality. In implementation though, the spirit of family is perhaps the most prominent value.

And these values are not only reflected in interactions with customers, but also realized through strong family ties between the company and its employees. At the heart of its success is a family oriented approach to personnel management, making Jollibee one of the most admired employers in the region. It recevied the Employer of the Year Award from the Personnel Management Association of the Philippines, Best Employer in the Philippines Award from Hewitt Associates, and a Top 20 Employer in Asia citation from the Asian Wall Street Journal (Jollibee Foods Corporation, 2016).

For its employees, Jollibee recognizes them by providing the highest compensation and benefits packages in the fast-food industry and modern and comprehensive training programs. Managers are regularly updated on the latest store operations systems, people-oriented management skills, among others. Service crews are trained on various store stations and food-service innovations. Jollibee also offers career opportunities for qualified and exceptional crew members to further their food-service careers as managers. And above all, employees are treated as part of a big family. This inculcation of family values into principles is duly maintained by Jollibee, no matter what the process is. Through internalization of such values into their employees themselves, Jollibee is able to consistently deliver care to its customers.

In addition to character and care, Jollibee also has a standard process that is implemented globally. It serves as a guide for the company when establishing collaborations with various parties, both upstream and downstream. Jollibee is very strict about implementing its standards, symbolized by "F.S.C.": Food (F) served to the public must meet the company's excellence standards or not be served at all; the Service (S) must be fast and courteous; and Cleanliness (C) in the kitchen and utensils must always be maintained. Each partner — local or global — who wants to collaborate with Jollibee must be able to meet these standards, to enable the company to consistently maintain the quality of products and service provided to customers.

Coordinated regional strategy: Confirming to different communities

Jollibee Foods Corporation engages in developing, operating, and franchising quick service restaurants in the Philippines and internationally. It operates through three businesses: food service, franchising, and leasing. The company operates quick service restaurants under the Jollibee, Chowking, Greenwich, Red Ribbon, Yonghe King, Hong Zhuang Yuan, Mang Inasal, Burger King, San Pin Wang, and 12 Hotpot names. The company is also involved in the leasing of store sites, digital printing and advertising activities, and provision of accounting, human resources, and logistic services, as well as business management services.

In terms of the consumer market, particularly in the food service segment, JFC aims to reach out to four customer communities: families, kids, adolescents, and thrifty people. The family makes a customer group that is willing to nurture the emotional bond and spend quality time with all its members. Kids form a customer group that wants a playground which can accommodate their adventure soul. Adolescents belong to a customer group that needs a large and comfortable place where they can share a laugh and tell a story through an affordable menu. Meanwhile thrifty people are the customers who come in group for certain events, such as office workers group, birthday treats, and reunions. Their requests are for high-standard clean and affordable food.

As for the overseas market, Jollibee uses somewhat different strategies. The company is trying to reach out to the Filipino community scattered around the world through the family values it offers (Dalgic, 2006). An example is Jollibee in the United States, which opened its first store in 1998 in California (Jollibee USA, 2014). Catering to the Filipino and Filipino-American families living in the area, Jollibee made them reminisce a familiar feeling from back home. In the East Asian region, Jollibee is trying to connect with the Chinese communities that represent a dominant culture there.

Customized local tactics: *Local menu and online initiatives*

The products offered by Jollibee appeal to the Filipinos' taste. By concentrating its resources on satisfying the Filipino palate, Jollibee has been able to serve localized dishes that are unlike any found in other fast-food chains in the Philippines. This is in addition to offering the usual french fries that accompany the meals found in McDonald's, KFC, Burger King, and so forth.

Outside the Philippines, Jollibee has crafted special menus tailored to local taste. For instance, fresh herbs and vegetables play a huge role in the Vietnamese cuisine and hence it's no wonder that a Garden Fresh Salad is found on Jollibee's menu. Along with Chicken Joy meals, they also offer Chicken Barbecue, Chicken Strips, and a Chicken Curry rice meal. In meat-loving Qatar, Jollibee has introduced pita sandwiches, with a choice of beef strips of chicken slices. With a menu similar to Qatar's, the Saudi Arabian version also offers Macaroni Salad and a Crispy Chicken Burger. Bruneian cuisine is heavily influenced by its neighbors Indonesia, Singapore, and Malaysia, so it's no wonder that a dish like chicken curry makes its way to the Jollibee menu.

To capture new opportunities from the rise of digital consumers, Jollibee has launched its online payment service with AsiaPay, an electronic payment solution and technology provider in Asia and the company behind PesoPay. It allows Jollibee's online delivery website (www.jollibeedelivery.com) to accept and collect credit card payments online. The integration of AsiaPay's payment platform for the Philippine market, PesoPay, allows Jollibee to offer its customers to pay online using their credit cards with confidence and ease. Additionally, PesoPay's anti-fraud management tools will enable Jollibee to facilitate online payments securely, thereby detecting and preventing fraud before it happens.

The implementation of online payment services for the local market could be seen as Jollibee's initiative to undertake "Currency Adaptation" (Chap. 11). Through the concept of this "new wave pricing", the company has set up transparent choices along with a mechanism to do customization. Jollibee can implement this by providing a variety of products and prices that are customizable online (e.g., by allowing the consumer to choose from a menu of burgers according to their needs or budget).

Jollibee has also made an attempt at integrating online and offline promotions. One example is their program called Amazing Aloha Champ Amazing Blowout, which was launched in 2015. Every customer in the Philippines who ordered the Amazing Aloha Champ value meal with pineapple juice could enter the contest. The participants could transmit personal data and the O.R. number on the receipt by entering details on their website http://www.amazingblowout.com/. The next challenge for Jollibee is to design creative online promotions, so as to create conversations that will spread from one consumer to another — both offline and online.

Honda

Short history

Honda's history is inseparable from the story of its founder, Soichiro Honda. Soichiro was born in a middle class family in a residential neighborhood in Shizuoka. To contribute to the family income, Soichiro used to help out his father at the bicycle repair shop.

Since childhood, Soichiro was quite keen in engineering sciences. Even as a teenager, Soichiro left the elementary school when he was only 15 because he was more interested in automobiles. Fortunately his father was supportive of Soichiro's interest. To that end, he introduced Soichiro to one of his friends, Kashiwabara in Tokyo, for work. Kashiwabara was a director at an auto repair shop called Art Shokai.

It is here that Soichiro learnt the mechanics and workings of automotive engines through practical work, despite no theoretical knowledge. Armed with the skills and expertise gained at the bicycle repair shop, Soichiro finally opened his own workshop where he eventually developed some automotive products. One of them was a motorcycle. The initial idea of the motorcycle occurred to him after he saw a bike milling about and tried to integrate the machine in the body of a bike.

In 1949, Honda launched a motorcycle named *Dream Type-D*. Because it was a breakthrough at the time, it did not take long for this product to become a best-seller in Japan. Honda went back to make improvements and in 1959 he unveiled a *Honda C-100* motorcycle, which eventually became the world's best-selling motorcycle at that time.

Honda today is one of the major players in the automotive industry not only in Japan but globally. The company not only makes cars and motorcycles, but has also created products based on other technologies. Examples include power equipment, boat engines, boats, lawn mowers, and many other such products. It is also taking huge strides in robotics research and is building the world's most advanced humanoid robot called ASIMO (American Honda Motor Co, Inc., 2016).

Global expansion

As part of its global expansion strategy, Honda has built assembly plants around the globe. These plants are located in China, the United States, Pakistan, Canada, England, Japan, Belgium, Brazil, México, New Zealand, Malaysia, Indonesia, India, Philippines, Thailand, Vietnam, Turkey, Taiwan, Perú, and Argentina. North America, led by US sales, is Honda's biggest market, generating nearly half its global revenue and operating income (Ohnsman, 2010).

After the 2008 economic downturn that severely hit the global automotive industry, several of Honda's markets are gradually recovering. The American market especially has shown encouraging signs, as can be seen from the improvements in the labor market, rising purchasing power of consumers, and growing investments in various sectors. The European market, although still stagnant, is no longer deteriorating.

On the other hand, the Asian market has become a source of positive growth for Honda, especially in the south East Asian region including countries such as Thailand and Indonesia. New auto sales in south East Asia are expected to grow for the next several years, clearly making business sense for Honda, akin to other Japanese automakers, to eye the market even more closely. Also, established automakers including Honda are increasingly looking toward developing economies to leverage the untapped potential and encourage business development in the future. In order to do so, the automaker is developing several products tailored to the needs of relevant markets.

Consistent global value: The three joys

Excellence and superiority of the Honda brand cannot be separated from the legendary visions of its founder and other prominent leaders. The personal values held by founder Soichiro Honda are seen to be deeply embodied in the basic business principles that are applied globally. The principles in question here are "Respect for the Individual" and "The Three Joys". Respect for the Individual reflects the company's desire to respect the unique character and ability of each individual, trust one another as equal counterparts, and try one's best at every opportunity. The principle of Three Joys includes "The Joy of Producing" (happiness felt by engineers in the company), "The Joy of Selling" (support from distributors and sales teams), and "The Joy of Buying" (customer delight).

In line with these basic principles, Honda has consistently continued to develop the highest quality products at affordable prices. A lot of effort goes into ensuring satisfaction of consumers from around the world. And it doesn't stop there; Honda also has demonstrated its commitment to continue to protect the environment and promote driving safety.

Coordinated regional strategy: Confirming the youth community

As discussed earlier, we recognize three subcultures that are increasingly dominant in today's world, particularly in Asia: youth, women, and netizens. Honda is making serious efforts to actively target these communities, especially in Asia and the youth market.

In the Indonesian market, Astra Honda Motor has launched *BeAT*, an automatic scooter targeting young buyers. For marketing communications, Honda roped in budding young artists and used songs that were popular among youngsters. Communities dominated by young people are also being targeted by specialized marketing programs from the company. *Honda BeAT*, meanwhile, has gained sizeable popularity in the Indonesian market and became one among the top two-wheeler models in terms of sales.

In Vietnam, Honda provides scholarships named "Honda YES Award", a form of appreciation for young people who excel in the country. With this program, Honda is aiming to make a place in the hearts of consumers in Vietnam as a brand that not only sells a quality product, but also possesses a character that can be readily embraced by youngsters.

An example of how Honda is targeting youth through its marketing strategies is evident from the concept of "Honda Big Fan Big Fun" in Thailand. It is a joint program with two English football clubs, Manchester United and Liverpool, with Honda as the regional partner. Thai A.P. Honda is the official motorcycle partner of Manchester United for Thailand while Liverpool has partnered with Honda on marketing campaigns. Under the Big Fan Big Fun program, Honda awards game tickets to lucky customers willing to watch their favorite teams play. The program was hugely successful following which in 2011, Honda restaged the "Honda Big Fan Big Fun #2".

Customized local tactics: Offline and online initiatives

Honda keeps a close watch on interesting trends in each country in order to draw up effective marketing tactics. An example is what Honda has done in India where motorcycles are a common means of commute to work. In recognizing this trend, a massive surge in demand for two wheelers is expected in the coming years. Considering such a trend, in 2012, Honda launched the *Dream Yuga* motorcycle in India. This low-cost single-cylinder motorcycle was especially targeted at suburban buyers in tier II and III cities. Even though the model was developed using a 100 cc engine, it still promised good performance at an affordable price. With this and other models targeted at young buyers, such as the best-selling *Activa*, Honda has emerged as the top motorcycle player in India, controlling a whopping 58 percent share of the scooters market in 2015 (Panday, 2015).

In Vietnam too, Honda offers a variety of products targeting all the segments ranging from lower class, middle to upper class, which are relatively affordable when compared with those of its competitors. For example, in 2002, Honda Vietnam sold a product under the name *Alpha Wave*, priced 40 percent lower than competitors. The subsidiary is able to capitalize on local production of spare parts to reduce production costs, hence gaining price competiveness.

In addition, Honda has begun to explore countries that have been out of its radar. It has set up a subsidiary in Bangladesh where the automotive market is expected to grow in the near future; Honda has also started selling well in Myanmar. Although there may be some looming challenges for the automotive market in Asia, Honda continues to maintain a high level of optimism for Asian markets.

In addition to offline initiatives, Honda is also using online tactics that are customized for each local market. As an example, Honda has kicked off a social media campaign as a build-up to the launch of the much-awaited *BR-V* in India. The *BR-V* marks Honda's entry into India's popular SUV segment where it looks set to rival the likes of the *Hyundai Creta* and *Maruti S-Cross*.

The social media campaign displays photos of the *BR-V* in various environments and on varied terrain, as suggested by the audience. Those interested are able to view the photos on the company's social media pages and the official website of *BR-V*. Honda says that the aim of the campaign is to create a connection with consumers prior to the SUV's India launch in the coming months (Mehra, 2016).

Samsung Electronics

Growth and global expansion

Samsung Electronics is a South Korean multinational electronics company headquartered in Suwon, South Korea. It is a part of the Samsung Group, accounting for 70 percent of the group's revenue in 2012. The company manufactures a variety of products including mobile phones, which is a core product. But apart from that, it makes semiconductors, televisions, home cinema, projectors, computers, home appliances, among others.

Samsung Electronics launched its first mobile phone in 1988 in the South Korean market. Sales were initially poor and by the early 1990s, Motorola held a market share of over 60 percent in the country's mobile phone market compared to just 10 percent for Samsung (Michell, 2010).

Samsung's mobile phone division also struggled with poor quality and inferior products until the mid-1990s.

After briefly turning its focus to component-manufacturing business during 1995–2008, Samsung Electronics finally returned to consumer products. In 2007, Samsung Electronics became the world's second largest mobile-phone maker, overtaking Motorola for the first time (Yoo-chul, 2007). In the first quarter of 2012, the company became the highest selling mobile phone company when it overtook Nokia, selling 93.5 million units compared to 82.7 million units sold by Nokia (Lunden, 2012). Today, in terms of revenue, Samsung continues to compete with Apple for the world's number one smartphone manufacturer position (Chowdhry, 2015).

As part of its business expansion plans, Samsung continues to spread its wings to almost all continents, not just in Asia. Based on 2013 data, Samsung Electronics has assembly plants and sales networks in 80 countries and employs around 370,000 people (Grobart, 2013).

Consistent global value: Innovation and collaboration

Although operating production and distribution facilities around the world, Samsung attempts to maintain its same, original character. And the keyword is innovation. The company wants to be perceived as a leader in innovation, especially in the field of digital products and services. This is what makes the innovation capabilities of Samsung at the forefront of the smartphone-manufacturing world.

Global vision is really taken quite seriously by Samsung. It is committed to inspiring communities around the world by developing new technologies, innovative products, and creative solutions. It even looks forward to exploring new territories, including health, medicine, and biotechnology. The company is also committed to creating a brighter future by developing new values for its core networks: industry partners and employees. Through these efforts, Samsung aims to contribute to a better world and a richer experience for all (Samsung, 2016).

The second keyword that is fast becoming a major contributor to its success is collaboration. Globally, Samsung collaborates with several key partners. One of the strategic initiatives undertaken by Samsung to enhance customer value is through collaboration with upstream providers of operating systems. Through such collaborations, Samsung allows users to stick with the Samsung brand while being able to choose from several different smartphone operating systems, including Android, Windows, and Bada.

Regional strategy and local tactics: *Product leadership and online channels*

In the rapidly growing market, one important strategy that Samsung recognizes is the need to constantly develop the best new products and be the first to market them. An example is the *85S9 television*, which was the first ultra-high-definition TV announced for Asia in 2013. Being the first company to launch such a product not only gave it a first-mover advantage, but also helped the brand to maintain its image for releasing new, high-end products.

Another important strategy Samsung undertakes is to localize its products and services to suit the market, and it works with each country within Asia to develop local content and services. The company came up with the term "Made for Asia" products that focus on the unique needs of its Asian consumers, including products like the *RT38 refrigerator*, which comes with customized placement for the integrated ice and water dispenser, as well as a basket specially made for storing medicine and cosmetics. Designed with Asian customers in mind, these products take into consideration the different preferences and habits that consumers may have (Kotler *et al.*, 2014).

In addition to product innovation, Samsung also pays special attention to the selection of its channels of distribution, particularly in targeting low-end market. Samsung Electronics uses limited marketing campaigns for its low-end smartphones to save costs and better compete with its Chinese rivals in emerging markets. It uses leading online commerce channels in India, Vietnam, and China to sell its handsets directly to consumers. If Samsung sells more of its smartphones via its online channels, then it can save a huge amount in costs. Finally, consumers will get Samsung's products at more affordable prices (Yoo-chul, 2015).

Tactical use of the online channel is adopted by Samsung, to deal with threats from its competitors such as Xiaomi — a fast emerging smartphone manufacturer from China — which has taken the smartphone world by storm through its low-cost high-end smartphones. One interesting point is that Xiaomi only sells its handsets via its official websites. Samsung management believes this strategy was one reason that helped the Chinese smartphone producer improve its bottom line in such a short time. But it's highly unlikely that Samsung will adopt this tactic in its key developed markets such as the United States and Europe, as well as Korea.

References

American Honda Motor Co., Inc (2016). http://www.honda.com/about (last accessed August 2, 2016).

Chowdhry, A (5 March 2015). Apple Surpassed Samsung as Global Phone Market Leader, Says Report. *Forbes*. http://www.forbes.com/sites/amitchowdhry/2015/03/04/apple-passes-samsung/ (last accessed May 7, 2016).

Dalgic, T (2006). *Handbook of Niche Marketing: Principles and Practice*. New York: Best Business Books.

Grobart, S (29 March 2013). How Samsung Became the World's No. 1 Smartphone Maker — and Its Plans to Stay on Top. *Bloomberg*. http://www.bloomberg.com/news/articles/2013-03-28/how-samsung-became-the-worlds-no-dot-1-smartphone-maker#p2 (last accessed May 7, 2016).

Jollibee USA (2014). About Us. http://www.jollibeeusa.com/about_us.html (last accessed August 2, 2016).

Jollibee Foods Corporation (2016). About Us. http://www.jollibee.com.ph/about-us/ (last accessed August 2, 2016).

Kotler, P, H Kartajaya and Hooi, DH (2014). *Think New ASEAN*. Singapore: McGraw Hill.

Lunden, I (April 27, 2012). Samsung May Have Just Become the King of Mobile Handsets, While S&P Downgrades Nokia to Junk. *Techcrunch*. http://techcrunch.com/2012/04/27/samsung-may-have-just-become-the-king-of-mobile-handsets-while-sp-downgrades-nokia-to-junk/ (last accessed May 7, 2016).

Mehra, J (6 April 2016). Honda Starts Digital Campaign for BR-V. *Autocar India*. http://www.autocarindia.com/auto-news/honda-starts-digital-campaign-for-br-v-401153.aspx (last accessed May 7, 2016).

Michell, T (2010). *Samsung Electronics: And the Struggle for Leadership of the Electronics Industry*. New York: John Wiley.

Ohnsman, A (20 August 2010). Honda's Dream of U.S. Production Protects Profits as Yen Surges. *Bloomberg*. http://www.bloomberg.com/news/2010-08-19/honda-founder-s-dream-of-u-s-production-protects-earnings-as-yen-surges.html (last accessed May 7, 2016).

Panday, A. (2015). Honda Increases its India Scooter Market Share to 58%. http://www.autocarpro.in/news-national/honda-increases-india-scooter-market-share-58-8848#sthash.BAohZjUd.dpuf (last modified July 13, 2015; last accessed August 3, 2016).

Samsung (2016). Values and Philosophy. http://www.samsung.com/us/aboutsamsung/samsung_group/values_and_philosophy (last accessed August 2, 2016).

Yoo-chul, K (26 December 2007). Motorola's Pain Is Samsung's Gain. *Business Week*.

Yoo-chul, K (22 March 2015). Samsung to Focus on Online Marketing. *Korea Times*. http://www.koreatimes.co.kr/www/news/tech/2015/03/133_175675.html (last accessed May 7, 2016).

Yoo-chul, K (January 9, 2016). Jollibee: Acquired Tastes. *The Economist*. http://www.economist.com/news/business/21685465-tenacious-filipino-burger-chain-tries-different-way-conquer-world-acquired-tastes (last accessed May 6, 2016).

Postface

Summary

Chapter 13. Asia's Local Champions

- Many local champions in Asia's developing countries mostly build thriving businesses by using preferential treatment from their respective governments. However, with the opening of the economy and the entry of new competitors, companies that are able to survive do so by building competitive advantages.

- The secret to success lies in local champions using their local wisdom to respond quickly to the anxieties and desires of local customers.

- The development of digital technology in Asia creates an opportunity for local champions to retain the loyalty of its customers in the face of invasions from regional players and multinational companies.

Chapter 14. Asia's Regional Player: Asia Vision, Local Actions

- Regional players in Asia are able to emerge as local champions when they can successfully cement their position in the domestic market and boldly spread their wings in neighboring countries.

- These companies are able to craft a well-defined vision at the regional level, but continue to use marketing tactics tailored to local conditions in each of the targeted countries.

- Online platforms are being used by regional players to support expansion into overseas markets, but their utilization in each country would be optimal only when using local content.

Chapter 15. Asia's Multinational Companies: Global Value, Regional Strategy, Local Tactics

- Multinational companies based in Asia generally aim to spread their wings to markets in developed countries such as North America and Europe.

- These companies adopt the same value globally to create a similar identity wherever they are. But underneath, they implement a coordinated strategy on a regional basis.

- To be able to face local champions who dominate market shares in their respective countries, Asia-based multinational companies should use customized local tactics, including leveraging on digital technology.

Printed in the United States
By Bookmasters